MAINSTREAMS OF *MUSIC*

by David Ewen

Opera

Orchestral Music

Solo Instrumental and Chamber Music

Vocal Music

MAINSTREAMS OF

MUSIC

Volume Four

1975

Vocal Music

Its Story Told Through the Lives and Works of its Foremost Composers

by David Ewen

Franklin Watts, Inc. 730 Fifth Avenue · New York, New York 10019

Illustration Credits

Staatsbibliothek, Berlin: pages 14, 43, 44, 89, 92, 145, 146
Foto Mas, Barcelona: page 16
The New York Public Library, Lincoln Center Collection: pages 24, 25, 204, 205, 226, 227
The New York Public Library, Picture Collection: pages 15, 42, 66, 88, 110, 111, 113, 124, 125, 169
The Mansell Collection: pages 40, 41, 63, 214
The Bettmann Archive: pages 123, 128, 144, 167, 168, 202, 203, 213, 215, 216
Scala, New York/Florence: page 183
H. Roger Viollet: page 190
Don Hunstein/Columbia Records: pages 132, 133, 228, 230
Diane Chadwick-Jones/Columbia Records: page 229
Columbia Artists Management: page 130
Philips Records: page 131
French Cultural Services: pages 39, 65, 112, 184, 185, 186, 187, 188, 189
German Information Center: pages 90, 91, 134, 147
R C A Records: pages 126, 127, 166
Hurok Attractions: page 129

Jacket photo by Don Hunstein, courtesy of
Trinity School Choir, New York City;
Westminster Choir, Princeton, New Jersey
Photo Research by Wesley Day

Library of Congress Cataloging in Publication Data

Ewen, David, 1907–
  Vocal music.

  (*His* Mainstreams of music; v. 4)
  SUMMARY: Traces the development of vocal music through the ages in discussions of its composers and their works.
  1. Vocal music—Juvenile literature. 2. Composers—Juvenile literature. [1. Vocal music. 2. Composers] I. Title.
ML1400.E9   784'.09   74-34115
ISBN 0-531-02829-1

Some Other Books by David Ewen

Dictators of the Baton

Music Comes to America

Music for the Millions

The World of Great Composers

The New Encyclopedia of the Opera

The New Book of Modern Composers

The Home Book of Musical Knowledge

The Encyclopedia of Concert Music

David Ewen Introduces Modern Music

The Complete Book of Classical Music

The World of Twentieth-Century Music

Leonard Bernstein

The Milton Cross New Encyclopedia of Great Composers
  (WITH MILTON CROSS)

George Gershwin: His Journey to Greatness

Composers of Tomorrow's Music

New Complete Book of the American Musical Theater

Great Composers: 1300–1900

Composers Since 1900

Great Men of American Popular Song

Panorama of American Popular Music

The Story of America's Musical Theater

American Popular Songs:
  From the Revolutionary War to the Present

Contents

Introduction

Distant Voices

What was the first music you heard? You do not remember, of course, because you were then just an infant. But it is more than probable that your first experience in music came from hearing the songs your mother sang to you.

The musical experience of the human race began similarly with songs. Nature endowed man with a wonderful medium for making music: the human voice. Long before man learned to fashion musical instruments he created music vocally. We do not know what kind of songs primitive man conceived, since he did not perpetuate them through notation, that is, a system of setting down musical ideas. (The earliest musical notation preserved is from the seventh century, and this notation is undecipherable.) We believe that man first used his singing voice to attract a mate, a theory propounded by Charles Darwin. Some anthropologists are of the opinion that songs were first devised for religious worship. Others say that song came into existence when man tried to imitate the warbling of birds or the call of animals. Whatever the origin or character of the earliest songs, we can be quite sure that love and religion were the dominant influences in the making of music. And so it remained long after music outgrew primitivism.

The first decipherable music notation is in signs called "neumes" found from the eighth to the fourteenth century. They were used for the earliest vocal music that today holds any meaning for us: plainsong or plainchant. These simple melodies in elementary rhythm were sung by two or more voices in unison. This music, unaccompanied by instruments (a cappella), was intended for the Catholic Church. It was crystallized in Rome between the eighth and the ninth centuries. But two centuries before that, Pope Gregory I had collected and standardized the early plainsong, and so it is often identified as "Gregorian chant."

In the ninth century, plainsong was known as "organum." Here a melody is duplicated by a second voice, note for note, but pitched either one fourth or one fifth below. By the eleventh century the two voices were moving in precise opposite direction from each other. This practice soon encouraged composers to adopt an altogether new voice either above or below the original instead of using the same voice in contrary motion.

In the ninth century, neumes consisted of dots, small curved, hooklike figures, and dashes. By the thirteenth century, square-shaped heads were adopted for the notes. Originally, neumes indicated only the general direction in which the voice moved, without indicating the precise pitch. This notation, then, was just a convenience to bolster the memory of a singer already acquainted with the melody. But in time the idea of placing neumes on a staff of one, two, and later four lines made it possible for pitch to be indicated and led eventually to the formation of the five-line musical staff.

We are now at the dawn of the polyphonic era, which grew and flowered for several centuries, contributing our first great composers and our first musical masterpieces. In polyphony several different melodies in independent voice parts are combined simultaneously, whereas in homophony a single melody is supported by an accompaniment.

The first music to come out of the Gothic era is referred to in history books as *ars antiqua* ("ancient art"). This is a term devised in the fourteenth century for music of an earlier period (twelfth and thirteenth centuries). The home of ars antiqua was Paris, specifically the Cathedral of Notre Dame, where the two most important composers of this ancient art were employed as music directors (*maîtres de chapelle*). They were Leoninus, or Léonin, in the twelfth century, and his successor, Perotinus or Pérotin. Leoninus was described as *optimus organista,* which at times has been erroneously translated as "the greatest organist." What this descriptive Latin phrase actually means is that he was the greatest composer of

organum music. Leoninus's masterwork was *Magnus liber organi,* a volume of some ninety two-part organums for the ecclesiastical year. Perotinus, on the other hand, was spoken of as *optimus discantor,* or the foremost composer of descant—descant being a florid, unmeasured improvisation used in early polyphonic music for a Gregorian melody in organum. Some of these organums were "clausulae," a development in which the upper voices were in a note-against-note style while the tenor voice ("cantus firmus") is set off from the others rhythmically with quick, lively sections. The clausula was the point of origin for the motet, later to become a major form of polyphonic music. Another important form in ars antiqua was the "conductus," in two or four voices, for festive occasions and set to a religious, political, or satirical text. Each part consists of a fluid melody, but the text is heard only in the tenor voice. The conductus is the earliest example of free composition independent of the Gregorian chant.

In or about 1325 Philippe de Vitry published a treatise called *Ars nova* ("New Art"). In this volume, de Vitry discussed only the notational practices of his period rather than the innovations. Nevertheless, some authorities regard de Vitry as one of the creators of "isorhythm" (or "equal rhythm"), a device in which a rhythmic pattern of notes and rests was repeated at fixed points throughout a composition, sometimes in the tenor voice, sometimes in all the voice parts. The age that took its name from de Vitry's volume is known for radical rhythmic and metrical developments. These introduced a flexibility and variety within the polyphonic texture that the organums of Leoninus and Perotinus had never known. Thus ars nova (together with a few other developments in the thirteenth century) helped to usher in a new age for polyphony that saw the emergence of the first composers with whom the history of Western music can well be said to have begun.

Guillaume de Machaut (c. 1300–77), another French composer, wrote a mass that is the earliest such work to have been preserved. The mass is the most important ritual of the Catholic Church, and by the same token the musical mass became one of the most important forms of church music. The musical portions fall into two categories: the Proper and the Ordinary. The Proper of the Mass, parts of which vary not only from season to season but sometimes even from day to day, includes an Introit, Gradual, Alleluia, Offertory, and Communion; these parts received plainsong treatment. The Ordinary of the Mass remained unchanged regardless of the season of the Church year. Normally, the Ordinary of the Mass consisted of five major sections: Kyrie, Gloria, Credo, Sanctus (which embraces the Benedictus), and Agnus Dei. This music was built from modes—modes antedating the major and minor scales of a later period, having been developed from the time of the Greeks, and bearing such names as Aeolian, Lydian, and Dorian. Before long, the five parts of the Ordinary of the Mass were combined into a single unified work. Originally, composers would select certain plainsongs that fitted a specific religious occasion and then would write a mass around them.

The mass by Machaut was for four unaccompanied voices. It used not only the five sections of the Ordinary of the Mass but a sixth section as well, Ite missa est. Some historians believe that Machaut may have written it in 1364 to honor the coronation of Charles V at Reims. In this work—which is sometimes called *La Messe de Notre Dame* (*Notre Dame* Mass)—Machaut uses a famous plainsong, ''David.'' The isorhythmic technique propounded by de Vitry is found throughout the composition, to connect one part to the next.

Another significant form of choral music developed by Machaut was the motet. This was a musical setting of a biblical text in Latin, sung chiefly at vespers, by four or five voices.

With John Dunstable (c. 1370–1453) ars nova traveled into England. He was England's first significant composer. His masses and motets brought fresh methods into early-fifteenth-century polyphonic music, in the way the melodic lines moved and in the freshness of the harmonizations. Dunstable was also a pioneer in trying to adapt the rhythms of his melodies to those of the spoken text.

The next important development in polyphonic music was contributed by the Burgundian and the Flemish schools of composers in the fifteenth century. The Burgundian school came first, within the duchy of Burgundy, made up of today's eastern France, Belgium, and the Netherlands. In this country there arose a group of highly gifted and innovative composers headed by Guillaume Dufay (c. 1400–74) and Gilles Binchois (c. 1400–60). The Burgundian school was succeeded by one in Flanders—the Flemish school—whose composers came out of the southern Netherlands, Belgium, and northern France. Its leaders were Jean d'Okeghem (1430–95), Jakob Obrecht (1452?–1505), Josquin des Prés (c. 1450–1521), and Orlando di Lasso (1532–94). These men, both the Burgundians and the Flemish, wrote masses and motets, and worked within other polyphonic forms as well. Dufay and Orlando di Lasso produced magnificats, settings of the song of the Virgin Mary in the Gospel of Saint Luke beginning with the line ''Magnificat anima mea Dominum.'' Josquin des Prés wrote music for the prayer ''Ave Maria,'' a hymn of praise to the Virgin Mary. He and Orlando di Lasso wrote settings of the

"Stabat Mater," a religious text describing the Blessed Virgin at the
Cross.

To their polyphonic writing the Burgundian and Flemish schools brought heightened emotion and color, a richer sonority, a greater clarity of phrases and cadences, and new embroidery in polyphonic writing. All this represents such a sharp forward movement from the earlier archaic styles that the leading works of Dufay, Josquin des Prés, and Orlando di Lasso are still performed and recorded. Even to our ears, unaccustomed though they are to the old church modes, there is much haunting loveliness in their compositions.

From Flanders we now progress to Italy, where the art and science of polyphony experienced further transformations. In Venice, Andrea Gabrieli (1520–86) and his nephew, Giovanni Gabrieli (1557–1612), were leaders of a polyphonic school of their own, the Venetian school. Ever more resplendent in color and sound, ever more ambitious in design does the tapestry of polyphonic music now become! With the chorus at the Cathedral of San Marco in Venice split up into two parts and placed around each of the two organs, the two Gabrielis—who at different times were employed either as organist or as maestro di cappella at San Marco—were able to achieve new brilliant and sonorous effects. The splitting up of the chorus into two parts at San Marco also enabled the Gabrielis to develop the technique of antiphony, in which one line of music is assigned to one choir and repeated by the second one in contrasting dynamics.

With the very next phase of development we arrive at the golden age of polyphonic music. This step takes place in Rome, where Giovanni Pierluigi da Palestrina, the greatest composer of his generation, and possibly the greatest before Johann Sebastian Bach, became the central force of the Roman school of polyphonic composers. This school followed the Venetian, and it included the Spaniard Tomás Luis de Victoria. With Palestrina and Victoria all the elements that thus far had gone into the writing of a cappella polyphonic music for the Church were swept to their ultimate fulfillment. With Palestrina and Victoria we scale the summit of the polyphonic age.

There was secular as well as liturgical music developing. Most of this was also polyphonic, for two or more voices. The principal form of a cappella secular music during the Renaissance was the madrigal, the secular equivalent of the sixteenth-century motet. It provided a musical setting for love or pastoral poems, and sometimes for poems with humorous or satirical subjects. The music was either sentimental or cheerful and lively. The word *madrigal* was used in vocal music as early as the fourteenth century, but the madrigals with which we are now acquainted come from the sixteenth century. In Italy magnificent madrigals were produced by such composers as Luca Marenzio (1553–99), Carlo Gesualdo, the prince of Venosa (c. 1560–1613), and Orazio Vecchi (1550–1605). Marenzio favored the love and pastoral verses of that great Italian Renaissance poet Petrarch. In "Io piango ed ella il volto," "Strider faceva," and "Solo e pensoso," all for five voices, Marenzio became one of the first to introduce pictorial images into his musical writing. Gesualdo was so concerned with the dramatic and emotional interest of his madrigals that he often used discords and bold modulations to enhance their effect. He also brought heightened attention to the melodic and harmonic content. His best madrigals were "Moro losso" and "Resta di darmi noia," both for five voices. Vecchi was an innovator in combining several madrigals into a unified sequence. His masterwork in this format is *L'Amfiparnaso,* made up of fourteen textually related five-part madrigals. It has such a fully developed plot that *L'Amfiparnaso* can be and has been staged. Two themes are woven into the story line. One involves the romance of Lucio and Isabella. When Isabella receives the false tidings that Lucio is dead, she contemplates suicide. But her servant soon brings her the happy tidings that Lucio is very much alive. This part of the work ends with their marriage. A subplot engages characters from the commedia dell'arte, while touching upon the amatory involvements of old Pantalone and a courtesan, Hortensia, and Lelio and Nisa. When *L'Amfiparnaso* was first heard—in Modena in 1594—it was sung as a madrigal cycle in a concert performance. Though entirely polyphonic, *L'Amfiparnaso* is the connecting link between polyphonic music and opera, the latter of which was born in Florence in 1597, the same year that *L'Amfiparnaso* was published.

The greatest madrigal composers appeared during the closing years of the sixteenth century and the early part of the seventeenth. They were Thomas Morley and Orlando Gibbons in England and, in Italy, Claudio Monteverdi. Their historic importance in secular choral music can hardly be overestimated.

Although major composers of the Gothic era and ars nova directed their principal creative efforts to choral music, secular music for a single voice was also getting a hearing at this time.

In France, in the twelfth and thirteenth centuries, troubadours and *trouvères*—poet-musicians—created words and music for a vast repository of love and pastoral songs and songs of war and adventure. Some three hundred troubadour songs and more than a thousand songs by the *trou-*

vères have survived. The troubadour was found in the Provence region of southern France even before the twelfth century. Gentlemen of the nobility, troubadours became the first known writers of the Western world to use texts in the vernacular. The *trouvères* originally took their songs from those of the troubadours, but with the text translated from Provençal to their own dialect. But, later on, the *trouvères* created their own songs, which were spread throughout northern France. *Trouvères* were responsible for evolving the strophic song—one made up of several stanzas in which each stanza uses the same melody. Strophic songs have continued to be in favor up to our present day.

The songs of the troubadours and the *trouvères* were known as "chansons" (*chanson* being the French word for "song"). They included such song forms as the ballade, the rondeau, and the virelay. Some chansons grew so popular throughout France that they were used by polyphonic composers for major compositions. "L'homme armé" is one of these chansons, a song of unknown authorship then believed to have been sung by the French military hero Roland as he led his troops into battle. Almost every significant polyphonic composer of the fifteenth and sixteenth centuries used this chanson in one version or another. The first book of masses that Josquin des Prés published included the *L'homme armé* Mass (1502), so called because it made such extensive use of this melody. In substituting a French chanson for a Gregorian chant, the *L'homme armé* Mass was a radical departure from the kind of masses Italians had written in the fifteenth century.

Machaut and his immediate successors during the ars nova period wrote secular compositions in the polyphonic style and in the forms of ballades, rondeaux, and virelays. Such songs by Machaut have historic importance, since they are among the first to be accompanied by instruments. The English composer Dunstable was also influenced by the troubadours to write ballades, just as Dunstable's ballades in turn stimulated Dufay to write chansons.

The impact of the songs of the French troubadours was also strongly felt in Germany between the twelfth and the fourteenth century by the minnesingers, and in the fifteenth and sixteenth centuries by the Meistersinger (mastersingers). The songs of the minnesingers usually had a strong narrative rather than a lyric character. This was the music heard most often in Germany during the Middle Ages. The mastersingers were members of craftsmen guilds who made a fetish of adhering to strict rules in the writing and singing of their songs, which they often presented in competitions. All this was the subject of Richard Wagner's only comedy opera, *Die Mei-* 7 *stersinger,* or *The Mastersingers* (1867), one of whose main characters was Hans Sachs (1494–1576), one of the most celebrated of all the mastersingers. The art song began to flourish in Germany, beginning with Hans Leo Hassler (1564–1612) and Heinrich Albert (1604–51), in whose songs we can detect the influence of both the minnesingers and the mastersingers.

England's music bloomed with the development of the art song. William Byrd (1543–1623) was the pioneer in the writing of songs for solo voice and accompaniment (his accompaniment being viols, predecessors of today's bowed stringed instruments). Thomas Morley wrote "ayres"—old English for "airs"—for solo voice and lute accompaniment. One of the rare surviving songs from sixteenth-century England is his setting of "It Was a Lover and His Lass" (the words come from Shakespeare's *As You Like It*).

In 1597 John Dowland (1563–1626) published a volume of ayres with lute accompaniment, which came to be known as "lute songs." This was the first such collection by an English composer. By virtue of these songs, and others in his later publications, Dowland has won the distinction of becoming the first significant composer of art songs in music history. The lute song is actually a simplified madrigal, sometimes for solo voice and lute, sometimes for solo voice and lute supplemented by other voices. The emphasis in the lute song, as distinguished from the madrigal, is on melody and not on polyphony (though the supplementary accompanying voices in lute songs may be used contrapuntally, that is, in a polyphonic style). Homophony—the counterpart of polyphony—is thus strongly suggested for the first time. Before long, homophony would displace polyphony as the style most favored by composers. In the process, the art song replaced the madrigal, which then went into total oblivion as a medium for vocal composition.

Dowland's first collection of ayres and songs enjoyed such success that within sixteen years of its publication it went into five editions and spread Dowland's name and music throughout Europe. Two more volumes of Dowland's songs were issued in 1600 and 1603 respectively. Dowland's best-known song, "Flow My Tears," appeared in the second volume, as did "Sorrow, Sorrow Stay" and "I Saw My Lady Weep." The third volume included "Say, Love" and "Weep You No More, Sad Fountains." With the exception of "Say, Love," which is in a carefree vein, these and other Dowland song gems are filled with melancholy and are characterized not only by the poignant emotion in the melody but also by the richness of the lute accompaniment. That is why such a distinguished twentieth-century musicologist as Ernest Newman was led to write that Dowland belongs with the half dozen or so of the foremost composers of songs in music history.

Though songs were written, sung, and even published throughout Europe between the twelfth and the seventeenth century, and though some of those songs have exceptional merit, music for solo voice played only a negligible role in the music of those years. The artistic fulfillment of the art song was comparatively late in coming. Between the twelfth and the seventeenth century, the musical scene in general and the vocal scene in particular was dominated by polyphonic writing, most of it for the Church, but some of it secular.

It is to the two greatest masters of polyphonic music for the Church that we must first direct our attention: to Palestrina and Victoria, creators of the glories of the age of polyphony.

The Power and the Glory
of the Renaissance

Giovanni Pierluigi da Palestrina,

Tomás Luis de Victoria

The sixteenth century was an age of creative giants and artistic and literary miracles. The Renaissance was at its height. Through the reintroduction of the heritage of ancient Greece and Rome, a flowering of culture and arts had begun in Italy, to spread throughout Western Europe. This was the century that presented to the world the work of Michelangelo, Raphael, Titian, Shakespeare (together with other distinguished poets and playwrights of the Elizabethan era), Montaigne, Erasmus, Tasso—to choose just a representative few from a conglomerate of geniuses with few equals in any other century before or since.

The sixteenth century also produced the greatest composer of the polyphonic age, the first composer in music history for whom the word *genius* is no overstatement.

Today we call him Palestrina, but his real name was Giovanni Pierluigi. ''Da Palestrina'' was added by his family to its name to indicate that for several generations the Pierluigis made their home in the little hill town of Palestrina, about twenty-five miles from Rome. It was there that Giovanni was born in or about 1525. Palestrina's father, who owned some modest properties, was well able to provide his family with physical comforts.

When the boy revealed talent for singing, he was recruited for the choir of the Sant' Agapit Cathedral in his native town. Cardinal Andrea della Valle, the bishop of Palestrina, became so interested in him that, upon being transferred to Rome as archpriest of the Church of Santa Maria Maggiore, the bishop took the nine-year-old Palestrina with him. For about five years Palestrina attended the choir school of Santa Maria Maggiore, where he also sang in the choir. After his voice broke, he returned to Palestrina in 1544 to begin a professional career in music by serving as choirmaster and organist at Sant' Agapit. His duties were to play the organ on feast days, train the choir for services, and teach singing to the choirboys. He held this post for about seven years, during which time, on June 12, 1547, he married Lucrezia Gori, daughter of a prosperous landowner.

The elevation of Cardinal del Monte, then the bishop of Palestrina, to the Holy See as Pope Julius III in 1550 was instrumental in bringing Palestrina to Rome in 1551 for an appointment as director of the Julian Choir, which performed at Saint Peter's Basilica. In gratitude, Palestrina composed a mass that he dedicated to his benefactor, the pope. Palestrina published it at his own expense, together with several other of his masses, in 1554. On the title page was engraved a picture of himself wearing priestly garb and kneeling before the pope while presenting him with this volume of masses. The pope, probably as a reward for this dedication, soon appointed Palestrina to the pontifical (Sistine) choir without requiring him to take the necessary examinations, which aroused a good deal of resentment among the other singers. They soon used their influence to have Palestrina removed from the choir when Pope Julius died in 1555.

Pope Julius was succeeded by Pope Marcellus II. The new pope demanded a reform in church music in which complexity of polyphonic writing would be reduced to the simplicity of oldtime plainsong. Some years later, the great church Council of Trent decreed that such a reform take place.

A legend was long circulated, and believed, about Palestrina and the Council of Trent. At that time he was the music director of Saint John Lateran Church in Rome, where Orlando di Lasso, whom we mentioned in the Introduction, had served a few years earlier. According to the story, Palestrina decided to write a mass in a complicated polyphonic style but filled with such religious ardor that the Council of Trent would be convinced no reform in church music was necessary. And so he created his magnum opus, the *Missa Papae Marcelli*. Its spiritual beauty was reputed to have convinced the council to rescind its demands for reform. This story, however, is apocryphal. There is no historic evidence to promote the belief that the *Missa Papae Marcelli* was in any way responsible for maintaining the status quo found in church music. (Nevertheless, in 1917, this legend was used as a subject for a fine German opera by Hans Pfitzner— *Palestrina*.)

What actually happened during the aborted reform movement was that the Council of Trent appointed a committee of cardinals to make an intensive study of existing church music. In the process they undoubtedly reviewed Palestrina's principal church compositions, and particularly his masses. It is also more than probable that the lofty inspiration of Palestrina's masses became a powerful contributory factor in the decision by the cardinals to make only perfunctory and highly generalized recommendations for changes.

Palestrina was not happy at Saint John Lateran. He encountered continuous opposition to his indefatigable attempts to raise the musical standards at that church, which had deteriorated sadly after Orlando di Lasso's resignation. In addition, Palestrina was as greatly concerned about money as he was about art. Underpaid for his services, he engaged in constant battles with the authorities to have his meager pay increased. Failing that, he fell into a fit of rage and handed in his resignation in July of 1560.

Less than a year later, he found a more lucrative and musically rewarding post as music director of Santa Maria Maggiore, where he had sung in the choir as a boy. His salary was the equivalent of $750 a year, a few hundred more than he had earned at Saint John Lateran. But he managed to supplement this income amply by receiving gifts from members of the congregation, by dedicating his music to powerful patrons, by teaching music to the rich, and by editing and rewriting the compositions of members of the nobility. Besides, he was entitled to an annual pension of about $250 because he had served in the pontifical choir. He was, then, financially well off, and he solidified his economic position through wise investments in valuable properties.

His years both at Saint John Lateran and Santa Maria Maggiore were creatively fruitful. He published masses and motets. Both of these polyphonic forms had been used by his predecessors and contemporaries, for Palestrina was no innovator in either devising new structures or experimenting with new techniques. He had thoroughly absorbed the methods of the Flemish masters. He was content to use the old church modes and the Gregorian chants the way other composers before him had done. But he went on from there to extend and transform their style through his extraordinary contrapuntal technique and through the power of a seemingly inexhaustible imagination. He was ingenious in the way he wove the voices

The title-page illustration of Palestrina's first collection of masses, printed in 1554. The composer is shown presenting his music to Pope Julius III.

Giovanni Pierluigi da Palestrina.

THOMAE LVDOVICI
DE VICTORIA ABVLENSIS
COLLEGII GERMANICI IN VRBE
ROMA MVSICAE MODERATORIS.

LIBER PRIMVS·

QVI MISSAS· PSALMOS· MAGNIFICAT·
AD VIRGINEM DEI MATREM SALVTATIONES,
ALIA'QVE COMPLECTITVR.

Venetiis apud Angelum Gardanum.
Anno Domini M· D· LXXVI.

The title page of a collection of compositions of Tomás Luis de Victoria, printed in Rome in 1576.

into a subtle contrapuntal fabric, and though his music was complex, it nevertheless possessed clarity, balance, and symmetry. A depth of religious feeling (for he was a very religious man), a sensuous beauty of sound, a glowing warmth of melody and harmony, and a radiant spirituality set his music above anything written up to his time. In his masterwork, the *Missa Papae Marcelli,* and in such other masses as the *Missa Assumpta est Maria* and the *Missa brevis*—as well as in his compositions in other forms including the motet and the "Stabat Mater"—he rises "to the highest flights . . . of spiritual ecstasy," as Sir Richard R. Terry, an English music scholar, has written. And, in the words of Palestrina's biographer Zoë Kendrick Pyne, he "penetrates depths of the soul."

Even while serving at Santa Maria Maggiore, Palestrina also held secular posts. For several summers he directed musical performances at the sumptuous estate of Cardinal d'Este at Tivoli, near Rome. He also taught music at a new Roman seminary, the Collegium Romanum, that trained young men for the clergy.

When he left Santa Maria Maggiore in 1567, Palestrina held no other church posts for about four years. He continued writing church music, of course, some of it on special (and highly profitable) commissions from the nobility. Among these works are a mass for the inauguration of a new church in Mantua and several motets honoring Saint Barbara.

In 1571 Palestrina resumed a church office by becoming once again the director of the Julian Choir at Saint Peter's Basilica. His preeminent position in Italian church music now became an accepted fact.

A series of epidemics devastated Rome and its environs in the 1570s, which greatly victimized Palestrina. Two of his sons died, and at about the same time, two of his brothers succumbed. For a while, in 1578, Palestrina's own life was endangered. Hardly had he recovered when in 1580 his wife became infected and died. Overwhelmed with grief at this succession of tragedies, Palestrina, seeking solace in his religion, decided to enter the priesthood. He received the necessary papal permission on the condition he did not desert his post with the Julian Choir. But after taking minor orders and submitting to the tonsure, symbolic of entrance into the clerical state, Palestrina had a sudden change of heart. He now became interested in a wealthy widow, Virginia Dormuli, whom he married on March 28, 1581. After her marriage, Virginia continued to carry on the highly prosperous business endeavors of her deceased husband with the cooperation of Palestrina, who, needless to say, did not neglect his musical activities. He continued to serve as director of the Julian Choir while writing some of his noblest masses, motets, and hymns, together with magnificats and Lamentations (the last using the "Lamentation of Jeremiah" from the Bible as text). The last volume of his works published during his lifetime was a book of madrigals in 1594.

His fame kept growing, and honors kept accumulating. Each successive pope considered him the composer of the papal choir, though he was never given that title officially. In 1592 Pope Clement VIII greatly increased Palestrina's pension out of gratitude for the many compositions Palestrina had written for the Julian Choir. A group of leading Italian composers honored him in 1592 by issuing a collection of their own psalms, which they dedicated and presented to Palestrina. Palestrina's response was to write for them a beautiful motet beginning with the words "You are my friends, if you do what I teach, saith the Lord."

In 1593 Palestrina planned to go into retirement in his native city. His bad health, however, kept him in Rome, where he died on February 2, 1594. Musicians, nobility, statesmen, high dignitaries of the Church attended his funeral ceremonies at Saint Peter's. His lead coffin bore the inscription "Musicae Princeps" ("The First Man of Music"). In one of many eulogies, a French priest said: "I pronounce him to be the father of music"—a tribute that the history book has since confirmed.

In sixteenth-century church music—that age of polyphony which the historian has described as "golden"—Tomás Luis de Victoria (or, as the Italians called him, Tommaso Luigi da Vittoria) holds a place second in importance only to the great Palestrina. Victoria was Spanish. But because of his long residence in Rome, and because of the influence Palestrina's music had on him, he is grouped with the "Roman school" of polyphonic composers of which Palestrina was the acknowledged head.

Victoria, like Palestrina, was a man of the deepest religious convictions and feelings who always dedicated his music, as he himself once wrote, to "the praise and glory of God." Almost all of Victoria's two hundred or so compositions are music for church use.

He was born in Avila, Spain, in or about 1549, and was a chorister at the Avila Cathedral while pursuing his early music studies. In 1565 he went to Rome to study for the priesthood, enrolling in the Collegium Germanicum, which Ignatius of Loyola had founded thirteen years earlier as a training school for German clergy. There Victoria sang in the choir. Meeting with and becoming a friend of Palestrina was a decisive factor in Victoria's deciding to abandon, temporarily at least, his training for the clergy and to give more of his time and energies to music. There is good reason to believe that for a time he even studied with Palestrina before assuming, in 1569, his first important music post, that of maestro di cappella at Santa Maria di Montserrato, a Roman church for Spaniards. Two years later Victoria succeeded Palestrina as the music master at the seminary, Collegium Romanum.

Victoria's first publication was a volume of thirty-three motets (the bulk of his production in this form) issued in 1572. What is remarkable about this music is the fact that, in spite of the obvious technical and stylistic echoes of Palestrina, these motets carried Victoria's own musical identity. In "O vos omnes," for four voices, for example, Victoria adds to Palestrina's polyphonic adroitness and Italian warmth and sensuousness a fervor, passion, and mysticism that would characterize his later best music. Here, as later, he revealed a rare gift for illustrating the text with vividly descriptive music. Palestrina himself must have been greatly impressed with these early motets, for when he wrote some motets of his own in 1584 he made a conscious effort to simulate Victoria's passionate expressiveness. Thus the master who had influenced his friend and pupil became, in turn, influenced by him.

In 1576 Victoria issued a collection of masses, motets, and magnificats; in 1581, two sets of magnificats; in 1583, two volumes, one of masses and another of motets and psalms; and in 1585, one of his supreme achievements, the *Officium Hebdomadae Sanctae,* music for Palm Sunday and the last three days of Holy Week.

While developing as a composer, Victoria left his post at the Collegium Romanum and took a similar position as maestro di cappella at the Collegium Germanicum. He was then ordained a priest in 1575. For seven years after that he served as the chaplain at the Church of San Girolamo della Carità.

In or about 1594, Victoria returned to Spain. There he served as organist and choirmaster at the Descalzas Reales Convent in Madrid, and as chaplain to the Empress Mother Maria, sister of Philip II. He completed a beautiful "Ave Maria" in 1603. His swan song, as he himself referred to it, was *Officium Defunctorum,* a mass for six voices, probably written in commemoration of the then recent death of the Empress Mother Maria, and just as probably sung at her funeral. Some musicologists look upon this as Victoria's finest composition. Its grandeur and ecstasy place it among the foremost accomplishments of the polyphonic age.

Though Victoria lived for another eight years after that, he wrote no more music. He died in Madrid on August 27, 1611. In the more than three and a half centuries after his death, Spain produced few, if any, composers of his equal.

Heyday of the Madrigal

Thomas Morley, Orlando Gibbons,

Claudio Monteverdi

The Elizabethan age, which spanned the forty-five years of the reign of Elizabeth I, was one of the greatest eras in English literature. In his famous allegory *The Faerie Queene,* Edmund Spenser named Queen Elizabeth I "Gloriana." "Glorious," too, is the word best describing a period that produced not only Spenser but also Shakespeare, Christopher Marlowe, and a host of immortal dramatists, poets, and writers of prose.

This was also a time of unparalleled achievement in English music, for this was the heyday of the English madrigal. The forty or so volumes of English madrigals published between 1588 and 1627 are, in the opinion of the English musicologist Ernest Walker, "the greatest music treasure England possesses."

The two foremost exponents of the English madrigal were Thomas Morley and Orlando Gibbons.

The madrigal first came to England in 1588, when an English publisher released *Musica Transalpina*. This was a volume of fifty-seven Italian madrigals with English words, including ten by Marenzio and four by Palestrina. In addition, four madrigals were the work of the Flemish Orlando di Lasso and one—"The Fair Young Virgin," for five voices—by an Englishman whom the publisher described as "a great master of

music.'' He was William Byrd (1543–1623). This one madrigal by Byrd marks the beginnings of a monumental epoch of English music. Byrd's most famous madrigal is the still-familiar ''Though Amaryllis Dance in the Green,'' which appeared in a volume devoted exclusively to Byrd's music, *Psalms, Sonnets and Songs of Sadness and Piety* (1588).

Important as Byrd's madrigals were in emphasizing melody and rhythm over counterpoint—and however lovely they are to listen to—the high-water mark of the English madrigal was reached not by him but by his two contemporaries Morley and Gibbons.

The place in England where Thomas Morley was born in 1557 is not known, but there is some conjecture that it might have been London. After singing in the boys' choir at Saint Paul's Cathedral in London, Morley went through a comprehensive period of music study with William Byrd, and after that, one at Oxford, where in 1588 he received his baccalaureate in music. In that same year he played the organ at Saint Giles' Church in the Cripplegate district of London.

In 1589 Morley became the organist at Saint Paul's Cathedral, where he remained until 1592. He left to become Gentleman of the Chapel Royal, a position requiring him to play the organ and direct the musical services at the royal palaces. During the decade from 1592 to 1602 Morley wrote all of his principal compositions, beginning in 1593 with a volume of canzonets (little polyphonic songs for three voices using lyric poems as texts) in which his later madrigal style is hinted at. That style had ripened one year later in his *First Book of Madrigals,* for four voices, where we find such delights as ''Now Is the Gentle Season'' and ''April Is in My Mistress' Face.''

A variation of the madrigal was the ''ballet,'' a volume of such pieces by Morley for five voices being published in 1595. The ''ballet'' differed from the madrigal in that its melody was usually lighter and more buoyant. It used a recurring refrain made up of the syllables ''fa-la-la'' (''ballets'' were sometimes spoken of as ''fa-la-las'') or other nonsense syllables. Morley's best-known compositions are actually ''ballets'' but are often designated as madrigals: ''Now Is the Month of Maying'' and ''Sing We and Chant It.''

The form, style, and character of the English madrigal was definitively established by Morley before the sixteenth century closed. This is polyphonic music that places more importance on beauty and sentiment of melody than on the skill with which voices are interwoven. It is music of surpassing charm and sweetness, whether the feeling be sad or gay; music that magically captures the effervescent or sentimental spirit of the English lyric poetry it uses; music that, in its serenity and gentleness, is a hallmark of English temperament.

The Triumphs of Oriana, edited by Morley in 1601 and published two years later, is one of the richest storehouses of English madrigals. This anthology contains two madrigals by Morley, together with others by some of his most distinguished contemporaries, of whom Orlando Gibbons is the most important. "Oriana" was a name used in the pastoral poetry of the Elizabethan era to identify Queen Elizabeth. Each madrigal in this set ends with the words "Long live fair Oriana," in honor of the queen.

Morley's health went into a decline along with the sixteenth century. As he wrote in 1597: "My health . . . has been so bad that if it had been the pleasure of Him who made all things to have taken me out of the world, I should have been well contented; and have wished it more than once." He was forced to relinquish his post at the Chapel Royal early in 1602, after which he led a solitary existence at his home (probably in London), where he died some time in October of the same year.

By publishing *Madrigals and Motets in Five Parts* ten years after Morley's death, Orlando Gibbons became his heir as the foremost madrigalist of his time. This was the only such volume Gibbons ever produced, but it would have been enough to make him equal to the immortals of Elizabethan music even if he had not also distinguished himself as a composer of instrumental music. For this volume contains some of the choicest specimens of madrigal music, on a level with the best by Morley. The most famous madrigals in it are "The Silver Swan," "What Is Our Life?" and "Dainty Fine Bird." For the most part, Gibbons's madrigals are sadder and more solemn than those by Morley, but, as Ernest Walker maintains, "none could be more polished in expression." Gibbons's favorite subjects were unrequited love, death, and renunciation.

Gibbons was born in Oxford in 1583 and was a member of the choir at King's College at Cambridge, where he matriculated in 1598. In 1605 he assumed the post of organist of the Chapel Royal. Gibbons's first compositions (fantasias for three viols and pieces of keyboard music) were completed between 1610 and 1611, the keyboard music appearing in *Parthenia,* a monumental volume of such music by him and some of his eminent contemporaries. With the publication of his madrigals and motets in 1612 he demonstrated that he was also a master of vocal polyphonic music.

In the year 1619 he became chamber musician for the king, James I, and four years later he was also appointed organist at Westminster Abbey. He died on June 5, 1625, at Canterbury, the victim of an apoplectic stroke, just two months after he had directed the music for the funeral of James I.

It is poetic justice that the final evolution of the madrigal should take place in Italy, the country where it had first been conceived. This happened with Claudio Monteverdi.

Monteverdi is now remembered by most music lovers principally for his operas. *La Favola d'Orfeo* (popularly called *Orfeo*), produced at Mantua in 1607, is not only his first but also his best-known work for the stage. This opera is also the oldest that is still occasionally performed today. But together with Monteverdi's significance in opera is his eminence as a madrigalist. His musical invention that seemed to recognize no boundaries, his dramatic instincts, and his compulsion for innovation—all those things which helped make him the greatest composer of operas up to his time—are also encountered in his madrigals.

He was the modernist of his time, a composer who was always experimenting with new techniques. He did not hesitate to use discords or other unusual harmonies, radical changes of rhythm and dynamics, unprecedented ways of combining voices, or any other then-still-untried method in order to enhance the theatrical effects and imagery of his writing.

In spite of the fact that his contemporaries held him in high esteem, since he was one of the foremost Italian composers of his age, they were also critical of the way he continually broke with tradition. But one has merely to look at Monteverdi's face, in his only existing picture, to recognize that this was not a man easily swayed by criticism or expedience. The face speaks of strength and determination. The lips are so tightly compressed that they are almost hidden by his mustache and beard. The eyes, below an imposing forehead, have a severe look. This is not a man to make compromises.

And throughout his long and active career as a musician he did not compromise. He wrote the best and the most original music of which he was capable whether or not it pleased his employers or patrons. Facility and fertility were demanded of him. But, though he wrote much, he was always painstaking. "I do most heartily pray your Most Serene Highness for the love of God, no longer to put so much work on me," he once pleaded in writing to an employer who was showering him with commissions, "and to give me more time for my great desire to serve you. Otherwise the excess of my fatigue will not fail to shorten my life." But, as once more we look at his picture, we know full well that not fatigue or overwork or the fear of physical collapse could prompt such a request, but only the stultifying fear that the excessive demands made upon him for new works would put a severe strain on his ability to maintain the highest standards.

Monteverdi was born in Cremona in 1567. His father, a physician, was   *23*

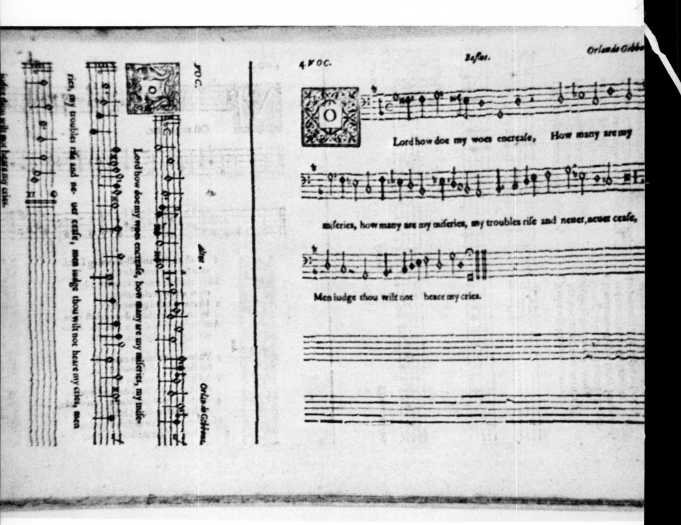

Musical composition by Orlando Gibbons, showing the four voice parts of a madrigal.

Lord how doe my woes encrease, how many are my miseries,

how many are my miseries, My troubles rise and neuer ceafe, and neuer

ceafe, men iudge thou wilt not heare my cries, men iudge thou wilt not

heare my cries.

Cantus. Orlando Gibbons.

Lord how doe my woes encrease, how many are my miferies, my miferies,

my troubles rife and neuer ceafe, Men iudge thou wilt not heare my cries, Men iudge

thou wilt not heare my cries.

a devotee of the arts who raised his family in a cultured household. He encouraged Monteverdi's bent for music. The boy received his musical training from one of the most reputable musicians in Cremona: Marc Antonio Ingegneri, a theorist and composer as well as the organist and chorus master at the Cathedral of Cremona. Young Monteverdi sang in his choir.

Monteverdi was unusually precocious as a composer. When he was fifteen he published his first volume of music, three-voice motets. A volume of canzonettas for three voices followed in 1584, and his first volume of madrigals in 1587. Beyond this work, almost nothing is known about his boyhood.

He first revealed his lifelong concern for musical tone painting in his second volume of madrigals (1590). In "Ecco mormorar l'onde," to a pastoral poem by Torquato Tasso, Monteverdi used various musical motives to portray dawn, the murmur of breezes, the rustle of leaves, and the gentle lapping of waves. He worked out these various motives with consummate contrapuntal skill.

This second volume of madrigals was dedicated to Senator Ricardi, through whose influence Monteverdi tried, but failed, to get a musical post in Milan. But another appointment soon came along at the court of Vincenzo Gonzaga, the duke of Mantua. There Monteverdi was given the humble, poorly paid post of violist in the court orchestra. But the job also offered some rewarding benefits. The duke modeled himself after the great Italian patrons of the Renaissance. He encouraged the arts and spent immense sums to build a cultural center in Mantua, which provided the young Monteverdi with considerable intellectual stimulation. Besides, the duke took Monteverdi with him on his travels to Hungary in 1595 and Flanders in 1599, enabling Monteverdi to become acquainted with the musical art of those regions.

While thus employed at the Mantua court, where he remained almost a dozen years, Monteverdi published his third volume of madrigals (1592), in which the voice of the rebel sounds loud and clear. Discords are used to portray anguish, angular melodic lines to create tension. More than before, Monteverdi indulges in musical imagery.

In 1595 Monteverdi married Claudia Cattaneo, a singer at the Mantuan court. Their union ended tragically with her sudden death twelve years later, but not before she had given birth to two sons.

In or about 1602 Monteverdi was promoted to the office of maestro di cappella at the ducal palace in Mantua. His salary was still meager and, worse still, it was not always easily collected. On one occasion he engaged the treasurer at court in a fight for the wages due him. Further adding to Monteverdi's distress was the fact that his employer showered him with more assignments than Monteverdi felt he could handle. More than once the unpleasantness of his life at Mantua induced melancholia, but all this did not interfere with his creativity. Two more volumes of madrigals appeared, in 1603 and 1605, each more remarkable than the other in the way new harmonic resources were tapped and structure was extended. Monteverdi's concern for his texts and his need to find the musical tones best able to interpret the words had by now become increasingly sensitive. In the preface to the fifth volume of his madrigals (1605) he explained how he had made a conscious effort to achieve a new style (*stile moderno*) by allowing his music to interpret the text, as opposed to the older style (*stile antico*) in which the composer was solely concerned with his polyphonic skill. Again and again, special effects were realized through ornaments, chromatic changes, and unexpected harmonies. "The fact is," Henri Prunières, the eminent French musicologist, has said, "he was constructing a new . . . language that threatened the foundations of polyphony by the introduction of a dramatic and personal sentiment."

Monteverdi first invaded what was for him a new arena—that of opera—with *La Favola d'Orfeo,* which we mentioned before. As long as he lived, Monteverdi kept on writing operas, a medium that was immeasurably advanced and enriched through his genius of musical expression. But he never deserted the madrigal. After becoming maestro di cappella at the Cathedral of San Marco in Venice in 1613—where he remained until the end of his life—Monteverdi published three more books of madrigals—in 1614, 1619, and 1638 respectively. Three laments find Monteverdi at the peak of his genius: the "Lamento d'Arianna" ("Lament of Arianna") and the "Lagrime d'amante" ("Tears of a Lover") in the sixth book (1614), and the "Lamento della Ninfa" ("Lament of the Nymph") in the eighth (1638).

The first is an adaptation of a lament for solo female voice ("Lasciatemi morire") in which the heroine grieves at being deserted by her lover. Monteverdi wrote it in 1608 for an opera, *Arianna,* of which the entire score (except for the lament) has been lost. In 1614 he used this poignant air as the basis of four deeply moving five-voice madrigals.

"Lagrime d'amante," the tears of a lover at the tomb of his beloved— a series of six madrigals—is one of the most inspired threnodies in early polyphonic literature. (A threnody is a song of lamentation for the dead.) In "Lamento della Ninfa," a soprano solo and three male voices sing

27

about the nymph Amor, who is wandering about in a meadow bemoaning her sad fate. Four descending notes in the bass, recurring throughout the composition, express the utter desolation of the nymph.

Thus, like Michelangelo, Monteverdi grew artistically profounder and more original with old age. His hand never lost its skill. His imagination continued to wander into formerly unexplored fields. His vocal writing continually gained in richness, beauty, and emotion. In his eighth book of madrigals he thoroughly explored all the artistic possibilities of the madrigal.

Aware that his life was drawing to a close, Monteverdi took a leave of absence from the Cathedral of San Marco in 1643 to revisit the cities where he had spent his earlier years. He was gone six months, spending much of that time in Mantua and Cremona. In the fall of 1643 he was back in Venice. There he was taken ill on November 20, and nine days later he died. "The news of such a loss upset and turned all the city to sadness and mourning," wrote Camberlotti in an obituary, "and was accompanied, not by singing from the choir of singers of St. Mark's, but by their tears and weeping." Funeral services were held in two churches—San Marco and Santa Maria dei Frari. Monteverdi was then buried in the mortuary of Sant' Ambrogio.

It can be said with justification that when Monteverdi died, the madrigal, as a significant form of vocal music, died with him.

Baroque Grandeur

George Frideric Handel,
Johann Sebastian Bach

The years from 1600 to about 1750 comprise the Baroque era in music. The birth of opera and the madrigals of Monteverdi usher in an age of vocal masterpieces that ended with the deaths of Johann Sebastian Bach and George Frideric Handel.

In architecture, "Baroque" referred to the grandiose, heavily ornamented structures then so much in vogue, particularly palaces and churches. The buildings designed by architect Giovanni Lorenzo Bernini (1598–1680) are masterpieces of that style. Music borrowed the term "Baroque" to identify older polyphonic forms that were greatly extended and amplified in the seventeenth and early eighteenth centuries, and also those new large forms which then became prominent and required the services of not only a chorus but also solo voices and an orchestra. Of these newer forms, the most significant was the oratorio.

In the closing years of the sixteenth century, Filippo de' Neri, founder of the congregation of the Oratorians, which met in a building in Rome called the Oratorio, felt the need to bring the Bible closer to young people. He asked composers to write music for parts of it, the text and the music to be presented in the Oratorio after the sermon. These biblical settings—

fragments set in the monotonous musical style of the plainchant—were first called "laude." The congregation soon got into the habit of referring to laude as oratorios after the building in which they were performed.

Laude were not oratorios in the Handelian sense, but their ancestor. The Baroque oratorio began with Giacomo Carissimi (1605–74). He used extended dramatizations of biblical or other sacred texts for musical settings for solo voices, chorus, and orchestra. His masterwork, *Jephte* (c. 1650) is looked upon now as the first "modern" oratorio—in other words, the first that comes closest to resembling a work by Bach or Handel. For the first time dramatic and lyric writing is stressed within this format. In the texts the story was told mostly in the recitatives. The recitative, sung by a narrator, allows the dramatic action to progress while the chorus becomes a commentator on what is happening. Melodic and emotional interest are localized in arias and duets.

With the style and structure of the oratorio now established, several composers formed the transition from Carissimi to the greatest of all oratorio composers, Handel. Among Handel's predecessors were the following: Alessandro Scarlatti (1660–1725) in Italy; Heinrich Schütz (1585–1672), whose *Seven Words from the Cross* (1645) is the first important oratorio written in Germany; and Johann Sebastian Bach, whose *Christmas Oratorio* (1734) and *Easter Oratorio* (c. 1736) are among the most significant such works before Handel.

It was through Carissimi that Handel first came to write oratorios. During the first decade of the eighteenth century, Handel, then in his early twenties, was traveling in Italy, where he heard and was deeply impressed by Carissimi's oratorios. Handel decided to turn his hand to the writing of religious music in the manner of Carissimi because he was unable to get a hearing for his operas in Rome. His first oratorio, *La Resurrezione,* had its successful premiere at the Palazzo Bonelli in Rome on April 8, 1708.

But not until late in his life as an Englishman did Handel turn the full force of his genius to the oratorio. He was led to do this because his former huge success as an opera composer had gone into a sharp decline in England. Convinced, and with justification, that his day as an opera composer was over, he came to the wise decision that if he were ever again to recoup his former triumphs it would have to be in another branch of music. He chose the oratorio. A series of masterworks representing the greatest epoch in the history of the oratorio now left his pen. It is for his oratorios—far more than for his operas or instrumental works—that we today honor Handel as one of music's immortals.

As if by some careful design of fate, the two supreme figures of vocal

Baroque music—Handel and Bach—were born in the same country and in the same year: in Germany in 1685. Handel was born in Halle on February 23. His father was a barber who combined this profession with that of surgeon, a dual profession practiced by many in those days. A highly practical man, with a healthy respect for money, the father was bent on having his son George become a lawyer, even though the boy had always revealed an unusual gift for music. In a studied effort to keep the boy from the "disaster" of becoming a professional musician, the father did whatever he could to keep his son away from music. Little George had to sneak up into the garret of his house every night to practice as quietly as possible on the old spinet stored there.

Since Handel's father was the surgeon of the court in Weissenfels, he had to make frequent trips to that German town. On several occasions he took George with him. The child was only seven when, on one of those trips, he tried out the chapel organ at the ducal court. The duke was so impressed by this performance that he showered the child with gold and persuaded the father to permit the boy to take music lessons. Thus it was that Handel, while pursuing his academic education at grammar school, was finally able to study music—with Zachau, organist of one of the principal churches in Halle. For three years, beginning in 1693, Handel received a solid training in violin, harpsichord, and oboe, as well as in harmony and counterpoint. In 1696 Zachau told the eleven-year-old boy that he was fully equipped to begin his career both as instrumentalist and composer.

For a reason never explained, Handel now paid a visit to Berlin, where his performances on the harpsichord so impressed the Electress Sophia Charlotte that she offered to finance a trip to Italy for Handel so that he might study Italian music at first hand. His father, still insistent upon Handel becoming a lawyer, refused to grant permission. A year later Handel's father died, leaving Handel completely free to chart his own course. He now accepted a post as assistant organist at the Halle Cathedral and began composing music in earnest. Some of his motets were sung at the cathedral during the Sunday services.

Probably out of respect for his father's memory, Handel entered the University of Halle in 1702 for the study of law. He followed two directions simultaneously—law and music—by assuming the office of first organist at the cathedral. But after one year at the university, Handel abandoned law for good to pursue his career in music more actively. At that time, Hamburg was a vital center of music-making, largely through the distinction of its opera house, directed by Reinhard Keiser. Since Handel felt that he could advance himself professionally in Hamburg, he went to that German city in 1703 and joined the opera-house orchestra as violinist.

Hardly had he taken on this job when he learned that Dietrich Buxtehude, then one of the most renowned composers and organists in Germany, was planning to relinquish his organ post at Saint Mary's Church in Lübeck. Handel paid a hurried visit to that city to compete for this desirable post. He gave such an outstanding exhibition of organ virtuosity that his acceptance was assured. Unfortunately, the rules in Lübeck specified that each new organist at Saint Mary's was required to marry the daughter of his predecessor. Handel discreetly withdrew from the competition and went back to Hamburg. (Two years later, young Johann Sebastian Bach turned down this post in Lübeck for the same reason.)

In 1704, during a performance of *Cleopatra,* an opera by the official harpsichordist of the Hamburg Opera, Johann Mattheson, Handel was asked to play the harpsichord while the composer appeared on the stage in the role of Antony. Since Antony dies early in the opera, Mattheson returned to the orchestra to take his place at the harpsichord, which Handel stubbornly refused to relinquish. This defiant act so enraged Mattheson that he challenged Handel to a duel. But for a button on Handel's coat, the career of this master might have ended even before it began. Mattheson's sword aimed at Handel's heart but split in two when it pierced the button—ending the duel then and there without inflicting any wound on Handel.

Handel's first opera, *Almira,* was produced by the Hamburg Opera early in 1705. It was a huge success, and so was his second, *Nero,* performed only seven weeks later. But Hamburg was a hotbed of rivalries, cabals, and jealousies. Handel's growing popularity as an opera composer did not endear him to Keiser, the director of the opera house, himself a prolific opera composer who did not take lightly such serious competition to his fame and position. He made Handel's life so miserable that Handel decided at long last to visit Italy.

Handel arrived in Florence late in 1706. There he played the harpsichord at the palace of Ferdinando de' Medici, and soon he produced a new opera, *Rodrigo.* He also completed some church music in the style of such Italian masters as Alessandro Scarlatti and Carissimi. In Rome, he wrote and had performed his first two oratorios, the second one (*Il Trionfo del tempo e del disinganno*) coming soon after *La Resurrezione.*

In 1710 Handel was appointed Kapellmeister to the court of the elector of Hanover. Since this post allowed him to make intermittent trips, Handel was able, soon after his installation, to go to England for the first time.

It did not take Handel long to establish his reputation in England as an opera composer. *Rinaldo,* first produced at the Queen's Theatre on February 24, 1711, was a giant success. A year or so later, Handel returned to England to supervise the production of several more of his operas. He lingered on longer than his leave from Hanover allowed. Meanwhile, his employer—the elector—was elevated to the throne of England as George I. Though originally annoyed by Handel's long absence from the Hanover court, the new king soon became reconciled with him and showered on him numerous royal favors, including a handsome annual pension. In 1727 Handel officially acquired British citizenship.

Handel's fluctuating fortunes from success to failure and back again to success belong to opera history and need not be detailed here. We need merely mention that few men of his generation soared so high and then plunged so low—not once but several times—both as a composer of operas and as an opera-house director. At one time he was acclaimed as the greatest opera composer in England, if not one of the greatest in the world. Then he saw fame and glory evaporate into mist. Initially, powerful enemies in England were the agents to drive him from the pinnacle to the lower depths. They hated him because he was a foreigner, and (it must be confessed) because he was boorish, tyrannical, hot-tempered, and foul of language. Those who hated him referred to him derisively as "the Bear" because of his huge frame and enormous hands and feet. As he grew older, he became more and more flabby, his jowls hanging loosely beneath a horselike face. His personal appearance was continually subjected to mockery.

With remarkable resilience, Handel lifted himself from the dust to scale mountains. Then he toppled again, destroyed not only by his extravagance in mounting his operas but also by the precipitous decline in their popularity. For even as an opera composer, Handel was his own worst enemy through his insistence on clinging to outmoded Italian patterns, formulas, and ritual of which his audience had grown weary.

Those of his enemies who gloated over this development did not reckon with his indomitable will, supreme self-control, and genius. It was true that as an opera composer he was through, though he continued writing for the stage until 1741. But his powerful creativity could not be permanently smothered; it merely had to be directed into another channel. He eventually found that channel in oratorio, a form he had more or less neglected for many years while focusing his gifts on opera and instrumental music.

After the two oratorios he had written in Rome in 1708, Handel did not   *33* return to this medium for another quarter of a century—and then only by chance. On February 23, 1732, to celebrate Handel's forty-seventh birthday, a private performance was staged at the Crown and Anchor Tavern in the Strand in London of his biblical production *Haman and Mordecai*, which he had written back in 1720 for performance at the private chapel of the duke of Chandos at Cannons. This London revival in 1732 was so well received that the work was repeated privately twice more at the tavern. This success inspired Handel to announce another staged production of *Haman and Mordecai*, this time for the general public, at His Majesty's Theatre. At this point the bishop of London stepped in and refused to allow the performance on the grounds that dramatizing a biblical subject with costumes and scenery was sacrilegious. Handel then revised his text so that he could present his work as an oratorio. Now renamed *Esther*, it was given publicly in London on May 2, 1732, with the royal family attending. London responded with such an outburst of enthusiasm that additional performances had to be given the same month.

Handel went on to write other oratorios with English texts, but still without altogether deserting opera. In 1733 came *Deborah* and *Athalia*. Then, for the next five years, Handel wrote no more such works. In that time he suffered one failure after another in the opera house. By 1738 he was faced with the grim reality that his operas had lost their audiences. Though he stubbornly continued writing operas for another three years (the last of which, *Deidamia*, was a disastrous failure in 1741), he showed increasing interest in the oratorio. His true greatness as an oratorio composer first became evident in 1739, with *Saul* and *Israel in Egypt*. *Saul* was written in just two months in 1738, and was a score in which Handel tapped new veins of tender lyricism (as in David's lament "In Sweetest Harmony") and power in writing for the chorus (the song of the Israelites "Welcome, Welcome, Mighty King"). The excerpt most frequently referred to from this music is the orchestral episode "Dead March," heard after Saul's death is announced. What is unusual about this instrumental elegy is that, unlike most such works, it is in the major key instead of the minor.

More glorious still is *Israel in Egypt*, on which Handel began to work only four days after finishing *Saul*. Swept by an irresistible momentum, Handel completed this monumental score in twenty-seven days. Haste, however, did not affect the quality of its inspiration. *Israel in Egypt* is one of Handel's mightiest oratorios.

Handel prepared his own text from those sections of the Bible dealing with the exodus of the Israelites from bondage in Egypt. Additional material was taken from the prayerbook version of the psalms. The oratorio begins without the preliminary of an overture. Instead, the narrator is heard in a recitative beginning with the line "Now there arose a new king over Egypt, which knew not Joseph." The narrator then serves as the agent to carry on the story line of Moses, as the deliverer of the Israelites; of the infliction by God of the ten plagues on the Egyptian people; and then of Moses as the leader of the Israelites as they leave Egypt, pass through the desert, cross the Red Sea, and approach the Promised Land. This narrative is continually interrupted by choral numbers, some of the latter of which have a stunning effect. The second part of this oratorio, called "Song of Moses," is a series of hymns to God and of songs of victory by the Israelites. Then the oratorio ends with a mighty eight-part chorus, "The Lord Shall Reign Forever and Ever."

With the sure brushstrokes of a master painter, Handel often creates the most vivid pictures. All the tools of his compositional trade are called upon to describe the ten plagues. But it is in his choral writing that he writes some of his most sublime music: "Sing Ye to the Lord" and "But as for His People, He Led Them Forth Like Sheep." The most popular episode of all, however, is the duet for two basses, "The Lord Is a Man of War."

Good as they are, neither *Saul* nor *Israel in Egypt* was in any way instrumental in effecting a change in Handel's then rapidly sinking fame. *Saul* was heard in London on January 16, 1739, and *Israel in Egypt* in the same city less than three months later. Both were received coolly. During this same period Handel's operas were faring even worse. By 1741 Handel stood ready to concede that his day—once blazing with the hot sun of triumph—was sinking into the chill of night. He was now a man broken in health, spirit, and finances.

Several times before this he had shown he could rise above crushing defeat to new victories. Sick and discouraged though he was in 1741, with his world around him seemingly crumbling, he was once again able to lift himself out of failure and despair, in fact to rise even higher than ever before. He did this by writing the greatest oratorio the world has known: the *Messiah*.

In 1741 Handel was invited to conduct one of his compositions for charity in Dublin, Ireland, where he was still held in high esteem. For this occasion, Handel proposed to write a new oratorio. Charles Jennens (who had previously prepared the text of *Saul*) wrote a script that took its material from the Bible, detailing the birth, suffering, and crucifixion of Christ. This subject stirred Handel as no other had done before. The moment he began to write the first measures, he became a man obsessed with a religious frenzy. He worked day and night, never leaving his house, refusing to see anybody but his servant, and frequently not even touching the food brought him. Often he worked right through the night. He seemed to be in a kind of spell or fever; his pen raced as if driven. Never had he known such exaltation and at times even fury. When he finished the last bar of the exultant "Hallelujah Chorus," he said, "I did think I did see all Heaven before me, and the great God himself." For twenty-four days and nights he labored this way. And then it was done. As Handel gathered the pages of his huge manuscript, his face lit up with a smile of satisfaction. He had completed his masterwork—and he knew it.

Dublin pulled out all stops in making the premiere of Handel's *Messiah* an occasion to remember. The city placed at his disposal the best singers and orchestral players that could be found. The Music Hall in Fishamble Street was completely sold out long before the first official presentation of the new oratorio, on April 13, 1742. People came with anticipation sharpened by the enormous publicity Handel and the *Messiah* had been receiving in the newspapers and by word of mouth. And that first-night audience was not disappointed. It underwent a rare spiritual as well as musical experience as one glorious section followed another.

"Words are wanting to express the exquisite delight it afforded," reported *Faulkner's Journal* about the *Messiah*. One Dublin music critic wrote: "The sublime, the grand, the tender, adapted to the most elevated, majestic and moving words, conspired to transport the ravished heart and ear."

One year later, on March 23, 1743, the *Messiah* was heard for the first time in London, with King George II himself present. He was so overwhelmed by the power and glory of the "Hallelujah Chorus" that, while it was being sung, he spontaneously rose to his feet and remained standing until it was over. One by one the members of the audience followed suit. It was on this occasion that a tradition was permanently established for the audience to stand throughout the "Hallelujah Chorus."

Since then, no oratorio—possibly no other musical work of similar dimensions—has been played more often and in more places. If even a modest royalty were paid each time the *Messiah* was given, it would have earned for its composer and his heirs over ten million dollars. Its universal fame through the years can easily be explained. Whether heard for the first time or for the twentieth, this is music that can melt a heart of stone with its compassion and radiance.

The fifty-odd numbers are divided into three sections. The first tells of the coming of the Messiah. In the second, the suffering and death of Christ are described. The subject of the third is the Resurrection.

The oratorio opens gently. After the overture, the tenor presents a tender recitative, "Comfort Ye," which becomes the preface for an ornamented melody, "Every Valley Shall Be Exalted." Then the chorus enters with a glowing song of praise, "And the Glory of the Lord." The majestic procession of recitatives, arias, a duet, and choruses follows without any slackening in the high inspiration. The mood changes from joy to overwhelming sorrow, from storm and stress to power, majesty, and religious fervor.

The glory of Handel's music does full justice to the glory of the Lord: in the touching aria for bass "But Who May Abide"; the wondrous chorus "For unto Us a Child Is Born"; the exquisite "Pastoral Symphony" for muted strings reverently portraying the Nativity; the affecting aria for alto "He Shall Feed His Flock." These are samplings from the first part. The second begins with a poignant chorus, "Behold the Lamb of God," and ends with the awesome "Hallelujah Chorus." In between we experience the overwhelming pathos of the alto aria "He Was Despised" and of the chorus "Surely He Hath Borne Our Griefs." In the concluding section, the beatific soprano aria "I Know That My Redeemer Liveth" sounds a new note of sublimity, while the closing chorus, "Worthy Is the Lamb," is a prayer that carries the oratorio to a blissful conclusion.

The writing of the *Messiah* helped to release a floodtide of creativity in Handel. One mighty oratorio succeeded another. Handel completed eleven after the *Messiah*, beginning with *Samson* (first performed in 1743) and ending with *Jephtha* (introduced in 1752). None of these eleven is another *Messiah*, to be sure, but each is a work of powerful imagination and invention. They are the source of some beloved arias and choruses: for example, the soprano aria "Let the Bright Seraphim" from *Samson* (1743); the tenor aria "Sound an Alarm," the chorus "See the Conquering Hero Comes," and the orchestral march from *Judas Maccabaeus* (1746); the orchestral sinfonia "Arrival of the Queen of Sheba" from *Solomon* (1748); and the tenor arias "Deeper and Deeper Still" and "Waft Her, Angels" from *Jephtha* (1751).

While working on his last oratorio, *Jephtha,* in 1751, Handel began experiencing the first symptoms of failing eyesight. When the condition worsened, he had to undergo three operations, which were unsuccessful. By 1753 he was totally blind. But not even total darkness could lay this giant low. He continued to give public performances both as organist and as conductor of his oratorios.

His last public appearance took place in London on April 6, 1759, in a performance of the *Messiah*. Midway he felt faint, but he continued to perform until the end of the work. Then he collapsed and had to be taken home and put to bed. He knew his end was near. "I should like to die on Good Friday," he whispered resignedly. His last wish was almost realized. He lingered on until the morning of Holy Saturday, on April 14, 1759. However, one other last wish could be carried out to the letter. He wanted to be buried in Westminster Abbey. There he now lies beneath a statue by Roubillac showing Handel standing with the score of the *Messiah* open in front of him with the following words clearly legible: "I know that my Redeemer liveth."

The amount of music Johann Sebastian Bach left behind him is as staggering as its quality. Somebody once estimated that it would take a copyist seventy years just to put down on paper all that Bach had written. When a Bach Society was formed in Germany in 1850 to collate and publish all of Bach's music, the project consumed fifty years and resulted in sixty volumes. Bach's own explanation for so prodigious an output was both simple and humble. "I worked hard," he said.

Hard indeed!—probably no composer ever worked harder. While piling up a mountain of manuscripts—so much of which contains some of the sublimest music ever conceived—he had to fulfill the exacting duties of a professional musician, which made excessive demands on his time and energy. He was also helping to raise a large family: seven children with his first wife, and thirteen with his second (though not all of the children survived infancy).

Music flowed from him, wave upon wave, like a measureless ocean. In retrospect we can only wonder that a man who was so extraordinarily gifted, and who produced so much, should have been so slighted by his employers, co-workers, and the general public. They all valued him as an organist—but that is about all. They tended to regard him and to treat him as if he were nothing more than a conscientious, hardworking musician who could always be counted upon to produce functional music for specific occasions. They saw him as a devout Lutheran who knew little save music and religion—something which, incidentally, happened to be true. Bach's intellectual horizon was so circumscribed that his reading experience did not extend far beyond the Bible. He traveled within a highly limited area and never outside Germany, and he spoke in an ungrammatical German and with poor diction. To most of those who rubbed elbows with him it was inconceivable that this plain man of limited intellectual attain-

George Frideric Handel.

A page from the manuscript of Handel's Judas Maccabaeus. *An autograph manuscript.*

Handel conducting a performance of one of his oratorios.

Johann Sebastian Bach.

The autograph title page of the Ascension Oratorio *of Johann Sebastian Bach.*

A page from Bach's Christmas Oratorio.
An autograph manuscript.

ments should be someone special. They surely would have been dumb- founded to learn that later generations would look upon him as the holy of holies in music, that many scholars and musicologists would consider him probably the most outstanding composer the world has known.

His musical genius branched out into all types of music except opera. Bach's orchestral and solo instrumental music is an enduring landmark. Yet if none of this other music survived, if Bach were today remembered exclusively for his choral music, he would still be one of the musical elect. In his Passions, masses, oratorios, motets, chorales, cantatas, and magnificats we possess music of incomparable majesty. Listening to it, we understand what Bach's eminent biographer Charles Sanford Terry meant when he wrote that Bach "saw the heavens opened and was prophetically oracular."

Bach brought polyphonic music and the Baroque tradition to their final stages of development. After Bach there *had* to come a new age in music—homophony and Classicism—because Bach had so completely exhausted the technical and artistic potentialities of the old age of polyphony.

Born in Eisenach, Germany, on March 21, 1685, Johann Sebastian early showed that he was a true and worthy Bach—the Bachs having produced highly esteemed professional musicians for generations. His father was his first music teacher. The child devoured his lessons as a starving man might food; his appetite for music seemed insatiable. Then, when his father died, Johann Sebastian, aged ten, was raised by his brother, who gave him a thorough musical training, especially in the playing of keyboard instruments, for which the boy showed unusual aptitude.

When he was fifteen, Johann Sebastian Bach sang in the chorus of Saint Michael's Church in Lüneburg. Four years later he filled his first important post as professional musician by becoming an organist in Arnstadt. In 1707 he occupied the organ chair at the Saint Blasius Church in Mühlhausen. This was the year in which he married his cousin, Maria Barbara Bach.

There ensued three major stages in Bach's professional growth. The first took place in Weimar, where, from 1708 to 1717, he was employed as organist and chamber musician at the ducal chapel. Some of his greatest organ compositions came to life during these years. The second stage, between 1717 and 1723, found Bach in Cöthen as chamber musician to Prince Leopold of Anhalt. This appointment required him to direct concerts of instrumental music for which he created many of his celebrated orchestral and solo instrumental compositions. (In Cöthen his wife, Maria

Barbara, died in 1720, and one year later Bach married Anna Magdalena Wülken.) Then came the last magnificent stage of his career, beginning in 1723 and ending with his death, as cantor at the Thomasschule in Leipzig. His many and varied duties included the writing of music for church services.

This Leipzig post was not an exalted one, certainly not one worthy of one of the greatest organists of his generation and a composer who for years had been shaking masterworks from his sleeve with incredible profusion. He had to write and direct music for two of Leipzig's leading churches, the Thomaskirche and the Nicolaikirche. He had to teach a boys' class in Latin and train singers and instrumentalists for the church services. Teaching proved a painful chore, since the boys were a poorly disciplined, unruly lot who made his life miserable. Bach's relationship with his employers (church officials and the town council) was no happier. Those in high places in Leipzig held him in contempt because they mistook his pride and idealism for arrogance, his indomitable will for stubbornness. They did what they could to humiliate him; at times they even tried to defraud him of income due him.

Nor was all this the sole source of Bach's grievances. The Thomasschule provided him with dark, cold, and disease-ridden lodgings. It is more than probable that the high mortality rate of his children was due to the unsatisfactory conditions in which they were raised; seven of Bach's ten children born in Leipzig died in childhood.

Such tragic circumstances would have stultified many a musician—but not Bach. Burdened though he was by overwork, dismayed by his living conditions, overwhelmed by the omnipresence of sickness and death in his own household, interminably harassed by employers and pupils, Bach nevertheless managed to complete a prodigious repertory of choral compositions: his beautiful cantatas and chorales; the Magnificat in D major; the *Passion According to Saint John* and the *Passion According to Saint Matthew;* the *Christmas* and *Easter* oratorios; the Mass in B minor. All this, in addition to a vast instrumental output of concertos, partitas, organ preludes and fugues, *The Musical Offering,* and *The Art of the Fugue.*

His genius made him invulnerable. "A Mighty Fortress Is Our God"—this is an adaptation by Martin Luther of the Forty-sixth Psalm, which Bach used as a theme both for an organ prelude and for a cantata. God *was* Bach's mighty fortress. But another mighty fortress was his genius, protecting his creative spirit from hostility, malice, pettiness, discouragement, and tragedy.

The first of his major church works that he directed in Leipzig was also his first setting to music of the suffering and crucifixion of Christ: the *Passion According to Saint John,* in 1723.

The design of the Passion that Bach adopted was one established by his eminent predecessor in Germany, Heinrich Schütz (1585–1672). Born in Köstritz, in Saxony, Germany, Schütz had received his principal training with Giovanni Gabrieli in Venice, where Schütz's first publication—a volume of madrigals—appeared in 1611. About a year later he returned to Germany. In 1617 he was made Kapellmeister at the electoral chapel in Dresden, and two years later he arrived at full maturity as composer of church music with *Psalmen Davids,* a book of psalms and motets. He then went on to write more psalms and motets, as well as other religious compositions for chorus that introduced some of the dramatic qualities of Italian music into German church music. In old age, Schütz completed an oratorio for Christmas and three settings of the Passion of Christ. In his Passions, Schütz used the narrator to tell the story in dramatized recitatives, had the chorus represent the crowd, and had Jesus, the Evangelist, and other religious figures connected with Christ's story speak for themselves in recitatives. But besides crystallizing the structure of the Passion for German composers, Schütz further developed the art of word setting and of pictorial writing and enhanced the ability of music to give voice to religious feeling. Thus Schütz became an all-important link between the choral music of the Renaissance and that of Bach.

In his *Passion According to Saint John* Bach used a text adapted from two chapters of the Gospel of Saint John relating the betrayal, arrest, crucifixion, death, and entombment of Christ. The Evangelist (tenor) serves as narrator. Recitatives are used for the Evangelist, Christ, Pontius Pilate, and Peter. But the score is dominated by sweeping choruses, such as the chorus's harrowing cry to crucify Christ (''Kreuzige!''), or its terrifying fanaticism in ''Wäre dieser nicht ein Übeltäter?'' Interspersed throughout the Passion are chorales, in the singing of which the congregation joined. The chorale was a hymn of the German Protestant Church; this form of hymn came into existence during the Reformation in the sixteenth century and was interpolated by Martin Luther into church services in order to encourage congregational singing. By Bach's time the chorale had become so well liked by the people that it was virtually the popular music of its time. Bach was the last and grandest composer of chorales. Besides introducing them in his Passions and church cantatas, he harmonized several hundred of them for church services. In the *Passion According to* 47

Saint John, solemnity and reverence are brought into the music through chorales, while profound emotion is embedded in such moving arias as one for contralto, "Es ist vollbracht," and one for bass, "Betrachte, meine Seele."

It is believed that Bach wrote four Passions in all, but only one other has survived, the *Passion According to Saint Matthew,* which took its text from the Gospel of Saint Matthew. Bach wrote it six years after completing the *Passion According to Saint John* and directed the first performance on April 15, 1729, in Leipzig.

The *Passion According to Saint Matthew* is the most spiritual, and structurally the most ambitious, of any Passion ever written. Where the *Saint John* emphasized both drama and the chorus, the *Saint Matthew* stressed religious and spiritual values in music for solo voices. One way in which Bach brought a more intense religious feeling to the *Saint Matthew* was to accompany the recitatives of Christ with strings. (Those in the *Saint John* had a background of chords in the keyboard instrument, as was then habitual with so-called "dry recitatives.") Another way in which Bach emphasized the spiritual over the dramatic is in the profusion of arias in which the suffering and tragedy of Christ becomes the main theme: in "Buss' und Reu' " for alto; "Blute nur" for soprano; "Erbarme dich" for alto with violin obbligato; and "Aus Liebe will mein Heiland sterben," also for soprano. The Passion ends on a note of surpassing pathos with the elegiac chorus "Wir setzen uns mit Tränen nieder."

The congregation hearing the *Passion According to Saint Matthew* for the first time was disturbed by some of Bach's pictorial writing. One of Bach's pupils recorded the reaction of the congregation as follows: "Some high officials and well-born ladies in one of the galleries began to sing the first chorale with great devotion from their books. But as the theatrical music proceeded, they were thrown into the greatest wonderment, saying to each other, 'What does it all mean?', while one lady exclaimed, 'God help us, 'tis surely an opera-comedy!' " Never again was the *Passion According to Saint Matthew* performed in Bach's lifetime; it had to wait a century to be heard again.

More grandiose still is Bach's mighty Mass in B minor. Two of its parts—the Kyrie and the Gloria—were completed in 1733. At that time Bach submitted them as "a trifling example of my skill" when, disgusted with conditions in Leipzig, he applied at the Saxon royal chapel for a post he did not get. Five years later he finished the other parts. Three sections (Kyrie, Credo, and Gloria) were heard in Frankfurt, Germany, between

1828 and 1831, and a condensed version of the mass was given by the Singakademie in Berlin in 1834. Not until April 24, 1861, was the complete mass given, performed by the Sternsche Gesangverein in Berlin.

The traditional five large sections of the Mass are in the Mass in B minor split into twenty-four parts: fifteen for chorus, the rest for solo voices. The Kyrie opens with a luminous four-measure introduction for full chorus and orchestra. After its main melodic subject has been elaborated upon by the orchestra, it evolves into a five-part choral fugue stretching for forty-three measures. The grandeur of this opening is sustained in the subsequent sections: the Gloria, Credo, Sanctus, and Agnus Dei. Tragedy darkens the pages of "Qui tollis peccata mundi," which is a section of the Gloria, and of the "Crucifixus," which is found in the Credo. A more personal note is introduced by solo voices in pages that range from pathos to spirituality: "Laudamus Te," for soprano accompanied by solo violin, in the Gloria section; the solo for baritone with obbligato of oboes, "Et in Spiritum Sanctum," within the Credo; the Benedictus, for tenor with solo-violin background; and the Agnus Dei, for contralto accompanied by the violins, which ends with that poignant plea for peace, "Dona nobis pacem." "We learn now," wrote Rosa Newmarch, the distinguished twentieth-century English musicologist, "if we have never learned before, the true meaning of the word 'sublime.' . . . As the music continues we hold our breath, marveling what can appropriately follow. . . . But Bach goes on from strength to strength."

The vast literature of church cantatas by Bach is as rich as it is varied. The cantata is actually a miniature oratorio, taking only from twelve to twenty minutes for performance. It is usually a work for solo voices, chorus, and orchestra, though some cantatas are for just one voice and orchestra. While a cantata does not boast a sustained narrative the way an oratorio does, it does have a unifying thought or idea, its text taken sometimes from the Bible, sometimes from the verses of hymns, and sometimes from a scriptural lesson. A cantata opens and closes with the chorus (whenever a chorus is employed), the concluding section being a chorale. In between we find recitatives, arias for solo voices, duets, instrumental numbers, and often chorales. Where a cantata is written exclusively for a solo voice and orchestra, the recitatives alternate with arias.

The cantata first comes into prominence with Giacomo Carissimi who favored writing in this format for the practical reason that small churches were incapable of summoning the large forces required for oratorios, nor was the time in which to perform such large works always available. *49*

Carissimi, consequently, wrote short and modest works retaining some of the features of the oratorio.

Bach wrote his cantatas for the Sunday and saints-day services. He completed almost three hundred such works, enough to fill the needs of a five-year church cycle; but about a hundred or so of these have been lost. The surviving two hundred are Bach music *in excelsis*. These cantatas (regrettable to say) are almost never given at concerts, but most have been recorded so that music lovers have had the opportunity to hear masterworks which, only a few decades back, were unknown territory even to sophisticated and knowledgeable concertgoers. Excerpts from the cantatas are undoubtedly more familiar than the complete cantatas themselves, however superb the rest of their music may be. These are among the most familiar parts of Bach's cantatas: the chorale "Jesu bleibet meine Freunde," which is surely better known to us by its English title, "Jesus, Joy of Man's Desiring," from *Herz und Mund und Tat und Leben* (1716); the beautiful tenor aria "Jesus Christus, Gottes Sohn," from *Christ lag in Todesbanden* (1724); the haunting sinfonia for strings and solo oboe from *Ich steh' mit einem Fuss im Grabe* (1730); the chorale "Gloria sei dir gesungen" from *Wachet auf* (1731); the soprano aria "Mein gläubiges Herz" from *Also hat Gott die Welt geliebt* (1735). Of the complete cantatas, besides those just mentioned, the most famous are *Aus der Tiefe* (1707), *Nun komm der Heiden Heiland* (1714), and two cantatas for solo voice and orchestra, *Jauchzet Gott in allen Landen,* for soprano (1731), and *Ich habe genug,* for bass (1731).

Bach wrote several more cantatas, this time for secular rather than church consumption. Since some of these have a story line, however slight, they have sometimes been staged—the closest Bach ever came to writing operas.

We never associate the name of Johann Sebastian Bach with humor, satire, or burlesque—do we? Yet in several of his secular cantatas he is both lighthearted and thoroughly witty. The *Coffee Cantata* ("Schweigt, stille, plaudert nicht"), written in 1732 for three voices (soprano, tenor, and baritone) and orchestra is almost a little comic opera. A tenor, merely an unidentified bystander, opens the work with an exhortation to the audience to be silent, to remain still, and not to applaud, but to listen to what has just occurred. He then goes on to reveal that Herr Schlendrian is a most unhappy man. Herr Schlendrian is then heard in a bass aria in which he complains that "children often are headaches." His problem is that his daughter, Lieschen, is addicted to coffee, which she stoutly refuses to give up in spite of her father's threats to deny her privileges. Their harangues are found in three duets, while, in an aria, Lieschen sings the praises of coffee, "which is choicer than ten thousand kisses." Only when her father refuses to allow her to get married is she willing to surrender coffee. But she is a wily sort and in the end manages to get not only a husband but coffee as well. The cantata closes with a trio that asks: If older folk are partial to coffee, why should not young girls be similarly inclined?

Throughout, the music is vivacious. This is equally true of two other secular cantatas rich with satirical overtones: *Phoebus and Pan* (*Der Streit zwischen Phöbus und Pan*) and the *Peasant Cantata* (*Mer hahn en neue Oberkeet*). The first—for solo voices, chorus, and orchestra—came in 1731. It is a retelling of an old Greek legend about a song contest between Phoebus Apollo and Pan. Bach uses another character, Midas, to satirize composers who favor writing ponderous scores for operas. In the end of this cantata the chorus sings the praises of simple music that brings joy to the hearts of gods and men.

Bach wrote the *Peasant Cantata* a decade later, in 1742, to a text celebrating the then recent appointment to the office of lord of the manor of a gentleman named Karl Heinrich von Dieskau. His duties entailed collecting various taxes. The cantata calls for only two characters, sung by soprano and bass. The opening instrumental sinfonia is made up of folk-dance melodies, beginning and ending with a Ländler, which was the predecessor of the waltz. This is followed by a duet for soprano and bass announcing that a new lord of the manor has been appointed. We next get a rather risqué interchange between these two, with the man trying to get the girl to kiss him, while the girl stoutly refuses on the ground that if she consents he would not stop with mere kissing. Some of the ensuing recitatives and arias make humorous comments on tax collecting. An exchange between bass and soprano describes the kind of man Dieskau is, while a recitative for bass gives us an insight into the personality of Dieskau's wife. A picture of the little town of which Dieskau is lord of the manor is found in an aria for soprano. After the concluding section expresses a wish that Dieskau and his wife might become the parents of "many fine sturdy sons, big and tall and stalwart," it urges the people to celebrate by drinking wine and dancing to the tunes of bagpipes in the town inn.

The *Wedding Cantata* (*Weichet nur, betrübte Schatten*), for soprano and orchestra (1720), has no plot at all and consequently does not lend itself to staging. The overall theme is a wedding. The cantata opens with a bucolic description of the vernal season. Four arias and four recitatives then speak about a wedding. The concluding section (in the style of a gavotte) wishes the young couple contentment and a good life.

Two of Bach's larger church works are identified as oratorios, but only one of them is more or less in oratorio form: the *Easter Oratorio,* for solo voices, chorus, and orchestra (1736). Here the story of the Resurrection unfolds in a series of recitatives, while emotion flows over into the arias. Two of the most tender arias are "Sanfte soll mein Todeskummer," a lullaby sung by Peter, and Mary Magdalene's aria, "Saget, saget mir geschwinde." The concluding section is a song of praise to God.

The other so-called oratorio by Bach is the *Christmas Oratorio,* for solo voices, chorus, and orchestra (1734). This is not an oratorio at all but the stringing together of six cantatas, each of which was intended for performance at one of the six church services between Christmas and Epiphany. The six cantatas were never performed as a single unit when Bach was alive. The Evangelist (tenor) binds the various arias, ariosos, and choruses together by relating through recitatives the story of Christ's birth as described in the Gospels of Saint Matthew and Saint Luke. One of the most memorable pages in this score is the gentle "Pastorale" (or "Shepherd's Music") for orchestra telling of Christ's birth. This lovely melody is repeated in the chorale that ends the "oratorio."

One other major choral work merits attention: the Magnificat in D major (1723). It uses a text from Saint Luke in which the Virgin Mary expresses delight upon learning from the angel that she will bear the Holy Child. Scored for solo voices, chorus, and orchestra, this magnificat (one of the greatest works in this genre) is in twelve sections made up of arias, a duet, a trio, and choruses. It was intended for performance at the Christmas service.

In about 1740 Bach began to have serious trouble with his eyes, which continued to worsen until he was virtually blind by 1749. Yet he never stopped composing. He worked on his last piece of music—a revision of eighteen choral preludes—just before his death. In 1750, at the age of sixty-five, he underwent an eye operation, which briefly restored his sight. But his general health had failed and Bach died in Leipzig on July 28, 1750.

Indicative of the low esteem with which Bach was regarded by his contemporaries is the fact that he was buried in an unidentified grave, in the churchyard of the Church of Saint John in Leipzig. More than a century later, the grave was finally discovered and identified. His remains were then placed in a sarcophagus and reburied beneath the church.

He was forgotten soon after his death. His music (of which only nine compositions had been published during his lifetime) was almost totally discarded. Not long after he was buried, a bundle of manuscripts of his cantatas sold for about forty dollars. Other manuscripts were used by local merchants as wrapping paper. The plates of his last masterwork, *The Art of the Fugue,* were sold for the price of the metal.

The shocking truth is that, upon his death, Bach was regarded as a "has-been." Most musicians, including Bach's own children, looked upon him as an exponent of the then dying Baroque era that had emphasized polyphony. To them Bach was a composer who had been made obsolete by the new age of homophony and Classicism. For many years, then, Bach's music was rarely performed, and his manuscripts were left unpublished. Whenever the name of Bach was mentioned, the man referred to was invariably one of Bach's sons, each of whom was a voice of early Classicism.

However little of Bach's music was available, some of it somehow managed to reach and to impress several farsighted musicians, including Mozart, Beethoven, Schumann, and Mendelssohn. Mendelssohn was the first to initiate a movement to revive Bach's long-neglected music. On March 11, 1829, when he was twenty, Mendelssohn conducted in Berlin the first performance of the *Passion According to Saint Matthew* since Bach's own time. To the attending audience, which knew so little about Bach or his music, the grandeur of this Passion came as a revelation. "Everyone was filled with the most solemn devotion," reported Mendelssohn in a letter to his sister. "One heard only an occasional involuntary ejaculation that sprang from deep emotion." Eduard Devrient, one of the performers that evening, remarked, "I felt that the thrill of devotion that ran through me at the most impressive passages was also felt by the hearers who listened in deadly silence." So enthusiastic was the response of the audience that Mendelssohn was encouraged to give the work a second performance.

In 1850 the Bach Gesellschaft was formed to publish all of Bach's compositions. By the time this giant project was consummated half a century later, Bach's towering greatness had become universally accepted. As more and more of Bach's works were played, the world stood ready and willing to agree with Robert Schumann, who had said that "music owes as much to Bach as religion to its founder."

4

The Triumvirate
of Classicism

Joseph Haydn,

Wolfgang Amadeus Mozart,

Ludwig van Beethoven

When, after the death of Johann Sebastian Bach, music passed from the Baroque to the Classical era, it experienced major changes. No longer was the church the focal point of musical activity. Attention had shifted to the opera house, the glittering salons in palaces, and the public auditorium. Composers became more interested in instrumental and operatic music than in choral music, more in the homophonic style than in the polyphonic. Classicism produced music that was graceful, clearly written, and elegant. Classical music fits into established forms and rules. Symmetry and balance are emphasized; emotion becomes subservient to controlled precision of design and style.

Nevertheless, some of the major forms of polyphonic music managed to survive, notably the cantata, the mass, and the requiem. Choral music was still being written within those structures, utilizing contrapuntal techniques. However much Haydn, Mozart, and Beethoven—that majestic triumvirate which dominated the Classical age—favored instrumental forms, they did not altogether neglect choral writing. Though most of their choral music is religious, a good deal of it was intended for secular performance.

Though Joseph Haydn (1732–1809) made his mark in music history as

one of the earliest masters of the symphony, string quartet, and piano sonata, he wrote a number of highly important choral compositions. He had
been well grounded in the religious music of the Baroque era. Born in
Rohrau, in Lower Austria, near the Hungarian border, Haydn spent his
boyhood years in Vienna at Saint Stephen's Cathedral, where, from about
1741 to 1749, he attended choir school and sang in its boys' choir. Religious music, then, was a potent influence during his formative years. In
1749, the breaking of his voice led to his dismissal from Saint Stephen's.
Left adrift in Vienna to make his way as best he could, Haydn was compelled to perform menial musical tasks to support himself, while at the
same time working long and hard on his music study. Even then he knew
that as a composer his destiny lay not in the Baroque music in which he
had been trained at Saint Stephen's but in the new Classical tradition that
was in its infancy. And so, as an employee in the musical establishment at
the palace of Baron Karl von Fürnberg, he wrote his first string quartet in
1755. Then, as music director and chamber composer for Count Max-
imilian von Morzin he completed his first concerto, his first symphony,
and his first piano sonata, all in or about 1760. While thus beginning to
face the future in music, he occasionally looked backward, too, by writing
a few religious choral works in the Baroque style, including a mass in
1750.

In 1761 Haydn became the second Kapellmeister to Prince Paul Anton
Esterházy in Eisenstadt. The prince died in little more than a year and was
succeeded by his brother Nicolaus Joseph. Haydn remained in the employ
of Prince Nicolaus for almost thirty years, rising to the post of full Kapellmeister in 1766. These were the years when Haydn's genius as instrumental composer made him the most celebrated composer of his generation and
one of the foremost exponents of musical Classicism. In those three decades, however, he did not desert religious choral music. But it was only
very late in his life—and only after he had left his post with the Esterházy
family in 1790—that he fulfilled himself in choral music as completely as
he had previously done in instrumental music.

By 1790 he had become a supreme symphonist, as he was once again
to prove decisively in 1791 and 1794 by writing a dozen new symphonies
for London, six in each year. He himself conducted them. To the Baroque
forms of the mass and the oratorio he was now also to bring that dramatic
power, that intensity of expression, that resourcefulness of technique, and
that originality of thought which had long since characterized his instrumental compositions. And though most of his late masses and his two
oratorios—all children of his old age—were not intended for church but   *55*

for secular performance, he carried over into his choral writing the profound convictions and the pious sentiments of a dedicated Catholic.

He was a deeply religious man who always began his manuscripts with the phrase "In nomine Domini" ("In the name of the Lord") and ended them with "Laus Deo" ("For the glory of God"). During the composition of *The Creation* he fell on his knees early each morning in prayer to God and the Holy Virgin that "I may succeed again today." He ended an autobiographical sketch with the following words: "I offer up to Almighty God all eulogiums [praises], for to Him alone do I owe them. My sole wish is neither to offend against my neighbor nor my gracious Prince but above all not against our merciful God." Once, when rebuked for including comparatively light music within a serious religious work, he replied, "I cannot help it. I give forth that which is in me. When I think of the Divine Being, my heart is so full of joy that the notes fly off from a spindle, and as I have a cheerful heart He will pardon me if I service Him cheerfully." To a man as religious as this, a religious text—even if intended for secular use—always inspired profound emotions.

Haydn's greatest masses came at the dusk of his life, between 1796 and 1802. The invasion of Austria by Napoleon's French army was the stimulant for the writing of the *Missa in tempore belli* (*Mass in Time of War*) in 1796. This work is also sometimes called *Paukenmesse* (*Drum Mass*) because of the prominence of the tympani in the Agnus Dei section. A quotation of a famous German hymn, "Heilig, Heilig," in the Sanctus is why the *Heiligmesse* (1796) is so called. *Nelson-Messe* or *Nelson* Mass (1798) got its name from the blare of the trumpets in the Benedictus, an effect interpreted as a proclamation of the victory of Admiral Nelson at the Battle of the Nile. *Theresienmesse* (1799) was probably named after Empress Maria Theresa of Austria. The title of *Harmonienmesse,* or *Harmony* Mass (1802) comes from its rich orchestral sonorities.

In each of these masses Haydn combined outstanding skill in contrapuntal writing with his command of orchestration. Religious sentiment is joined with dramatic power, emotional intensity with radiant spirituality.

Haydn wrote only two oratorios. Both were among his last works, and both have become classics in choral music.

He first became imbued with the ambition to write an oratorio in 1791 in London, where his lifelong admiration for Handel was further nurtured through the hearing of several of Handel's oratorios. From then on he knew he would find neither peace nor rest unless he channeled his deep religious feeling into the form that Handel had elevated to such a pinnacle of greatness. It was some years, however, before Haydn went to work on his first oratorio. He was driven to his work table by an excellent text, *Die Schöpfung (The Creation)*, which was believed to have been originally prepared for Handel, who was not interested in it. The text told the story of the Creation—parts taken from Genesis in the Bible, and parts from Milton's *Paradise Lost*. To set the story of the Creation to music became for Haydn an exciting spiritual as well as artistic adventure. "I felt myself so penetrated with religious feeling," he revealed, "that before I sat down to the piano, I prayed to God with earnestness that He would enable me to praise Him worthily."

When in his mid-sixties, Haydn finally realized his ambition to write a Handelian oratorio. Indeed, *The Creation* is the greatest oratorio since Handel. But there is more of Haydn in this music than of Handel: Haydn in the daring harmonies and exciting dynamics; Haydn in the breadth and scope of the orchestration; Haydn in the vividness of the tone painting. The orchestral opening is something that would have been inconceivable during the Baroque era. It is something of a tone poem about the Creation, as chaos is resolved into order and darkness is dissipated by light. Then, after a recitative by the baritone, the chorus raises its voice in the resplendent music of "And the Spirit of God." In that chorus, as the words tell us of light invading a dark world in "and there was light," Haydn hurls the thunderbolts of piercing chords whose effect is as startling and magnetizing as the sudden outburst of blazing light they describe. "It was not I but a Power above who created that," Haydn said. This same telling realism pervades the three-part score as Haydn uses every resource at his command to describe thunder and lightning, rain and snow. But however noteworthy are the theatricalism and pictorialism, it is Haydn's glorious lyricism that is most unforgettable. One of the most famous arias is that for soprano, "With Verdure Clad," whose gentle rustic beauty comes as a relief from the tensions that preceded it. It is found in the first part of the oratorio, a part that also includes the majestic chorus "The Heavens Are Telling."

The second part describes animals coming to life, their voices recreated in descriptive music. After a recitative, we hear the delicate cooing of pigeons in violins and bassoons as the accompaniment to the soprano melody, "On Mighty Pinions." Equally picturesque is the way the fructification of the earth is suggested by divided violas, cellos, and double basses accompanying the recitative "Be Fruitful and Multiply." The tenor tells of the wonder of the creation of the first man and woman in the deservedly celebrated air "In Native Worth."

Adam (bass) and Eve (soprano) are heard in the concluding part of the oratorio. Their love duets, "Sweet Wife, Dear Husband" and "With Thee   *57*

Every Joy Is Heightened,'' are among the most glorious pages Haydn ever wrote for the voice.

Haydn himself conducted the first public performance of *The Creation* at the Burgtheater in Vienna on March 19, 1799. The audience was shaken with emotion throughout the performance, at the end of which outcries of approbation were heard. But nobody was more deeply moved than Haydn. ''Sometimes my whole body was ice cold and sometimes I was overcome with burning fever,'' he confessed. ''More than once I was afraid that I should suddenly suffer a stroke.''

Haydn's last oratorio was a far different work from *The Creation*. Where *The Creation* had been the music of a pious Catholic in awe at the miracle of the Creation, its successor—*Die Jahreszeiten (The Seasons)*—is the voice of a man in love with nature. Haydn completed it in 1801. Its first public performance—in Vienna on May 29, 1801—was a triumph. Using a poem by James Thomson, whose paean to the glories of nature anticipated the Romantic poems that followed, Haydn sang about the wonder and beauty of the four seasons, beginning with spring. Springtime is hailed in the chorus for peasants ''Come, Gentle Spring,'' which is followed by a bucolic air, ''With Joy th' Impatient Husbandman.'' (In this air Haydn quotes a passage from the slow movement of his *Surprise* Symphony.) With strong strokes of the brush, Haydn then paints the beauty of the countryside drenched with springtime rain, of the lambs playing in the fields, of the buzzing of bees and the murmur of brooks, of the play of the fish in the sea, and the flight of birds in the air. Summer gives Haydn further opportunities for tone painting, particularly in a section depicting a thunderstorm. In the section about autumn Haydn calls forth pictures of a harvest and a stag hunt. Winter leads him to write melancholy music, for to Haydn wintertime was a symbol for old age. But in the closing part of the oratorio, optimism replaces regret and sorrow. The closing chorus, ''Let Our Labours Still Unwearied to That Glory Only Lead,'' is an exultant affirmation of the glory of God and the miracle of nature.

Haydn's last appearance as conductor took place in Vienna on December 26, 1803, in a performance of his *Seven Last Words of the Saviour on the Cross*. This was a work he had written in 1785 for the Cádiz Cathedral in Spain for performance during Lent. After his Vienna appearance in 1803, he withdrew into seclusion at his house in a suburb of Vienna. His faculties now began to fail him—first his hearing, then his speech, and after that his memory. Feeble though he became, he nevertheless was able to be present at a performance of *The Creation* in Vienna on March 27, 1808, when he had to be carried into the auditorium in an armchair. Seeing the audience springing to its feet to do him homage, Haydn was unable to control his tears.

Not long before his death, Haydn was visited by a French officer from Napoleon's army, which was then invading Vienna. He had come to pay the master his respects. When the visitor sat down at the piano and sang the opening passage of "In Native Worth" from *The Creation,* Haydn embraced the officer. He said, "God bless you my son! You have made me very happy today."

The best arias in Haydn's masses, oratorios, and operas prove that he had a skillful hand in shaping melodies for the voice. After all, as a young man struggling to make his way as a musician, he had worked as house servant and piano accompanist for Niccolò Porpora, one of the most famous singing masters in Vienna, in return for singing lessons. Haydn's spongelike capacity to absorb musical knowledge enabled him to master the art of vocal music, a lesson that he continually put to use in later years.

Though the writing of songs for solo voice and piano was not an activity engaging the prime interest of the composers of the Classical period, Haydn did write a few songs. His best-known one is "My Mother Bids Me Bind My Hair." This is one of twelve songs (or, as Haydn labeled them, canzonettas), gathered into two sets of six each, which Haydn completed in London in 1794–95. With one or two exceptions, the poems used by Haydn in this series are not distinguished; Haydn was never a connoisseur of poetry. "My Mother Bids Me Bind My Hair" is characteristic of these numbers, and characteristic of Haydn's song-writing ability. The melody is ingratiating and neatly molded; the accompaniment is discreet and formal. It cannot be said that in this department Haydn had profited from the songs of Mozart in giving the piano part an individuality of its own or in having the melody respond to the demands of the text. Nevertheless, "My Mother Bids Me Bind My Hair" still makes for pleasurable listening; and so does another song in these sets, "She Never Told Her Love," a setting of a verse from Shakespeare's *Twelfth Night.*

Far more often remembered than any of these concert songs is the melody Haydn wrote as an Austrian national anthem, "Gott erhalte Franz den Kaiser" ("May God Protect Franz the Emperor"). Feeling the need of a strong stimulus with which to arouse the patriotism of the Austrian people, the Austrian minister of the interior asked Haydn to write a patriotic song. Keeping in mind the British anthem "God Save the King," Haydn complied with "Gott erhalte," to the words of a German poet, Haschka. On February 12, 1797, it was sung in every theater in Austria on the occasion of the emperor's birthday. In gratitude, the emperor told Haydn, "You have expressed what is in every loyal heart. Through your melody Austria will always be honored.'' From then on until 1918 it served as the Austrian national anthem and subsequently—to the words, ''Deutschland, Deutschland über alles''—it was also used similarly for many years in Germany. Haydn loved this melody so much that he used it as the theme for variations in the slow movement of his String Quartet in C major, op. 76 no. 3 (1797), which, for this reason, has come to be known as the *Emperor* Quartet.

There was no composer of his time Haydn admired more than Wolfgang Amadeus Mozart (1756–91). Mozart—born in Salzburg, Austria—was almost a quarter of a century younger than Haydn. He had learned much from the older man about Classical structure, the sonata form, and the *galant* style (the *galant* style being an elegant, aristocratic manner of fashioning music favored during the Classical era). Haydn had proved to be the beacon light to illuminate for Mozart his direction during his formative years. But once he had learned his lessons from Haydn, Mozart had to think and write only as his own conscience and intuition dictated. Always he had to find new techniques, idioms, and methods with which to enhance the poetic, dramatic, or emotional nuances of his music. Now it was Haydn's turn to learn from his much younger and far less famous colleague: how to mold musical conventions to his own artistic specifications; how to achieve an exquisite balance between structure and content; how to heighten and extend the articulateness of music through unconventional harmonies and modulations; how to introduce surprise through unexpected procedures; how to convey every possible shade of human feeling; and how to vary and expand musical thought through thematic development and transformation. All this, which could be found in Mozart's music, had an overpowering effect on Haydn. By studying Mozart, he was able late in his life to open up for himself new artistic horizons. The reason why Haydn's last symphonies, quartets, and choral compositions have the kind of breadth, scope, dimension, and profundity they possess is that Haydn had come to understand, appreciate, and emulate Mozart so well.

There was no medium in music that Mozart did not touch with magic. This was true of his religious music, to which, too, he brought his extraordinary musical sophistication. Though raised in a strict Catholic household, and though long employed at musical tasks in the archbishop's palace in Salzburg, where he was further subjected to religious influences, Mozart did not have the deeply confirmed religious convictions of a Bach or Haydn. Yet, because of his powers of imagination, his religious music is nonetheless filled with a beatific spirit that at times is breathtaking.

Because of his religious upbringing and his affiliations, Mozart began to write religious music early. As the amazing child whose musical endowments inspired the wonder of all Europe, he had written several short choral works between his tenth and twelfth years. When he was twelve he completed two short masses. (*Missa brevis* is the official designation for these simpler masses, a missa brevis being less pretentious in ceremonial form and less demanding in musical technique than a full mass and used for less formal church services.) When he was thirteen, Mozart completed a full-length mass. He continued producing religious compositions thereafter, including some during his triumphant visit to Italy between 1769 and 1771, when honor after honor was heaped upon him.

During a return to Italy in 1773, Mozart wrote a motet for soprano and orchestra, *Exsultate, jubilate,* K. 165. This is a three-part composition. The last section is so famous that it is often performed separately, jubilant music whose entire text consists of the single word *Alleluia.*

(The letter *K* with a number following it identifies Mozart's compositions and places each one in proper chronological sequence. *K* stands for *Köchel,* and the number represents the place of the composition in the official catalog of Mozart's compositions that Ludwig von Köchel, a Viennese musicologist, compiled and had published in 1862.)

Back in his native Salzburg in 1773, Mozart soon discovered to his distress the wisdom of the biblical adage that a prophet is not without honor except in his own country. The archbishop of Salzburg, who employed him, was a proud, overbearing, intolerant man. In matters concerning music he was both uninformed and unperceptive. Toward Mozart he behaved with the cold-blooded brutality of a feudal lord. For the next few years Mozart suffered abuse and insult at his hands. However much the world outside Salzburg might acclaim Mozart's genius, to the archbishop he was still a little scrub of talent to be treated no better than a footman or a valet. Mozart continued to work for him as court organist and composer at a pitiful salary of about two hundred dollars a year. But he dreamed of the time when he could once and for all free himself from his employer's tyranny. While waiting for liberty he composed as never before—string quartets, concertos, symphonies, other orchestral compositions, sonatas, operas, and vocal music—much of it idiomatically, structurally, and technically far in advance of its times.

One of his choral works was a gesture of defiance to his hated employer. Commissioned by the archbishop to write a mass, Mozart complied with the

Spatzenmesse (*Sparrow* Mass), K. 220 (1775). This was not a full-length mass but a missa brevis, in which, with tongue in cheek, Mozart created a parody of a mass. A repeated violin figure in the Credo sounds like the chirping of a sparrow—hence the name of the work.

Much more serious both in content and intent is the *Krönungsmesse* (*Coronation* Mass), K. 317, for solo voices, chorus, and orchestra (1779). This is a full-length mass. The ''Coronation'' in the title refers to the crowning of the image of the Virgin Mary that had appeared miraculously on the Maria Plain near Salzburg in 1751. Each year after that there took place in that holy shrine a service commemorating this coronation; Mozart's mass was intended for such a service. There is high drama in the stirring pages of this masterwork, and exaltation in its more serene ones. In the former category belongs the Credo, and in the latter, the Benedictus.

Some of the best of Mozart's concert arias belong to the 1770s. In all, Mozart was the composer of more than fifty such compositions. Most are for soprano and orchestra; others, for tenor, bass, or alto and orchestra. Mozart's concert aria is a self-sufficient piece of music with an Italian text; it is the concert equivalent of the opera aria and, like it, has a recitative preceding the main melody. The two written between 1776 and 1777 are among the most rewarding of Mozart's works in this form. Both are based on texts from eighteenth-century operas by other composers. The words of *Ombre felice,* K. 255 (1776), for contralto and orchestra, come from an opera by a long-forgotten composer that is a retelling of the pathetic love story of Dido, Queen of Carthage, and the Trojan hero Aeneas. Aeneas must leave Carthage—and the arms of his beloved Dido—to fulfill his destiny of founding the city of Rome. Mozart's *Ombre felice* is Aeneas's farewell to Dido.

Ah, lo previdi, K. 272 (1777), for soprano and orchestra, is the most extended of all of Mozart's concert arias. It has two recitatives instead of one, besides the basic aria. And it has a concluding cavatina. In the first recitative Andromeda accuses Perseus of destroying her love with the same sword he had formerly used to save her life. In the aria, ''Ah, t'invola agl' occhi miei,'' Andromeda consigns Perseus to live with wild beasts. Then comes a second recitative in which Andromeda expresses her torment in living without Perseus. The concluding cavatina, ''Deh, non varcar quell' onda,'' is Andromeda's message to Perseus of her determination to join him in the lower world at the banks of the river Lethe.

In 1781, following an ugly exchange of words with the archbishop, Mozart finally made a permanent break with his employer. At that time Mozart came to the decision once and for all to brush the dust of his native

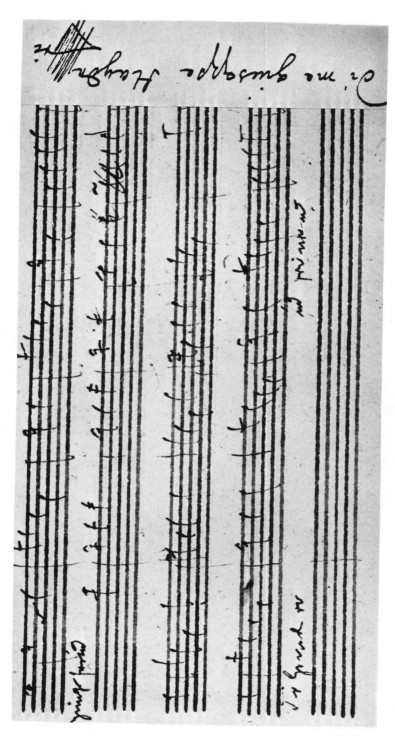

A sketch of part of the chorus "The Heavens Are Telling" from Haydn's Creation. *An autograph manuscript with Haydn's signature in Italian.*

Joseph Haydn.

Wolfgang Amadeus Mozart.

Beethoven at age thirty-three.

Salzburg off his boots, to make a new, independent life for himself in Vienna. He had good reason to be optimistic about his future. His opera commissioned by the emperor of Austria—*The Abduction from the Seraglio*—was a huge success when given on July 16, 1782. Besides he was in love, with Constanze Weber.

In 1782 Constanze fell seriously ill. Mozart made a vow that if his betrothed recovered, he would write a grand mass as his token of gratitude. Constanze did recover, and on August 4, 1782, Constanze and Mozart were married. Early in 1783 Mozart started to work on the mass he had sworn to write. By midsummer of that year he had finished the first sections: the Kyrie, Gloria, and the Sanctus, with the Benedictus. Then, for some unexplained reason, Mozart abandoned the composition after completing only the first section of the Credo and making just a sketch of the "Et Incarnatus est." He never even made an attempt to put a single note of the concluding Agnus Dei on paper. When this mass was performed for the first time (at Saint Peter's Church in Salzburg on August 25, 1783, with Constanze herself singing the soprano part) sections of earlier Mozart masses were used to fill in the missing parts. Today this mass is given the way Mozart wrote it, ending with the Benedictus.

Why did Mozart fail to complete a work that contained some of the noblest choral music he ever wrote? Some say that, early in their marriage, friction had developed between Mozart and his wife that made him lose enthusiasm for a composition honoring his wife. This explanation makes sense, since Mozart was a composer whose musical inspiration never failed him.

This mass, in C minor, K. 427, for solo voices, chorus, and orchestra (1783) has deservedly been called the "Great." The grandeur of its architectonic structure, the contrasts between surging power and serene eloquence, the subtlety of detail, all make this one of the noblest such works written between Bach's Mass in B minor and Beethoven's *Missa Solemnis*.

Things did not go as well for Mozart in Vienna as he had anticipated. His enemies were musicians in high places who envied his genius and feared the competition he gave them. They used their power to obstruct him in every way they could devise. Mozart's fine opera *The Marriage of Figaro,* a success at its premiere in Vienna in 1786, was soon forgotten because of their cunning machinations. For years Mozart was unable to get a post at court. When he finally did, it was for a miserly salary. Thus poverty was compounded on frustration, and eventually bad health joined them both in making his life miserable. Yet not poverty, debts, despair, or illness could stunt his continual growth as composer as he kept on tapping new veins of creativity and revealing new powers.

It was in his darkest moment—when, more than ever, he seemed lost in the maze of misfortunes—that, in the middle of July in 1791, a mysterious stranger dressed in gray appeared at his home to ask him to write a requiem. The fee was generous; the only condition imposed upon Mozart was that he make no attempt to inquire after the source of the commission. In reality, the stranger was the messenger of a count who made it a habit to commission musical works from composers which he passed off as his own. But Mozart—oppressed by thoughts of death and harassed by care and illness—suddenly became obsessed with the idea that this mysterious stranger was a messenger from the next world come to beg him to compose his own requiem. Mozart set to work feverishly upon a composition that became more and more associated in his mind with his own death. "I cannot remove from my eyes the image of the stranger," he is believed to have said. "I see him continually. He begs me, exhorts me, and then commands me to work. I continue, because composition fatigues me less than rest. . . . I thus must finish my funeral song, which I must not leave incomplete."

Mozart knew he was dying. Though racked by pain, he continued to work on the Requiem. When he realized that his wasted strength made further work impossible, he explained to his pupil Süssmayr how the work was to be completed. On December 4, 1791, Mozart asked to be propped up in his bed. Then, calling his friends closer to him, he gave them the manuscript of the Lacrimosa from the Requiem and begged them to join him in singing it. In the midst of this impromptu performance, he burst into tears. That night a priest was called to administer Extreme Unction. At midnight Mozart bid his family farewell. Then he turned to the wall. When they touched him, they found he was dead.

He had not lived to complete the farewell he had been writing for himself. He was able to get down on paper nine of the twelve major parts, the Requiem and Kyrie completed, the other parts in sketches. No sketches in Mozart's handwriting exist for the remaining sections—the Sanctus and Benedictus and the Agnus Dei. But, apparently, Mozart had detailed his musical intentions to his pupil so meticulously—instructions which, obviously, Süssmayr followed to the letter—that the Requiem remains an integrated masterwork from beginning to end, with the three concluding sections as thoroughly Mozartean as those that precede them.

A requiem is a mass for the dead in the Catholic liturgy. Instead of beginning with a Kyrie as a regular mass does, the music begins with an

Introit—"Requiem aeternam dona eis, Domine"—which precedes the Kyrie. The Gloria and Credo sections of the mass are supplanted by a Dies Irae and other parts in a Latin text that varies with different requiems. Requiems had been written by such early polyphonic masters as Victoria, but Mozart's is one of the first such that is still frequently heard.

Because Mozart wrote it as his own elegy, the Requiem is his most personal document—a deeply moving religious work with tragic overtones. There are, at times, a conflict and turbulence that almost touch on terror. But there is in this score grief as well (in the Lacrimosa) and a beatific calm (in the Benedictus and Agnus Dei).

Mozart wrote one other remarkable choral work in his last year—a short piece called *Ave Verum*. This is a motet for chorus and strings, a simple four-part harmony of a serene, devotional melody. This is the voice of one who, having plunged into the depths of suffering, has finally found solace.

One of Mozart's finest songs dates from 1787, the lament "Das Lied der Trennung" ("The Song of Separation"), K. 519. In all Mozart wrote thirty-six songs. The best are "Das Veilchen" ("The Violet"), K. 476 (1785), "An Chloe" ("To Chloë"), K. 524 (1787), and "Abendempfindung" ("Feelings at Evening"), K. 523 (1787). In his songs Mozart was often influenced by his experiences in opera; they frequently have the character of opera arias. But in Mozart's gift for exquisite lyricism, in the richness of his accompaniment, and in the way music adapts itself to the written word, he anticipated practices of the later art songs by German and Austrian masters.

In July of 1792 Haydn made his long return journey to Vienna from London after having conducted the six new symphonies he had written on commission there. En route home, as he had on his way to London, he stopped off at Bonn, where he met Ludwig van Beethoven (1770–1827), then already something of a musical celebrity in that city of his birth. For, from his early boyhood on, Beethoven had given testimony of exceptional gifts: as organist at the court of the elector; as a pianist; and as a composer, some of whose works had already been published and performed.

During his meeting with the great Haydn, young Beethoven showed him the manuscript of a cantata he had written in 1790 as an elegy for the death of Emperor Joseph II of Austria. Haydn found the young composer to be "a man of great talent" and urged him to come to Vienna to study with him.

Beethoven arrived in Vienna later the same year, in November, and *69* forthwith made arrangements to study with Haydn. But those lessons did not go well. The elegant, courtly, well-mannered Haydn did not take kindly to Beethoven's uncouth behavior, brusque manners, and rebellious attitudes toward authority. Haydn soon lost patience with him; and young Beethoven, for his part—though his admiration for Haydn's music was unbounded—looked upon his teacher with disdain as a representative of a decaying aristocratic society. Beethoven soon left Haydn to take up with other teachers, none of whom understood him any better than Haydn had done. Then, impatient with the rules that governed the musical thinking of his teachers, Beethoven finally gave up formal study to initiate his professional career. He soon made his mark as a piano virtuoso. He also composed some instrumental and vocal music, some of which got published.

In his early Viennese compositions Beethoven was still strongly influenced not only by Haydn but also by Mozart; he was still the apprentice learning from masters whose work he respected. This is evident in the love song "Adelaide," op. 46, for voice and piano (1795). This is more of an opera aria than an art song, extending for some ten printed pages. Friedrich von Matthisson's poem consists of four verses each ending with the word "Adelaide." They describe the trembling and swaying of blossoming branches, the whispering of leaves, the sound of silver bells in the grass, the chant of nightingales—pictures that were continually suggested by Beethoven in his accompaniment to a romantic melody.

Still clinging to the creative apron-strings of Mozart is Beethoven's "scena" and aria, for soprano and orchestra, *Ah, Perfido!,* op. 65 (1796). This is in the style and structure of a Mozart concert aria, with the orchestra almost as much a protagonist in the proceedings as the voice, both projecting a miniature drama. The scena, which is a preliminary recitative, is an electrifying outburst of a woman who has been betrayed by her beloved. This leads into a grief-stricken aria beginning with "Say not words of farewell, I implore you. How shall I live without you?"

Starting in 1800, when Beethoven's first symphony was introduced in Vienna, the giant began to stir restlessly in his music. This is the beginning of the so-called second of Beethoven's three creative periods, the time when he shook himself loose from derivative influences and allowed his own turbulent personality to express itself in music that defied conventions. This was the time when, stricken by deafness, he withdrew into isolation and found strength and solace within himself and his art. This was the time when he permanently broke with the system of royal patronage, under which for so long musicians had been treated like menial hirelings, playing the tunes the wealthy pipers paid for. Henceforth Beethoven would yield to just one master in the making of his music: his own severe conscience. (He would continue to get generous benefactions from such noblemen as Prince Lobkowitz and the Archduke Rudolph, but he accepted their money because they were his friends, who revered him for his genius and who made no demands or placed no restrictions on his art.)

This was the time, finally, when Beethoven's writing was governed by poetic concepts, no longer concerning itself primarily with elegance of form or beauty of sound, but rather with the voicing of high ideals and ideas. Beethoven the democrat, who violently opposed authoritarian rule and dreamed of the brotherhood of man, now made his music reflect his social and political ideologies. The great humanitarian that was Beethoven now sang out in his music.

As a man who also worshiped nature, Beethoven speaks out in the song "Die Ehre Gottes aus der Natur" ("God's Glory in Nature"), op. 48 (1803). "The heavens proclaim the glory of the Lord" is the opening line of a verse by Christian Gellert for which Beethoven wrote a majestic melody richly harmonized with chords. This is the fourth in a set of six songs.

In an arietta, "In Questa tomba oscura" ("In This Dark Tomb"), op. 239 (1807), there resound the echoes of the torment Beethoven often carried into the slow movements of his symphonies, quartets, and sonatas. The music of this song is lugubrious, speaking of the yearning for the peace of death and pleading that rest might not be disturbed by tears. On the other hand, in "Lisch aus" ("Resignation"), op. 252 (1817), Beethoven has come to terms with life and fate. "You must learn to do without it," says a line in the poem in speaking of the extinguishing of light. Lyricism here gives way to declamation as Beethoven forcefully pronounces his resignation to deafness.

Beethoven's foremost contribution to song literature came through the song cycle *An die ferne Geliebte (To the Distant Beloved)*, op. 98 (1816), for this is the first song cycle ever written. A song cycle comprises several independent songs, each of which can be heard and appreciated without the others, but which are unified by a single subject, mood, or idea. The precise German word used in the publication of Beethoven's cycle was *Liederkreis* ("song series"); the word *cycle* does not come into usage until Schubert's *Die schöne Müllerin,* which is called a *Cyclus.* But *Liederkreis* is just another word for *Cyclus,* and *An die ferne Geliebte* is as much a song cycle as *Die schöne Müllerin.*

The central theme of this cycle of six songs is the poet's reaction to the woman he loves. In the first number he is on a mountain peak, looking down in the valley where his beloved resides. In the second, he yearns to be with her, and in the third and fourth he beseeches the clouds, the brook, and the breezes to carry tender messages of love to her. He speaks of his pain in being separated from her in the fifth song, contrasting his pain with the joy of the birds flying above him. The cycle ends with the poet presenting his verses to his beloved as a token of his feelings.

In his second creative period Beethoven produced one oratorio, *Christus am Ölberge* (*Christ on the Mount of Olives*), op. 85 (1802), for three solo voices, chorus, and orchestra, and the Mass in C major, op. 86 (1807). In both, Beethoven's style is more dramatic than religious, and more emotional than mystic. In his greatest choral composition—the monumental *Missa Solemnis* in D major, op. 123 (1823), which came in Beethoven's last creative phase—he utilizes a religious text as his point of departure for a personalized document glorifying not religion so much, or God, as the human spirit. As the eminent American critic Lawrence Gilman explained, Beethoven ''fixed his mind and heart less on churchly rubrics than on the immemorial human realities that lie behind and below and above the missal text—upon the pitiful and everlasting soul of man, suffering, fearing, longing, pleasing, hoping, worshiping, praying.''

In his last period of creativity, Beethoven's poetic concepts become spiritualized and his music goes beyond that of his second period in surmounting the limitations of formal structure and traditional techniques to lay bare the inmost secrets of his soul. ''It comes from the heart, may it go to the heart'' are the words that Beethoven fixed over the opening of the Kyrie of the *Missa Solemnis* (1818–23). The entire mass indeed springs from the depths of Beethoven's heart. Rarely before had he been so emotionally involved with a composition. While he worked on this score, as his friend Anton Schindler revealed, he sang, howled, stamped. ''After we had been listening a long time to this most awful scene, and were about to go away, the door opened and Beethoven stood before us with distorted features, calculated to excite fears. . . . Never, it may be said, did so great an art work see its creation under more adverse conditions.''

Beethoven returned to religious music after an absence of over a decade because he wanted to contribute an appropriate composition for ceremonies attending the installation of his royal friend and benefactor, the Archduke Rudolph, as archbishop of Olmütz. That installation took place in 1820—but without the benefit of Beethoven's mass, upon which he had begun work two years earlier. As he labored, the composition assumed under his fingers such Gargantuan dimensions that it took him five years to complete the project.

Again and again in this eloquent work a noble humanitarian passionately espouses the cause of peace, freedom, and the equality of man. In the ''Dona nobis pacem''—that plea for peace—we get the sounds of rumbling drums and martial trumpets, with tremolos in strings to contribute to the agitation. This is Beethoven's battle against the forces of oppression and destruction. As the mass progresses to its grandiloquent conclusion— passing from the Benedictus, with its exalted violin obbligato to the voice, and continuing through the Agnus Dei, which Beethoven himself described as ''a prayer for inward and outward peace''—Beethoven appears confident of his victory, for the music achieves a blissful state of serenity as if the troubled heart had found that eternal peace for which the spirit had fought so bravely.

5

The Golden Age of Song

Franz Schubert, Karl Loewe,
Robert Schumann, Robert Franz,
Felix Mendelssohn

The Romantic movement in music, which replaced Classicism, sprawled across the entire nineteenth century. The Romantic composer was concerned with subject matter at the expense of structure. Extramusical subjects fascinated him to the point that he often preferred programmatic writing (that is, music written for a descriptive or narrative theme) to abstraction as he liberally tapped poetry, prose literature, plays, legends, folklore, and national sources for subjects for musical treatment. Subjective expression of feelings, rather than objectivity, became his prime concern.

One of the more significant developments during the Romantic era was the cultivation of the art song, inspired by Romantic lyric poetry. The song now became for the first time a major art form receiving the most serious consideration from Romantic composers, whereas with Haydn, Mozart, and Beethoven it had been more or less neglected. This development took place mainly in Austria and Germany. This is why the Romantic art song is called a "lied," the word *Lied* being German for "song." Strictly speaking, a lied is an art song with German words, so that the songs of minnesingers and mastersingers, and folk songs (*Volkslieder*), as well as the songs of Haydn, Mozart, and Beethoven, are all lieder. But the term *lied* acquired a specialized connotation. It now refers to a German-language art song in which new avenues of expressivity and methodology are opened through the marriage of words and music.

Structurally, early German art songs were strophic, which means that all the stanzas of the poem were sung to the same melody. The lied can be strophic, but it can also be "through-composed" (*Durchkomponiert*). Through-composition is the process in which the melody changes, chameleonlike, with each verse, the better to interpret faithfully the emotional and dramatic context of a poem.

In the lied, the Romantic composer fills his music with personal sentiments. He seeks out the precise musical equivalent for every suggestion or nuance of his text. He assigns such an importance to the piano accompaniment that it becomes a major contributor to the emotional, atmospheric, or dramatic interest of a song.

The lied first comes into its own with Franz Schubert. Many a historian looks upon him as the greatest lieder composer of all time. He is a phenomenon in music, since he had virtually few precedents to guide him when, in his eighteenth year, he brought altogether new methods and values to the writing of songs. He was guided exclusively by a God-given instinct; in his hands, the art song changed character completely, literally overnight with the writing of a single song. On October 19, 1814, Schubert wrote "Gretchen am Spinnrade." That was the day the golden age of the lied began.

As had formerly been the case with Mozart, the making of music was as natural a function with Schubert as breathing. Born on the outskirts of Vienna on January 31, 1797, Schubert began to study music in early boyhood, first with his older brother, after that with the parish church organist. Both stood in awe of the effortless way in which the child learned his lessons, be it on the piano or violin, or in singing. At the so-called Konvikt School, which trained boy singers for the imperial chapel choir, Schubert was looked upon by both his fellow students and his teachers as a "genius." Here is how one of his fellow pupils, Josef von Spaun, described Schubert's passion for music at school: "As he was already rather proficient on the violin, he was taken into the small orchestra. . . . Very soon, I noticed that the little musician far surpassed me in rhythmic surety. This aroused my interest and made me realize with what animation the lad, who otherwise seemed quiet and indifferent, gave himself up to beautiful symphonies. Once I came upon him in the music room, sitting at the piano which his tiny hands could already play passably. . . . Under my friendly encouragement he played me a minuet of his own invention. He was shy and red with shame; but my approval made him happy. The lad confided to me that he often secretly wrote his thoughts down. . . . After that I sometimes slipped him music paper.''

Schubert was fourteen years old, and still a student at the Konvikt, when he committed to paper his first art song, "Hagars Klage" ("Hagar's Lament"). This was an extended song in thirteen sections in a through-composed style. Through-composition can be found in some German songs antedating Schubert. In fact, a now forgotten composer by the name of Johann Rudolf Zumsteeg (1760–1802) had preceded Schubert in writing music for the poem "Hagars Klage"—and in a through-composed style. Nevertheless, it is still remarkable to find that Schubert, a mere boy writing his first song, should produce not a strophic miniature but an art song in an extended format in which the music changes character resiliently with the sentiments of the text.

When Schubert's voice broke in 1813, he had to leave the Konvikt. During the years between 1814 and 1818, he was on and off a teacher in a school owned and directed by his father. His heart, however, was not in teaching (which he detested) but in composition, in which he indulged every free hour he could find. Together with numerous other compositions, he completed in 1814 his first mass, and his first song masterpiece, "Gretchen am Spinnrade."

"Gretchen am Spinnrade" ("Marguerite at the Spinning Wheel"), utilized verses from Goethe's epic *Faust* describing Marguerite's romantic dreams about the handsome Faust as she works at her spinning wheel. Listen to the piano accompaniment and you will hear the whirring of the spinning wheel, now and then coming to a full stop as Marguerite's intense emotions compel her to pause momentarily in her spinning. Notice the subtle changes of key in which the changing feelings of Marguerite find such an accurate reflection. Notice, too, how wonderfully Marguerite's exquisite bliss is projected when she allows herself to dream of being kissed by her beloved. Then the song ends in the same tender vein with which it began, as the sad opening line is repeated: "My peace is gone, my heart is heavy."

Schubert's first mass—in F—introduced him as composer to a Viennese public. It was heard on October 16, 1814, in a little church in the district where Schubert was then living and teaching. The mass was liked so well that ten days later it was given a second performance in another church.

The one who sang the solo soprano part was a sixteen-year-old girl named Therese Grob. She was not very attractive, since her face was pockmarked and her mouth and nose were oversized. But she sang beautifully. This may very well have been the reason why Schubert fell in love with her. Many years later he confessed to a friend that she had been the only female he had ever loved. Therese was aware of Schubert's infatuation, was flattered by it, and apparently found the cherubic-faced, diffident young composer much to her liking. She waited for a proposal of marriage, which never came, either because Schubert was too shy to pursue her or both too young and too poor to consider matrimony. In any event, after six years of frustrated waiting, Therese married another man, much to Schubert's distress. He never married.

Schubert wrote six Latin masses and one in German. They are more secular in spirit than religious. Since Schubert's strong suit was melody, the masses are generally characterized more by their rich-blooded lyricism than by polyphonic skill or architectonic structure. Their best pages are those for solo voice and orchestra. The earliest Schubert mass still to interest us is his second one, in G major, completed during a five-day period in 1815, and introduced in the same church where his first mass had first been heard. Schubert's last mass, in E-flat major—written six months before his death—was his longest and most ambitious. There is mystery in this music, and with it a good deal of tragedy, for Schubert was deathly sick when he wrote it. But what distinguishes this mass from its predecessors is Schubert's command in writing for the chorus. Together with melodies of surpassing beauty, we here come upon stirring choral pages such as the fugues that close the luminous Gloria and the stirring Credo.

Schubert's genius for creating a miniature drama within the song form, first revealed in "Gretchen am Spinnrade," once again comes to the fore in the remarkable lied "Erlkönig" ("The Erlking") in 1815. Again the words are by Goethe. In this dramatic poem a father is riding through the night and wind carrying his child in his arms. The terror-stricken child insists that he sees the Erlking (symbol for death) and hears his pleas that the child join him. The father insists that the child has seen an apparition, a streak of mist. The pleas of the Erlking alternate with the agonized fears of the child trying to convince his father that it is indeed the Erlking who is beckoning to him, trying to seize him. The father rides swiftly through the dark, clutching the moaning child. When they reach home, the child is dead.

In creating music for this grim poem in the through-composition technique, Schubert's instincts were unfailing. For every change of mood and feeling in the poem, for every image and suggestion, Schubert finds the appropriate music. The storm rages in the piano accompaniment. Declamation alternates with haunting melody to contrast the terror of the boy with the enticements of the Erlking. Measure by measure, the drama unfolds with compelling force until the closing lines, where the melody gives way entirely to declamation, and consonance in the accompaniment yields to dissonance.

Josef von Spaun, who had been a fellow student at the Konvikt, left an account of how Schubert wrote the "Erlkönig." "One afternoon . . . I called on Schubert who was then living in his father's house. . . . I found him all aglow, reading the 'Erlkönig' out of a book which he carried several times to and fro across the room. Suddenly, he sat, and in the shortest possible time the magnificent ballad was put down on paper. As Schubert had no piano, we ran with it to the Konvikt; and there that evening the 'Erlkönig' was sung . . . and received with enthusiasm. Ruzicka [Schubert's teacher at the Konvikt] . . . was appreciative; the music moved him deeply. When some of the hearers criticized a recurring dissonance, Ruzicka sounded it on the piano and explained how it mirrored the text; more than that, how beautiful it was and how happily it was resolved." (The dissonance here referred to is the notes G flat and E flat sounded concurrently to the words "My father, my father, he's seizing me now!")

The "Erlkönig" is one of Schubert's few art ballads, and by far his best. An art ballad is an extended song dealing with historical, legendary, medieval, or fantastic subjects. It owed a strong debt to poems and songs developed in England and Scotland from the sixteenth century on. August Herbing is most credited with introducing the ballad into German vocal music, and Johann Zumsteeg with developing it. But it was with Schubert's "Erlkönig" that the ballad form comes fully into its own as a significant vocal form.

Because he could not allow any dikes to hold back the floodtide of his creativity, Schubert gave up teaching in 1818 to throw himself completely into composition. His father violently opposed this move, seeing in a composer's life nothing but penury and suffering. He was not wrong—as far as his own son was concerned. From his music Schubert earned almost nothing. (His total income from *all* his compositions for his entire life was about five hundred dollars!) Except for two brief summer assignments as music teacher for a private family in Hungary, music jobs were never offered to him. Those for which he applied were time and again refused him because he was an unknown.

All his life, from 1818 on, he depended upon the bounty of his friends to provide him with life's necessities, even with the music paper on which he scribbled his masterpieces. His friends were not affluent by any means, yet they never seemed to hesitate to share what they had with him. Through the years, Schubert wandered from one lodging to another, living now with one friend and now with another.

Among his closest friends were Johann Michael Vogl, a distinguished opera baritone; Johann Mayrhofer, an indigenous poet of modest talent; the friend from the Konvikt, Josef von Spaun; Franz von Schober, an aristocrat who was part connoisseur, part poet, part actor, and part gallant; Anselm Hüttenbrenner, a musician; Moritz von Schwind, a painter; and the Fröhlich sisters. Music was the tie binding them to Schubert in close intimacy. Schubert was the fixed star around which all revolved. He held them together with his inner strength, his lovable nature, and, most of all, his genius. They would all meet regularly at whatever lodgings Schubert occupied at the time, mainly to listen to or perform his latest compositions. These evening sessions were called *Schubertiaden* ("Schubert evenings"). Hour after hour Schubert sat listening to his friends making music—*his* music. As Kathi Fröhlich later recalled, he would fold "his hands in deep emotion as if in prayer, pressing them to his mouth." He sat there "as if in ecstasy." Sometimes he would sit on the sofa and confide to Kathi (he who was always so chary of words): "Today I have something with which I believe I have been really successful." Then he would be coaxed from his silent corner and brought to the piano. Simply, unostentatiously, he would play—invariably something he had composed one day before—and play for hours at a stretch. The music-making over, the group would indulge in horseplay, their spirits warmed not only by Schubert's music but also by wine. Schubert would take a comb, and whistle a melody through the teeth. There would be an exchange of humor and much uproarious laughter; sometimes even dancing. Then they would all go off to a nearby café for more talk, more gaiety, more laughter.

It was during these Schubert evenings that most of Schubert's songs were heard, usually performed by Vogl with the composer at the piano. Schubert wrote in all over six hundred lieder, only a minute handful of which ever came to the notice of the public outside Schubert's most intimate circle. One of them, "Am Erlasfee" (1817), a setting of a poem by Mayrhofer, appeared as a supplement to a magazine in 1818 to become Schubert's first published song. Twenty songs, for whose publication Schubert's friends had raised the necessary funds, appeared in 1821 and included "Erlkönig" and "Gretchen am Spinnrade," among other master-pieces; these were Schubert's official op. 1 and 2. After that, a scattered few of his songs were issued by a commercial publisher. But the bulk of his fabulous song production remained in manuscript at the time of his death, so that only a few of his friends were in the least aware of Schubert's incredible song productivity.

The performance history of Schubert's songs was just as pitiful. Not until 1819 (by which time he had written hundreds of songs, including some of his best) did one get heard in public. This was "Schäfers Klag-lied," which Schubert had committed to paper in 1814. In 1819 Vogl and Schubert embarked on a vacation walking trip through Austria, during which they gave a number of public concerts of Schubert's songs. They did this again in 1825. "The way in which Vogl sings and I accompany him, so that for the moment we seem to be one, is something quite new and unexpected to these good people," Schubert reported to his friends. (These concerts probably represent the first time that a tour was undertaken by a lieder singer and his accompanist.) Then in Schubert's last year, 1828, an all-Schubert program in a Viennese public auditorium offered seven of his songs.

These scattered publications and performances did nothing to lift Schubert from the obscurity that enveloped him. But in his own circle Schubert's greatness was both recognized and worshiped. "We must all bend the knee before Schubert's genius," said Vogl, adding, "We must creep after him on our knees." As his friends were introduced to one after another of Schubert's songs they felt each time as if they had witnessed a miracle.

With what unbelievable facility those beautiful melodies poured from him as he turned from one poem to the next! Sometimes he wrote as many as six to eight songs in a day. A song could even come in a single sitting. In one year alone—that of 1815–16—he completed some two hundred songs. He knew only one master—work. He would get up early and labor from six in the morning until one in the afternoon, oblivious of everyone and everything around him. That is what his friends marveled at most. *They* groped and spun their imaginary dreams and barely got things down on paper. But for Schubert there was no diversion, no distraction, only the single oneness of creation.

The poem always dictated the character of Schubert's lyricism, which was seemingly infinite in the wide gamut of its expressiveness. As his friends listened to each of his new songs, they were able to divine new meanings and subtleties in the poem that Schubert cloaked with his me-

Von Stade beguiles with the charm, candor of her singing

By John von Rhein
TRIBUNE MUSIC CRITIC

Classical review

Frederica von Stade's song recital Thursday in Ravinia's Martin Theatre was so wonderful that afterward one felt the urge to wrap up the concert hall and plunk it down in the middle of Symphony Center downtown, where a suitably intimate showcase for artists such as her is still sadly lacking.

The great American mezzo-soprano has reached the stage of her career where she can sing anything she wants and know exactly how it will sound and the effect it will produce in her adoring listeners. Yet, paradoxically, the effect is never of calculation but of the utmost spontaneity, as Von Stade reaches across the stage to gather her audience in the warmth, charm and simple candor of her singing. She inspires instant affection, a gift given to very few singers.

With her trusty, longtime accompanist, Martin Katz there to share in the fun and to provide his customary insights at the piano, Von Stade beguiled a sold-out house, including stage seats, with a delightfully diverse program, sung in four languages. Songs by Gabriel Faure and Richard Strauss shared the first half with Alberto Ginastera's rhythmically charged "Five Argentine Popular Songs." The second portion brought a world premiere, that of Jake Heggie's "Songs to the Moon," along with Joseph Canteloube arrangements of French folk songs.

"Songs to the Moon," a cycle of children's fairy tales drawn from writings by Vachel Lindsay, is the third and latest in a series of song collaborations between the San Francisco composer and Von Stade. Musically the idiom slips in and out of classical, blues and jazz styles; song, speech, scat-singing and rhythmic clapping make surprisingly happy bedfellows. Never mind that the cycle boasts more facile theatricality than musical substance. Heggie has captured Von Stade's personality, as artist, entertainer and mother. The performances of the singer and pianist were just like the songs—clever, charming, amusing, eager to please. The composer was present to share in the audience's enthusiastic response.

Von Stade's voice was never large but it retains its velvety nap and seamlessness over a wide range. Its generous tonal palette and crystalline clarity she exploited to telling effect in the French songs. Her Faure "Roses d'Ispahan" had the radiant rapture this singer communicates better than just about any recitalist. The four colorful Canteloube settings also were beautifully delivered, a refreshing sorbet after the meal that had come before.

So securely placed is her instrument that Strauss' soaring melodic trajectories held no terrors for her. If "Wiegenlied" requires a warmer, richer sound than Von Stade was able to produce, she brought out the peasant humor in the Mahlerian "Muttertaendelei" and sustained "Morgen" with rapt tonal beauty and deep feeling. Of the four encores, the highlights were her signature bonbons, Carol Hall's tenderly maternal "Jenny Rebecca" and the tipsy waltz from Offenbach's "La Perichole," which gets broader though no less hilarious every time Von Stade sings it.

Correction: Readers have reminded me that Bryn Terfel has indeed sung Wagner previously at Lyric Opera — Donner in "Das Rheingold" in 1993.

MOTION PICTURE DIRECTORY

lodic inspiration. Did not his friends Mayrhofer and Schober insist that whenever Schubert set one of their own poems to music, new facets of those poems were revealed to their authors of which they themselves had not been aware? Schubert's genius seized upon a poem and translated it immediately into musical terms true to every phrase and emotion of the words. When he read a poem that moved him, the suitable melody and its accompaniment came to him full-grown in a flash. He was at a café reading Shakespeare's *Cymbeline* when he came upon the words of "Hark, Hark, the Lark." Then and there he scratched out staves on the back of a menu and wrote the song from beginning to end without making a single change.

With lyrical or romantic poems Schubert usually used the strophic form; dramatic or atmospheric ones generally were through-composed. But whatever structure and style he chose, the music was invariably so beautifully adjusted to the text that words and music seemed to be the work of the same man, created in one piece with a kind of inevitability. For his texts, Schubert drew copiously from the rich repository of German poetry—from Goethe and Heine, Klopstock and Schiller, Schlegel and Friedrich Kind, Rellstab and Müller, as well as from the writings of many lesser poets, including poems by his personal friends.

Who among us does not have a favorite in Schubert's treasure trove of songs? It might be one with the simplicity and charm of German folk music, where the main interest is contained in the loveliness of the melody: say, "Heidenröslein" ("Meadow Rose"), to a poem by Goethe, or "Who Is Silvia?" (Shakespeare). It might be a buoyant, exuberant song like "Die Forelle" ("The Trout"), which the composer used as a theme for variations in his Quintet in A major, op. 114, or "Auf dem Wasser zu singen" ("To Sing on Water").

Perhaps it is a song with the peace and calm of "Du bist die Ruh' " ("You Are Rest") or "Wiegenlied" ("Cradle Song"); perhaps one throbbing with dramatic impulses, as in the dialogue between Death and a maiden, Death speaking with solemnity and determination and the maiden with febrile emotions—"Der Tod und das Mädchen" ("Death and the Maiden"). This last, too, was used by Schubert for variation treatment, in his String Quartet in D minor.

Then there are other kinds of songs: ones with the brooding atmosphere and mystery of "Der Wanderer" ("The Wanderer"), the melody of which Schubert extended into a large fantasy for solo piano in C major, op. 15; songs memorable for their fervor, such as "An die Musik" ("To Music"); songs filled with devotional or spiritual feelings, such as "Ave Maria," to words by Sir Walter Scott, "Litenei" ("Litany"), or "Der Musensohn" ("Son of the Muses"), the last to a poem by Goethe.

In these and many, many other song masterpieces, pictorial images, emotional states, atmospheric suggestions are all felicitously projected through subtle key changes, unexpected chromaticisms, syncopated figures, declamatory passages, unusual rhythmic patterns and accentuations, and unexpected chords and progressions in the accompaniment. Always there was the piano to add to the realism or pictorialism: the strumming of the lyre in "An die Leier" ("To the Lyre"); the monotonous tune of a hand organ in "Der Leiermann" ("The Organ-Grinder"); the mystery of the shadow in "Der Doppelgänger" ("The Double").

The last two songs mentioned above come out of song cycles, the first from *Die Winterreise,* the second from *Schwanengesang.* Schubert wrote three major song cycles, from which we get some of his best-loved songs. Indeed, perhaps the most famous love song ever written is "Ständchen" ("Serenade"), which can be found in *Schwanengesang,* where there can also be found "Die Stadt" ("The Town"), "Das Fischermädchen" ("The Fisher Maiden") and "Am Meer" ("The Sea"). "Der Lindenbaum" ("The Linden Tree"), "Frühlingstraum" ("Dream of Spring"), and "Die Post" ("The Post") come from *Die Winterreise;* "Ungeduld" ("Impatience"), "Wohin?" ("Whither?"), and "Das Wandern" ("Wandering"), from *Die schöne Müllerin.*

The song cycles belong to Schubert's later years. Like Mozart and Beethoven, he spoke most eloquently toward the end of his life. There was no sense of creative exhaustion, though his physical strength was rapidly depleting, and his feeling of despair did not dry up the springs of his imagination. On the contrary! It seemed there was so much to say, and so little time in which to say it, that Schubert wished he could run on and on. One senses his desire to communicate everything in the immortal length of his last instrumental works: the great Symphony no. 7 in C major; the last three piano sonatas, published posthumously; the last three string quartets; his two piano trios; his C major String Quintet, his last mass. Similarly in the song form he had to expand his horizons.

Die schöne Müllerin (The Lovely Miller Maid), in 1823, is a collection of twenty songs to poems by Wilhelm Müller. There is still much optimism in these songs, though, from time to time, a note of sadness is introduced, while in the closing songs sadness gives way to gloom like some menacing cloud hinting at imminent storms. This cycle narrates the story *82* of a miller, his daughter, and the miller's apprentice who is in love with the girl. In the first song a miller tells of his delight in wandering. Songs follow touching on the loveliness of a brook, of the feeling of peace that the miller experiences after a good day's work, and the dreams and hopes of the apprentice for his future. Then the apprentice entreats the brook to find out for him if the miller's daughter is responsive to his love, and he becomes impatient because the brook fails to reply. The apprentice stops off at the banks of the brook to pick flowers for his beloved. The lovers meet at the brook, but their meeting is interrupted by a storm. The apprentice knows now that he is loved, and his joy is for the time being unbounded. But soon a hunter appears as a rival for the girl. Grief-stricken, the apprentice decides to go wandering and seek solace. But he finds no relief from his sorrow. He begs that the flowers he had once picked for his beloved be placed on his own grave. Then, after returning to the brook, he sings to it a gentle lullaby. Only then does he find repose: by falling asleep at the edge of the brook.

The theme of wandering that courses through *Die schöne Müllerin* is a dominant theme in *Die Winterreise* (*The Winter Journey*), written in 1827, once again to poems by Müller. By 1827 Schubert had come face to face with the conviction that never would he receive the recognition his genius deserved, that he was doomed to permanent failure, that he would have to remain forever a pauper dependent for his subsistence on the charity of friends. In addition, his health was rapidly failing him, and he was obsessed with loneliness because he had never found a woman to love him constantly. All this plunged him into a chronic despondency. He poured out his distress in the two dozen songs of *Die Winterreise*. Death stalks through the pages of many of these songs, in some of which we sense the yearning for the peace that only death brings. The chill of loneliness is felt in "Einsamkeit" ("Loneliness"), the searing pain of grief and despair in "Wasserflut" ("Flood") and "Gefror'ne Tränen" ("Frozen Tears"). The cycle opens with "Gute Nacht" ("Good Night")—possibly Schubert's farewell to the world.

But he was not yet through, not by any means. More and more wondrous became the music of his last year. It included the fourteen songs of *Schwanengesang* (*Swan Song*). These have no unifying theme. In setting poems by Rellstab and Heine, Schubert had no intention of combining them into a single unit. This was done for him by his publisher. Nevertheless, since that publication, these fourteen songs (each of which Schubert had intended to be autonomous) are often performed as a cycle. The cries of anguish quiver in "Abschied" ("Farewell") and "Der Atlas"

("Atlas"); and with "Der Doppelgänger" ("The Double") the cycle ends in the depths of despond. If there is any single element that characterizes these songs, it is the expression of a fathomless grief.

Schubert, however, did have one glimpse of the promised land—one brief taste of success—before his end came. This happened late in March of 1828, when a concert of his works (including songs) was given in Vienna. It seemed that now at last that city had suddenly awakened to his presence. The concert took place before "more people than the hall had ever been known to hold," said one of his friends. The enthusiasm was great. His day, his friends insisted, was at hand.

It had come too late: Schubert was mortally sick. In September of 1828 he went to live with his brother in a suburb of Vienna. From there he wrote to his friend Schober on November 12: "I am ill. For eleven days I have neither eaten nor drunk anything. I am tottering from the chair to the bed, and vice-versa. . . . Whenever I eat anything I promptly bring it up again." Six days later he became delirious. He babbled endlessly. Late in the afternoon of November 19, at three o'clock, he died.

There are two famous musical settings of Goethe's "Erlkönig." The first, as we have already seen, was by Schubert. The other was by Karl Loewe.

Loewe's "Erlkönig" was written three years after that of Schubert. But since Schubert's art ballad was not published until 1821, Loewe knew nothing about it when he made his own setting.

Karl Loewe's name is prominent in song history through his German-language art ballads, for which he revealed so marked a gift that musicologists look upon him as one of the creators of this song form. Born in the town of Löbejün, near Halle, in Germany, on November 30, 1796, Loewe received his first lessons in music from his father, the village schoolmaster and the choir leader at the local church. Karl became a church chorister in Cöthen when he was eleven. Two years later he went to Halle, where he received instruction in singing and theory and where his singing attracted the interest of several of the city's notables. In Halle, Loewe wrote his first two songs, neither one of which was an art ballad.

While studying music at the Singakademie in Halle, Loewe also attended the university, where he specialized in theology. At this time he joined a vocal group that gave public concerts. He wrote his first two art ballads in 1818, both of which are now considered his greatest compositions. One was "Erlkönig" and the other "Edward."

It is surely a strange coincidence that the two versions of the "Erl-könig" should both have been the first opus numbers of their respective composers; that each is in the same key (G minor); that each employs a low range of voice for the father, a high range for the child, and a major key for the Erlking. But Loewe's concept of the Goethe poem was different from that of Schubert. There is less interest in declamation in Loewe's ballad, and much more in lyricism; less concern for the piano accompaniment, and much more for the voice. Nevertheless, Loewe's simpler and less sophisticated style is also faithful to the words. The storm that sweeps so relentlessly in the rapid bass figures of the Schubert song is suggested by Loewe discreetly in the first two measures, where an ascending figure in the bass conveys the image of the fatal ride by father and son. An arpeggio figure is used effectively to evoke a feeling of the supernatural character of the Erlking. An elementary rhythmic pattern or an ingratiating melody helps to delve into character. Had Schubert never written his "Erlkönig," that of Loewe would undoubtedly have been heard more often than is regrettably the case. Though certainly not in the class of Schubert's, Loewe's "Erlkönig" is an outstanding art ballad.

One year after he wrote his "Erlkönig," Loewe visited Jena to present a copy of his ballad to the great Goethe. Loewe was effusive in his praises of Goethe, who responded affably by speaking kindly of the setting. Goethe had been far less gracious to Schubert. When Schubert's friend Josef von Spaun sent Goethe a copy of the manuscript of the composer's "Erlkönig" (together with several other Schubert songs), the poet returned the bundle unopened. Goethe never knew anything about Schubert's ballad until 1830, two years after the composer's death. At that time a famous singer, Schröder-Devrient, performed it for him. It cannot be said that Goethe had the slightest perception of the greatness of Schubert's song. All that Goethe said was: "So sung, it becomes a veritable picture"—apparently far more impressed by the performance than by what had been performed.

Good as Loewe's "Erlkönig" is, his art ballad "Edward"—also in op. 1—is better still. The poem comes from an old Scottish ballad (translated into German), a dialogue between Edward and his mother. There is blood on Edward's hands and, in response to his mother's persistent queries, he has to confess he has killed his father. When his mother asks what penance he will do for this terrible crime, Edward responds he will never again find peace or rest but will wander beyond the sea, never to see home again; he will allow his wife and child to become beggars. Then when the mother

wishes to know what *she* is to do, Edward exclaims bitterly that "the curse
of hell shall fall on you, for it was you who counseled me!"

In a structure that makes a compromise between strophic and through-
composition writing, Loewe here produced a strikingly dramatic art ballad.
Each of the stanzas of the poem ends with the exclamation "O!" One of
the strong points of this song is the varied ways and colorations in which
this "O!" is presented to build up tension.

In some of his later art ballads Loewe further revealed his gift for tone
painting. We can feel the stress of battle in "Prinz Eugen, der edle Ritter"
("Prince Eugene, the Noble Knight"); we can visualize goblins dancing
nimbly in "Hochzeitslied" ("Wedding Song"); we are given a continually
changing pictorial panorama in "Tom der Reimer" ("Thomas the
Rhymer"); we get the effects of trumpets and drums in "Der Mohren-
fürst" ("The Moorish Prince"). In these and other ballads, Loewe rarely
loses sight of subtle details as he spins his beautiful melodies.

In 1820 Loewe became professor at the high school and seminary at
Stettin, Germany. A year later he also assumed the post of organist and
choirmaster at one of the city's churches and that of musical director of the
municipality. On September 7, 1821, he married Julie von Jacob, with
whom he had long been in love. Their idyllic marriage was shattered by
her death only two years later. When recovered from his grief, Loewe
married a second time in 1850, this time one of his pupils, Augusta Lange.

Honors came his way. The crown prince of Germany presented him
with a gold medal in 1834, and in 1837 he was appointed a member of the
august Academy of Berlin. After that he was honored by the emperor with
the Order of the Red Eagle and received an honorary doctorate from the
University of Greifswald.

His last years were somber. By 1864 he began to suffer from a pro-
tracted trance that compelled him to give up his jobs in Stettin at the
request of the authorities. His last dismal years were spent in Kiel, where
he was oblivious to the world around him and where he died on April 20,
1869.

The art song was close to the heart of Robert Schumann (1810–56).

He was the son of a literary man, a publisher, author, and bookseller,
who instilled in him a deep love for the printed word. Though Schumann
early revealed an unusual gift for music, literature was his first love. In his
childhood he wrote some dramatic sketches; in early boyhood he avidly
read Greek classics and Romantic poetry. He organized a literary society
with several friends to read and discuss literature. His own dream was to

become a poet. "Whether I am a poet . . . posterity must decide," he said at the time. He was only thirteen when he contributed articles to a journal published by his father; soon after that, he edited a volume of poems that included some of his own verses. Between his fifteenth and eighteenth years he continued writing poems, besides making poetical translations from the Greek. All his mature years he kept devouring the German lyric poetry of Goethe, Heine, Kerner, and Eichendorff—but Heine most of all. Many a composer has written music to his lyric poems, some of the most beautiful in the German language, yet it is the name of Robert Schumann that comes most often to mind when we associate the verses of Heine with music.

Fate in the end decided that Schumann become a composer, indeed one of the foremost of the German Romantics, the creator of symphonies, quartets, concertos, and a vast, treasurable library of piano music. In the writing of his remarkable songs the poet in Schumann had to be sublimated to the Schubert ideal of creating a oneness out of words and music.

Once he became a composer, Schumann made it a practice to concentrate on one branch of composition before proceeding to the next. From 1830, the year when he completed his op. 1, the *Abegg Variations,* up to about 1840, he specialized in music for solo piano. The year of 1841 was mainly devoted to orchestral music, and 1842 to chamber music. His year of song was 1840, when he married Clara Wieck. Since so many of his songs were inspired by his love for Clara and his marital happiness, any consideration of his lieder must include an account of his tempestuous romance.

He first realized with finality that he would be a professional musician in 1829, after having made tentative efforts to prepare himself for law at the University of Leipzig, to which he went in 1828. By this time he had long since given up the dream of becoming a poet. He began to study the piano with Friedrich Wieck with the hope of becoming a world-renowned virtuoso. In his passionate zeal to develop his digital technique, he used an exercise device to strengthen his fingers, which brought on paralysis of the hand. His virtuoso career thus permanently shattered, he began thinking seriously for the first time of devoting the rest of his life to composition. And so he began writing music for the instrument that he could never again sound as a performer, including such masterpieces as the *Études symphoniques* (1834), *Carnaval* (1835), and the Fantasy in C major (1836).

Clara Wieck, the daughter of Schumann's teacher, was just nine years old when she met Schumann, then eighteen. She was a piano prodigy,

Franz Schubert.

An engraving showing a Schubert evening in a private home in Vienna.

Karl Loewe.

Robert Schumann.

Felix Mendelssohn.

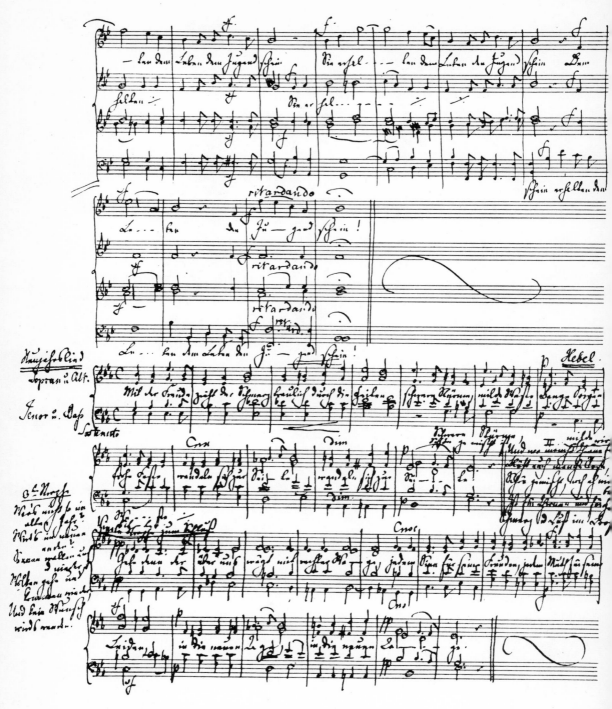

A page from Mendelssohn's motet Am Neujahrstage.
An autograph manuscript.

trained by a demanding and ambitious father to become a virtuoso. Schumann first noticed her when he heard her play some of his piano pieces. He became fond of her, played childish games with her, told her stories. By the time Clara was twelve she was completely in love with him, even though Schumann still regarded her as only a lovable, shy, and extremely gifted child.

One day, when Clara was sixteen and Schumann twenty-five, she was on the eve of embarking on a concert tour. Schumann came to say goodbye. Instinctively and impulsively he took her in his arms and kissed her. Clara was beside herself. "Everything went black before my eyes," she later confessed. "I thought I would faint."

It was at this point that Schumann came to recognize for the first time that he loved Clara not as a child but as a woman. Once Clara returned from her tour, they were overwhelmed by the joy of reunion. They were now deeply and irretrievably involved with each other emotionally. One insurmountable obstacle, however, blocked the way to marriage. Wieck had no intention of having his daughter marry an indigent composer. Besides, the father was convinced that marriage could only hinder his daughter's development as a concert pianist. He therefore enlisted all the resources and wiles of which he was capable to break up the love affair. He dispatched Clara to Dresden and ordered her not to have any further communication with Schumann. Then, when he discovered that Schumann had followed her to Dresden, Wieck threatened to kill him. He so intimidated his daughter that, for over a year, Clara and Schumann avoided all contact, in spite of a mutual love that had not faltered for a moment. After that, from time to time—in spite of Wieck's lies, threats, and deceit—they managed to exchange secret letters or to arrange brief, furtive meetings, ephemeral moments of ecstasy separated by months upon months of the black despair of separation. "I say to you again," Clara confided to Schumann, "that my love knows no bounds. If you wanted my life today I would give it up." Schumann wrote to Clara: "Some day my turn will come. Then you will see how much I love you."

The nerve-racking love affair exacted a heavy toll on Schumann's ever-delicate nervous system and brought no end of grief to Clara. It dragged on for about four years. Finally Schumann decided to sue Wieck in the law courts for the right to marry Clara. The trial compounded ugliness upon bitterness, but in the end Schumann emerged victorious. He was now free to claim his bride. Clara and Schumann were married near Leipzig on September 12, 1840. "My whole self was filled with gratitude to Him who had brought us safely over so many rocks and precipices," Clara confided to her diary. "Even the sun which had hidden his face for so many days, shed his warm beams upon us as we drove to the church, as if to bless our union. It was a day without a jar, and I may thus enter it in this book as the fairest and most momentous of my life."

Their happiness, as they settled down in their first home in Leipzig, was like a benediction. Schumann's joy was channeled into songs, a medium to which he had thus far paid scant attention. "Clara," he told his wife, "what a joy it is to write for the voice, a joy I have lacked too long!" This joy brought on a remarkable creative flood. In the first year of his marriage he produced over half the total of his life's output of some two hundred and fifty songs. They are among the best he ever wrote. Clara was his inspiration; his overwhelming love was the irresistible driving force. Love songs are, of course, prominent in this catalog. In the greatest lyric poets of the Romantic movement, Schumann found the verbal spark to set his musical imagination flaming. Soaring melodies reflected the ardor of his emotions—wondrous melodies like those to the twenty-measure "Du bist wie eine Blume" ("You Are Like a Flower") or "Im wunderschönen Monat Mai" ("In the Lovely Month of May"), both to the words of Heine and both among the most exquisite love songs in the lieder repertory; or "Liebeslied" ("Love Song"), words by Goethe; or "Frühlingsnacht" ("Spring Night"), words by Eichendorff. In these and other of Schumann's love songs, his lyricism proclaimed, as if from mountaintops, that Clara was his.

But not all the songs of 1840 were of love. Some contained the bittersweet taste of sorrow, as in "Stille Tränen" ("Silent Tears"), poem by Kerner. Sometimes the feeling is even bitter, as in the famous "Ich grolle nicht" ("I Bear No Grudge"), to Heine's words. Sometimes the mood is placid or contemplative, as in "Sehnsuchtnacht der Waldgegend" ("Longing"), verses by Kerner.

Schumann's gift for musical narrative can be found in the highly familiar art ballad "Die beiden Grenadiere" ("The Two Grenadiers"). In Heine's poem, two French soldiers of Napoleon's army are going home after confinement in a Russian prison camp. They hear of Napoleon's defeat at Waterloo. When one of the soldiers begins to talk about his wife and child, the other upbraids him for thinking about his family in the face of the overwhelming tragedy of the capture of Emperor Napoleon. This patriot then says he wants nothing better than to be buried in France with his gun, sword, and Cross of Honor, and in death to await the return of his emperor so that he may rise from his grave and defend him. The melody is

initially martial, then dramatic, then sorrowful as it faithfully follows the story line. It ends with a quotation of the French national anthem, the "Marseillaise."

Schumann's songs never lack for lyrical beauty in which the melody continually catches the essence of the poem. But however important the voice may be, it rarely takes the spotlight from the piano. It must be remembered that, by the time he wrote these songs, Schumann had already proved himself one of the most original composers for the piano in music history. The piano continued to dominate his thinking even when he turned to vocal music. He allows a climactic point in a salient phrase to be taken away by the piano from the voice. He sometimes prefaces his songs with beautifully sculptured piano introductions to set the stage for the appearance of the voice; and sometimes, too, the piano goes on for a final commentary when the voice part is over. The bitterness of "Ich grolle nicht" realizes an increasing intensity in its pathos in the brief concluding statement of the piano after the closing line of the poem has been sung by the voice, "I saw, my love, how miserable you are."

Nevertheless, when his artistic instinct made him conscious that the voice was of primary importance, he does not hesitate to give it dominance. In the song "Ich hab' im Traum geweinet" ("I Wept in My Dream"), words by Heine, Schumann achieves a wonderful effect by having no piano accompaniment whatsoever for almost half the song.

Some of the songs mentioned above—and a good many others hardly less noteworthy—come from three song cycles completed in 1840. One is a touching tribute to his wife: *Frauenliebe und -leben* (*Woman's Love and Life*), op. 42. Chamisso, aged forty, wrote for his eighteen-year-old bride these poems that sentimentalized over the unselfish and devoted love of woman for man. Flushed as he was with the glow of Clara's adoration, Schumann responded to the tenderness and romance of Chamisso's poems almost as in a reflex action.

The cycle *Dichterliebe* (*Poet's Love*), op. 48—settings of sixteen poems by Heine—contain such Schumann gems as the romantic "Im wunderschönen Monat Mai," with which the cycle opens; the pathetic "Aus meinem Tränen" ("From My Tears"), which follows; the tender "Wenn ich deine Augen seh" ("When I Look into Your Eyes"); the exquisite mood picture "Im Rhein, im heiligen Strome" ("In the Rhine, the Sacred Stream"); the dramatic "Ich grolle nicht"; the light and airy "Ein Jüngling liebt ein Mädchen" ("A Boy Loves a Girl"); the lugubrious "Ich hab' im Traum geweinet"; and the funereal "Die alten, bösen Lieder" ("The Old Evil Songs"), which ends this group.

The best numbers in Schumann's third famous song cycle—*Liederkreis* 95

(*Song Cycle*), op. 39, twelve poems by Eichendorff—are two versions of "In der Fremde" ("In Foreign Places"), "Mondnacht" ("Moonlight Night"), and "Auf einer Burg" ("In a Castle").

Myrthen, op. 25, is not a song cycle, since there is no central mood or thought. It is, rather, a collection of twenty-six songs with words by various poets, including Goethe, Heine, Rückert, Byron, and Robert Burns. It is here that we come upon one of Schumann's most exquisite songs, "Du bist wie eine Blume." Many a composer has written melodies for this Heine love poem, but none is more touching or lovelier than that of Schumann. "Die Lotosblume" ("The Lotus Flower"), "Widmung" ("Dedication"), and "Der Nussbaum" ("The Nut Tree") are three other memorable songs.

From time to time after 1840 Schumann continued to write songs, though few are of the caliber of the fabulous output of that year. Schumann's main creative efforts after 1840 were devoted to the symphony, the concerto, and the string quartet. Above and beyond his compositions, Schumann was active as the editor of a distinguished music journal that he had helped to found in 1833, the *Neue Zeitschrift für Musik;* as teacher of piano and composition at the Leipzig Conservatory; and as music director of the city of Düsseldorf, where he conducted orchestral concerts. In Düsseldorf his memory began to falter, an ominous sign that a terrible tragedy was hovering over him: the loss of sanity. "The night is beginning to fall," he wrote prophetically to his friend, the great violinist Joseph Joachim. Night fell upon him in 1854, when he tried to commit suicide. Soon afterward he was confined to an asylum near Bonn, where he remained two years in a hopeless state of mental disorder and physical pain. Death brought merciful release from his suffering in 1856.

When Robert Schumann wrote music articles for the *Neue Zeitschrift für Musik,* he used two pseudonyms for his pieces: "Florestan" and "Eusebius." He invented these two imaginary characters to symbolize two facets of the Romantic personality. Florestan was passionate and dynamic; Eusebius, the dreamer. There was a good deal of both in Schumann, as his songs betray, and as he himself fully realized when he used them as characters of self-portrayal in his piano compositions *Carnaval* and *Davidsbündlertänze.*

There are Eusebiuses and there are Florestans in the royal line of lieder composers that succeeded Schumann. In their lieder the Eusebiuses favored gentle, lovely melodies undisturbed by overwrought emotions; melodies that had both a haunting lyricism and spontaneous feeling and lay beautifully for the range of voice for which they were written. These composers were not concerned with the psychological probing, with the searching for deeper meanings of a poem, that we encounter so often in Schubert or Schumann. The songs of these Eusebiuses are rarely self-revelations. With these composers it was the voice that was in complete command of every situation. An accompaniment was often just that, a discreet and unobtrusive formal background for the voice. These Eusebiuses rarely departed in their songs from formal harmonic or tonal procedures, and structurally they more often than not preferred strophic songs to through-composition.

Robert Franz and Felix Mendelssohn were the Eusebiuses of the lied. If a pun be permitted, Robert Franz is the ''unsung'' hero of the lied. He is rarely represented on today's song programs, although a quarter of a century or so ago his songs were basic to the repertory of most famous lieder singers. More's the pity! For Robert Franz was born with the gift of lyricism. His melodies were admirably suited for the German lyric poetry he was setting. He was partial to the mezzo-soprano range, for which he wrote colorfully and masterfully. In comparison to Schubert and Schumann, he might appear disarmingly forthright and simple. Yet how much richer is the lied because Franz contributed these delectable items: ''Für Musik'' (''To Music''); ''Widmung'' (''Dedication''); ''Liebesfrüh-ling'' (''Love's Springtime''); ''Im Rhein, im heiligen Strome'' (''In the Rhine, the Sacred Stream''); ''Im Herbst'' (''In Autumn''); ''Ein Stüdlein-wohl vor Tag'' (''Before Daybreak''); and ''Mein Schatz ist auf der Wanderschaft'' (''My Treasure Is a-Wandering'').

Robert Franz was born in Halle, Germany, on June 28, 1815. Songs made a deep impression on his musical consciousness when he was still a child—not art songs but the church hymns and chorales that he heard both at home and in church. He soon found a sympathetic teacher in the local church choirmaster, who gave him lessons in organ and piano playing and introduced him to the choral masterworks of Handel and Haydn. For a time, Robert Franz served as a piano accompanist in performances of choral compositions. Then in 1835 he went to Dessau, where he was a pupil of Friedrich Schneider in harmony and counterpoint.

Two years later he was back in Halle, eager to make his way as a professional musician but unable to find a suitable opening. With free time on his hands, he devoted himself assiduously for half a dozen years to the study of such music of Bach and Schubert as was then available, and to the masterworks of Beethoven. He also read literature omnivorously, mostly philosophy and romantic poetry. And he did some composing.

The reading of poetry, combined with a frustrated love affair, sent him to write his first songs. Since by now he had become an admirer of Schumann, he collected the manuscripts of his first songs and dispatched them to Schumann, then living in Leipzig. Schumann was so delighted with them that he sent them on to a publisher without telling Franz about it. This is how Franz's op. 1 came into being in 1843: a collection of twelve songs, including "Lotosblume" ("Lotus Flower"), "Schlummerlied" ("Slumber Song"), and "O säh ich auf der Haide dort" ("Oh, Do I See There on the Hearth?"). Op. 2 was issued the same year. It contained his fine setting of Lenau's "Schilflieder" ("Songs of the Reed").

When Schumann reviewed these songs in the *Neue Zeitschrift für Musik* he said that they bore "an inward relationship to the whole development of our art during the last ten years" and hailed their composer as the creator of "a noble and new style" that required the services of "a poet as well as a singer." Mendelssohn and Liszt were also impressed by op. 1 and 2. And with good reason! These songs represent Robert Franz at his best, even though he wrote a good many others after these. When Franz himself remarked that "my opus 1, I consider no better and no worse than my opus 52," he recognized that his artistic identity had changed very little in that intervening period.

Following the publication of op. 1 and 2, Franz became organist of the Ulrichskirche and the conductor of the Singakademie, a choral group. In 1859 he was named music director of Halle University. Economic security made it possible for him to travel. In 1846 he visited Vienna, where he met Franz Liszt for the first time and heard from his lips words of praise. In 1848 Robert Franz married Maria Hinrichs, a song composer in her own right.

He had been suffering from an ear ailment since 1841. As the years passed, it was aggravated into total deafness and was supplemented by nervous disorders. By 1868 he had to withdraw from his posts in Halle and go into retirement. For a time he experienced intense poverty. Then several notable musicians (including Joachim and Liszt) came to his help by forming a committee to raise funds for his support. These musicians gave benefit concerts all over Europe, with the result that, in 1873, they were able to make Franz financially secure for the rest of his life through a present of about $25,000.

Franz published his last volume of songs (op. 52) eight years before his death. Composition had to end when, in his last years, he became a complete invalid. Robert Franz died in Halle on October 24, 1892.

In the sweetness and purity of his melodies, in the way the voice took precedence over the piano accompaniment, and in avoidance of any deep emotion, Felix Mendelssohn (1809–47) was also a Eusebius of the lied. Listen to the best-loved of all his songs, his setting of Heine's "Auf Flügeln des Gesanges" ("On Wings of Song"), which he wrote in 1834 and dedicated to Cécile Jeanrenaud, who later became his wife. Its enchanting melody (familiar, too, in Joseph Achron's arrangement for violin and piano, as well as in many other arrangements), gliding over the smooth surface of the accompaniment, is like a graceful swan in calm waters. Here you find both the strength and the weakness of Mendelssohn. He wrote with inordinate charm, but rarely with any degree of depth or profundity. You may be bewitched by his graceful music, but rarely are you stirred to the roots of your being.

Heine's opening line to "On Wings of Song" is "On wings of song, my dearest, I shall transport you." In his best lieder, Mendelssohn transports the listener to realms of beauty on wings of melody, and little else. This holds true for "Gruss" ("Greeting"), words once again by Heine; for "Volkslied" ("Folk Song"); for "O Jugend" ("Oh, Youth"), which was based on a Rhenish folk tune; for "Schilflied" ("Reed Song"); for "Nachtlied" ("Night Song"); for "Jagdlied" ("Hunter's Song"); and for "Lieblingsplätzchen" ("Drop of Love").

For all the loveliness and tenderness of songs like these, Mendelssohn uncovers far deeper and richer strains of beauty and poetry in his choral music. As the phenomenal prodigy who had invited comparison with the child Mozart, Mendelssohn became a member of the Singakademie, a choral group in Berlin, when he was ten. This chorus was directed by Zelter, a thorough musician who had a vast knowledge of choral literature, including some music by the then little remembered and rarely performed Johann Sebastian Bach. Through his affiliation with this group, Mendelssohn was introduced to the world's greatest choral literature, including parts of the neglected *Passion According to Saint Matthew* by Bach. These musical experiences with the Singakademie were a prime influence in making Mendelssohn conduct in 1829 the first complete performance of the *Passion According to Saint Matthew* since Bach's own day—a concert that led to the first reevaluation of Bach and marked the beginnings of the Bach revival that would sweep the world in the next half century. And it is equally true that Mendelssohn's early experiences with the Singakademie filled him with a love for choral music that led him to write the Psalm 115, op. 31, completed in 1830, and from then on to continue writing choral music as long as he lived.

Mendelssohn's choral works embrace motets, psalms, hymns, anthems, sacred pieces, and oratorios, among other religious compositions. To the secular field he contributed many part songs, a cantata, the *Festgesang,* or *Festival Hymn* (out of which comes the melody of the frequently sung Christmas hymn "Hark, the Herald Angels Sing"), and music to texts by Goethe and Schiller. Greatest of all his choral creations are his two oratorios: *Saint Paul,* op. 36 (1836), and *Elijah,* op. 70 (1846). The first, based on the New Testament, is the work of the convert to Christianity; the second, derived from the Old Testament, comes from the pen of one born a Jew.

With the help of Eduard Devrient, Mendelssohn prepared his own text for *Saint Paul.* It follows the career of the saint from the time he persecuted Christians and cooperated in the stoning of Saint Stephen through his conversion to Christianity and his own martyrdom. In two contrasting sections, this oratorio begins dramatically, but then goes on to be primarily lyrical. An overture opens and closes with a quotation of the famous Protestant hymn "Wachet auf." Midway, a fugal section is intended to describe the successful struggle to convert Paul to Christianity. In the first part, the most salient sections are the tenor recitative describing the stoning of Saint Stephen and the choral lament "Happy and Blessed Are They"; and the prayer for baritone, "O God, Have Mercy upon Me." Particularly noteworthy in the second section are the meditative chorus "How Lovely Are the Messengers" and Saint Paul's poignant farewell, "Be Thou Faithful unto Death."

Saint Paul scored an impressive success when introduced at the Lower Rhine Festival in Düsseldorf, Germany, on May 22, 1836. But this was only an echo compared to the thunder of acclaim meeting Mendelssohn's second oratorio, *Elijah,* at its premiere at the Birmingham Festival in England on August 26, 1846. "The reception . . . from the assembled thousands . . . was absolutely overwhelming," wrote a friend of Mendelssohn. Mendelssohn himself reported: "No work of mine ever went so admirably at the first performance, or was received with such enthusiasm both by musicians and the public as this."

England has ever since then kept *Elijah* close to its heart. Only Handel's *Messiah* has been heard more often. Elsewhere, too, *Elijah* has won the distinction of being received as one of the three or four greatest oratorios ever written.

Mendelssohn first thought of writing *Elijah* as soon as the ink was dry on the manuscript of *Saint Paul*. But it took an invitation from the Birmingham Festival a decade later to send him to work. Pastor Julius Schubring prepared the text about the biblical prophet Elijah; but it was Mendelssohn himself who dictated what the nature of that text should be. Mendelssohn insisted that the dramatic and not the epic character of Elijah's life be stressed. "I should like the representation . . . to be as spirited as possible," he told the pastor. Then he added, "The personages should be introduced as acting and speaking with fervor; not, in Heaven's name, to become mere musical pictures, but as inhabitants of a positive practical world, such as we see in every chapter of the Old Testament."

The oratorio opens not with the overture but with Elijah's recitative announcing that a drought will be inflicted upon the people of Israel for having abandoned God for Baal. Only then does the orchestra strike up an overture, whose somber character reflects the people's anguish. That anguish is then expressed vocally in the resonant chorus "Help, Lord, Wilt Thou Destroy Us?" Effective recitative, melodic arias and duets, and sweeping choruses then relate how Elijah brings back the widow's son from the shadows of death (a miracle to which the people respond with the chorus "Blessed Are the Men That Are Free") and how Elijah proves victorious in his challenge to Baal and the false prophets whose doom he foretells in the recitative "O Thou Who Makest Thine Angels Spirits." The first part of the oratorio ends with the joyous chorus of the people, "Thanks Be to God."

The second part begins with the beautiful soprano aria "Hear Ye, Israel" and contains Elijah's eloquent plea for death, "It Is Enough," and the beatific song of the angel sung by an alto, "O Rest in the Lord." After Elijah overcomes his enemies with the help of God and is carried heavenward in a chariot, the people intone a mighty hymn, "And Then Shall Your Light Break Forth."

Elijah was Mendelssohn's last oratorio. He began a third one, *Christus,* but did not live to finish it. On February 20, 1847, he wrote four part-songs for male voice, op. 120. Less than three months later he received the shattering news that his beloved sister, Fanny, had died. This loss disturbed him greatly. From then on he could write little, and then only by fits and starts. He suffered an attack while accompanying a singer in his "Nachtlied" ("Night Song"), which he had written on October 1, 1847.

After a night of restful sleep he appeared to be recovered. On October 7 he wrote another song—his last piece of music: "Altdeutsche Frühlingslied" ("Old German Spring Song"). Less than a month after that he died in his sleep in Leipzig. His last words were "I am tired—terribly tired."

The Romantic Spirit
in France and Italy

Hector Berlioz,

Henri Duparc, Gabriel Fauré,

Francesco Paolo Tosti, Giuseppe Verdi

The German Romantics developed the lied; the French, the "mélodie."

The mélodie was one of two kinds of French art songs. The other was the "romance," a carryover from the songs of the French troubadours. The earliest romance bore the same relation to the French art song that the German folk song did to the lied. It was, as the famous French philosopher Jean Jacques Rousseau once wrote, "in a simple, touching style, with a somewhat antiquated flavor, the tune . . . in keeping with the words: no ornaments, nothing mannered, a simple natural rustic melody which makes its effect . . . without depending on the way it was sung." "Plaisir d'amour" ("Pleasure of Love"), composed by Jean Paul Égide Martini and published in 1784, is representative of the romance.

The mélodie first became prominent with Hector Berlioz (1803–69). It concerned itself more with rhythm and harmony than did the romance; its melodic line had greater subtlety and complexity. The mélodie is the French equivalent of the German lied, but less dramatic and more sensitive in feeling and atmosphere.

Berlioz, the first of the great Romantics in French music, began his songwriting career in 1825 by writing romances, some of which he published at his own expense. From time to time thereafter he continued writing such songs. His interest in the romance was further revealed in 1849, when he adapted ''Plaisir d'amour'' for voice and orchestra. But beginning with *Irlande* (1829–30)—nine songs that are settings of French translations of poems by Thomas Moore—the style of the mélodie became clarified. Berlioz's finest songs after that were all mélodies. The most famous are *Les Nuits d'été* (*Nights of Summer*), op. 7, written in 1834–41 to six poems by Théophile Gautier. In 1856 Berlioz finished orchestrating these songs, and it is in these versions for voice and orchestra that they are best known.

Berlioz did not write many songs, though some of his are exquisite examples of French art songs. Berlioz is far more successful in his choral works and orchestral compositions. He breathed into them the brave, fresh new wind of Romanticism with his unbridled imagination and independence, passion and theatricalism. In true Romantic fashion, Berlioz was stimulated by his texts, many based on great literature. Romantic, too, was the way he liked to express himself within huge designs of unorthodox structure and enlisting immense forces. His earliest large choral work was an oversized oratorio in 1823 that was scheduled for but never reached performance. A huge mass in 1825 did get a hearing in a Paris church and was well received. Later choral compositions came from an artist unafraid to dream big dreams, and not reluctant to give voice to overemotionalized sentiments.

Directed to the study of medicine by his father, a physician, Berlioz went to Paris from his native town of La Côte-Saint-André in 1821. There he divided his time between medical studies and his overpowering musical interests, which had absorbed him from childhood. As he put it so picturesquely, he was torn between ''death and sensuality, between frightful death and hideous corpses and enchanting dancers.'' Sensuality won out over death, enchanting dancers over death and corpses. In spite of his father's violent objections, Berlioz, after he had received his Bachelor of Science degree in 1824, finally brushed medicine aside. He entered the Paris Conservatory in 1826, staying there two years. He supported himself by giving guitar lessons and singing in a theater chorus. Neither poverty nor his failures as a composer could shake his now fixed determination to become a composer.

His first important work was a remarkable symphony, the *Symphonie fantastique* (1830), whose freedom of form and expression, together with programmatic literalness, marked the beginnings of French Romanticism in music. He wrote several more gifted orchestral works after that (including *Harold in Italy* in 1834, a symphony for orchestra with solo viola) to which he brought the daring imagination and the instrumental virtuosity encountered in his first symphony. Meanwhile, between 1830 and 1832, he lived in Italy as the recipient of the Prix de Rome, and in 1833 he married the English actress Harriet Smithson. He had first fallen in love with her in 1827 from his seat in the theater watching her appearance with an English company as Ophelia in *Hamlet*. He pursued her relentlessly until he finally broke down her resistance. The *Symphonie fantastique* had been inspired by this turbulent romance, and so was the last song in the *Irlande* group, "Élégie."

Several outstanding musicians in Paris, including Liszt and Paganini, became aware of his immense talent. The French minister of the interior was also impressed by Berlioz' music. He commissioned Berlioz to write a new large work for the 1837 commemoration of the dead of the French Revolution of 1830, in which Charles X had been overthrown, to be replaced by Louis Philippe. This composition was to be performed at a special service. Berlioz conceived a giant choral work for this occasion: the *Grand Messe des morts* (*Grand Mass of the Dead*), a requiem for solo tenor, chorus, and orchestra, op. 5. Red tape and political intrigue frustrated all attempts to get this requiem played at the service for which it had been intended. It was heard, instead, at the Church of the Invalides in Paris on December 5, 1837, as funeral music for the death of a French general killed earlier that same year in the Algerian campaign.

The requiem is awesome music. Berlioz himself described it as "overwhelming" and "of a horrifying grandeur." In ten sections, it is scored for a chorus of 400 voices. The orchestra of 110 instrumentalists was supplemented by four small brass choirs (ranging in number from 8 to 14 instruments) placed at the four corners of the stage. Already having given evidence of his mastery at orchestration and harmony, Berlioz here filled his music with unusual sound textures and striking effects. The grandeur of the work is immediately sounded in the opening pages, which begin with the dirgelike music of the "Requiem" and continue with the compelling drama of the "Dies Irae." It is in the latter section that the four small brass choirs are used—to sound the call of the Last Judgment. This effect is highly theatrical, and so is the music of the "Tuba mirum," which the writer Alfred de Vigny described as "beautiful, queer, wild, convulsive, and sorrowful." Later, an extended "Lacrimosa" releases an outpouring of sorrow through unusual rhythmic and instrumental devices, as well as through the emotional content of its main melody. Unusual is the way a two-note phrase is used throughout the "Offertorium," a chorus of souls in purgatory. After that, the requiem proceeds to the majestic strains of the

"Sanctus" and the sublimity of the "Agnus Dei." In the latter the dirge-like music of the opening brings the requiem to a peaceful ending.

The requiem is a landmark in French choral music. Berlioz regarded it as his chef d'oeuvre. He once said, "If I were threatened with the burning of all my works except one, it is for the requiem that I would ask for mercy."

Though solo voices and chorus are used extensively with the orchestra in *Romeo and Juliet,* op. 17 (1839), this work is neither an oratorio nor a cantata but a dramatic symphony. As such, it does not fall within the province of this volume. But *La Damnation de Faust* (*The Damnation of Faust*), op. 24, does. Berlioz called it a "dramatic legend," and it has been performed in two ways: as an oratorio in the concert hall, and staged as an opera.

The idea of writing *The Damnation of Faust* occurred to Berlioz almost two decades before the work was finalized. In 1827 he read a French translation of Goethe's *Faust.* His imagination was seized. "I could not put it down," he wrote. "I read it constantly, at my meals, in the theater, in the streets, everywhere." At that time he wrote the music for eight scenes. The ambition of completing the entire project was rearoused some fifteen years later. With the help of a collaborator, he developed an appropriate text, which frequently transformed and greatly modified the original Goethe source. He used only four of Goethe's characters (Faust, Mephistopheles or Mephisto, Marguerite, and Brander). He completely deleted Goethe's philosophic concepts and interpolated a good deal of his own material. He placed the opening scene on a Hungarian plain, a setting that does not appear in Goethe. Marguerite is imprisoned not for killing her illegitimate child, as occurs in the legend and in Goethe's version, but for unwittingly having poisoned her mother. In Goethe, Faust achieves salvation; with Berlioz, he is doomed to perdition.

The four sections (or acts) are further divided into numerous episodes loosely strung together. In the opening part the best-known excerpt is the Hungarian march, the "Rakóczy March." There are two other famous orchestral episodes in later sections: "The Dance of the Sylphs," after Faust has been lulled to sleep on the banks of the Elbe; and the "Dance of the Will-o'-the-Wisps," the music with which the image of Faust is evoked before Marguerite. But the vocal parts are more treasurable still, and far more numerous: Brander's mocking tune about a rat in the kitchen, "Certain rat, dans une cuisine," and Mephisto's song of a flea who is pampered and loved by a king as if it were his son, the "Chanson de la puce," both heard in a scene set in Auerbach's cellar in Leipzig, haunt of carousing students; Mephisto's hymn to the beauty of the countryside by the Elbe River in "Voici des roses"; Faust's rapturous air "Merci, doux crépuscule," in Marguerite's boudoir, followed by her medieval-style song as she braids her hair, "Autrefois un roi de Thulé"; Mephisto's serenade "Devant la maison"; the love duet of Faust and Marguerite, "Ange adoré"; Marguerite's grief-stricken romance in the last section when she becomes convinced Faust has deserted her, "D'amour l'ardente flamme"; Faust's invocation to Nature, "Nature immense"; and the chorus of angels singing of Marguerite's salvation and welcoming her to heaven ("Remonte au ciel") after Faust has been consigned to join the devils and the damned souls of hell.

Berlioz conducted the world premiere of *The Damnation of Faust* in a concert presentation in Paris on December 6, 1846. Not at that time, nor in two later performances, was the glory of this work appreciated. Nor did this happen in Berlioz' lifetime. Then, in 1877, his *Faust* was revived in Paris in two different performances by two different conductors. From this time on, the masterpiece began what the French critic Adolphe Boschot called "its prodigal triumphal career." The first staging of *The Damnation of Faust* took place in Monte Carlo in 1893. It has since been given occasionally in the opera house, but it is as a concert work that it is most familiar.

In his Te Deum (1849) Berlioz once again becomes the architect of a huge design. A Te Deum is a Christian liturgical hymn of praise and rejoicing. It probably dates from the sixth century. From the seventeenth century on, its text was used by many composers both for church services and as a secular song of thanksgiving in celebration of some festive event, such as a victory in battle. Such a composition was Handel's Te Deum in 1743, commemorating the victory of the English over the French at Dettingen during the War of the Austrian Succession.

Berlioz first planned his Te Deum in 1832 to celebrate the victory of the French in Italy. But the composition remained bare sketches for seventeen years. Finally, in 1849, Berlioz had the entire work in manuscript, but its premiere had to wait until 1855.

As first conceived, the Te Deum was a work calling for Gargantuan forces: a thousand performers including two choirs (of a hundred voices each), a third chorus of children (numbering six hundred), and a greatly expanded orchestra. Eventually Berlioz came to realize that such an army of musicians would never be mustered. If he wanted this work performed, he would have to reduce it to more modest proportions. He then wrote it for 130 voices supplemented by a large, but not oversized, orchestra.

Here Berlioz combined his enormous resources in the science of orchestration and harmony with profound religious feelings. The work opens fugally and surges to a mighty climax in the seventh section with "Judex crederis." In between there are many pages of devout moods and poetic sentiments.

Another reverent work both in subject matter and in its projection was Berlioz' oratorio for solo voices, chorus, and orchestra, *L'Enfance du Christ* (*The Childhood of Christ*), op. 25 (1854). This composition had a curious origin. In 1850 Berlioz conducted a choral composition, *The Flight into Egypt,* which he identified as a "mystery" by the "seventeenth-century composer Pierre Ducré." The critics praised it highly. But those among them who did not favor Berlioz' music went out of their way to suggest snidely that Berlioz could have learned many a lesson on how to write religious music from this "remarkable work by Ducré." Such a gratuitous slap at Berlioz induced him to come forward with the startling confession that there existed no such composer as Ducré, but that Berlioz himself had written both the music and the text.

Four years later, Berlioz completed two new large choral sections: *Herod's Dream* and *The Arrival at Saïs*. With *The Flight into Egypt* placed between them, Berlioz now provided this choral trilogy with the new title of *The Childhood of Christ*. In *Herod's Dream,* Herod dreams that he orders his army to destroy the children of Judea and that the angel has come to Joseph and Mary with a warning about the Holy Child. The middle part, *The Flight to Egypt,* describes how a host of angels warns the Holy Family to flee to Egypt as shepherds gather to bid them farewell. The setting of the concluding part is the Egyptian city of Saïs, where Joseph, Mary, and the young Jesus are cruelly rejected before finally finding a haven with the Ishmaelites.

Like so much else by Berlioz, this is a highly individualized composition. It is not in the oratorio mold used by Handel, Haydn, the early Beethoven, and Mendelssohn. Instead of arias and duets and ensemble numbers, Berlioz makes extensive use of recitatives that are more often introspective and poetic than dramatic or programmatic.

The Childhood of Christ is one of the few works for whose performance a special auditorium was built. This happened in the city of Strasbourg, some years after the 1854 Paris premiere. An audience of some eight thousand music lovers in the new auditorium were moved to outbursts of enthusiasm.

Though he had become successful both as a composer and as a conductor, Berlioz' last years were unhappy. His first marriage had proved from its beginnings a continual clash of fiery temperaments. After ugly quarrels the two separated and lived apart until Harriet's death in 1854. A second marriage the same year—to a singer, Marie Recio—was no better for Berlioz and was terminated by her death in 1862. After that, Berlioz suffered loneliness. He led a monastic existence in his apartment in Paris. Broken in spirit and suffering from intestinal neuralgia, he was driven to write passionate love letters to a woman he had loved half a century earlier and had not seen since. One can only imagine the consternation of this woman on reading these letters. She was now sixty-seven and the mother of four grown children. But to the ardently romantic Berlioz, this ridiculous quest for a long-lost love, and for his youth, did not appear unnatural.

The death of his son in Havana of yellow fever in 1867 was the last blow to his will to live. In anticipation of death, for whose tranquillity he now yearned, he destroyed manuscripts, letters, and personal papers that he did not wish to have survive him. In Nice, in March of 1868, he was attacked by cerebral congestion. He traveled back to Paris, where he died on March 8, 1869.

Among the more familiar mélodies in the second half of the nineteenth century is one that is a curiosity and two more that were not originally intended for voice. The curiosity is the "Ave Maria" (1859) by Charles Gounod (1818–93). Gounod here superimposed a spiritual melody over an accompaniment comprising the music of Bach's Prelude in C major from *The Well-Tempered Clavier* without changing a note of Bach. The remarkable thing about this hybrid product is that Bach's prelude serves so admirably as an accompaniment that it almost seems as if it were written for the Gounod melody.

The two mélodies that are actually adaptations are the "Agnus Dei" (1872) by Georges Bizet (1838–75) and the "Élégie" (1873) by Jules Massenet (1842–1912). The melody of the "Agnus Dei" was first used by Bizet for his incidental music to Alphonse Daudet's play *L'Arlésienne;* it appears as a second-movement Intermezzo in the Orchestral Suite no. 2 arranged from this music. We do not know today who actually joined the words of the Catholic liturgical text to Bizet's reverent melody (though we do know this was not done by the composer himself). All the information we have is that this was accomplished during Bizet's lifetime and that the work was sung at Bizet's funeral.

The melody of Massenet's "Élégie" (which started out as a piano piece) also appeared in incidental music to a play, in this case *Les Érinnyes* by Charles Marie Leconte de Lisle, based on Aeschylus. Called the

Hector Berlioz.

A caricature of a performance of the music of Berlioz.

Gabriel Fauré, a portrait by John Singer Sargent.

Giuseppe Verdi, from a sketch by E. Tito.

"Invocation," this plangent melody was scored for strings; somewhat later, however, Massenet arranged it for cello and piano, at which time he provided it with the new title of "Mélodie." It was this arrangement that led a poet, Louis Gallet, to write sentimental words for this lugubrious melody. Now named "Élégie," it achieved world renown.

Bizet, Massenet, and Gounod were three of the foremost opera composers in France in the latter part of the nineteenth century, Bizet being the composer of *Carmen* (1875); Massenet, of *Manon* (1884) and *Thaïs* (1894); Gounod, of *Faust* (1859). As opera composers, all three knew well how to write for the voice and possessed to an uncommon degree the gift of melody. All three wrote songs, though these are by no means as well known as the more popular excerpts from their operas. Bizet's best songs were "Adieux de l'hôtesse arabe," to words by Victor Hugo, "Chanson d'avril," and the vocal bolero "Ouvre ton coeur." Both Massenet and Gounod were more prolific as songwriters than Bizet. Massenet wrote "Ouvre tes yeux bleus," "Pensée d'automne," and "Sérénade du passant," among numerous other mélodies. Gounod wrote "Jésus de Nazareth," "Où voulez-vous aller?" (words by Gautier), "Sérénade" (words by Victor Hugo), and "There Is a Green Hill Far Away" (with English words).

In addition to his songs, Gounod wrote several large choral works, all of them religious, and all done toward the end of his life, when he became imbued with religious ardor and mysticism. Unfortunately, the enormous fame of Gounod's operas has thrown this religious choral music into a shade it does not deserve. The most significant of his choral works are two oratorios—*La Rédemption* (*Redemption*), in 1881, and *Mors et Vita* (*Death and Life*), in 1884—a mass in 1887 honoring the memory of Joan of Arc, and a Te Deum in 1886. Just before his death Gounod worked on a requiem, which he did not live to finish.

César Franck (1822–90) was still another French Romantic composer whose religious and mystical nature found outlet in vocal music. This simple, humble, devout man spent the last thirty-two years of his life playing the organ at the Sainte-Clotilde Church in Paris where music lovers of every kind would sit in awe at his performances. He also taught music for pittances. All the while he completed masterworks for the orchestra, chamber-music combinations, piano, and the organ, the departments through which he acquired a niche all his own in French music. His vocal music is of equal distinction. His most often sung vocal piece is the religious song "Panis angelicus," in 1872, originally for tenor, organ, harp, cello, and double bass, but subsequently adapted both for chorus and also for orchestra. (Before its publication in 1872, the "Panis angelicus" was interpolated by the composer into his Mass.) His principal choral composition, however, is the oratorio *Les Béatitudes* (*The Beatitudes*), completed in 1879. This is a setting of the Sermon on the Mount. It took Franck ten years to write this oratorio. He invited several outstanding musicians to his home to hear him play and sing parts of it. Most of them withdrew quietly from the apartment while the music was being performed. Not until 1893 was this oratorio given a public presentation. At that time it proved to be a triumph, but one that had come too late for Franck, since he was no longer alive to enjoy it.

Franck influenced several of his French contemporaries. One of them was Henri Duparc, whose principal contribution to French music was his mélodies. He was born on January 21, 1848, in Paris. He seemed headed for a career in law until he took piano lessons from César Franck at the school where Duparc was then receiving his academic education. Franck brought to the surface Duparc's latent interest in music by taking him to concerts, teaching him harmony and piano, and encouraging him to compose. In 1867 Duparc completed a cello sonata, in 1869 he published some piano pieces, and in the next few years he produced several orchestral works that were performed in Paris. Duparc later destroyed most of this early music.

He allowed his earliest songs to survive because he knew that it was in the art song that his main strength lay. His first five songs came in 1868, two of which are numbered with his masterpieces: "Soupir" ("Sigh") and "Chanson triste" ("Sad Song"). There is here a freshness of lyricism, a romantic fire, and a purity of expression that forthwith placed him with the best French composers of art songs of his time, even though his output was pitifully small. After 1868, and up to 1884, he wrote only nine more songs, but each is an unblemished jewel. They are settings of poems by Gautier, Baudelaire, and Leconte de Lisle, among others, and include "Élégie" ("Elegy"), "Extase" ("Ecstasy"), "L'Invitation au voyage" ("Invitation to a Voyage"), "Sérénade florentine" ("Florentine Serenade"), and "Testament" ("Testament"). Duparc's last song was "La vie antérieure" ("Former Life"), in 1884. Though he lived for another half century, he wrote no more songs and almost no other music either. From 1884 he suffered from a neurasthenia. "The least little thing finishes me," he confided to a friend in 1888. He made futile attempts at writing music, even planning operas, but all these proved useless gestures. Neither the spirit nor the flesh was willing to cooperate with him. As the years went by, both his mental and physical condition degenerated. Toward life's end he tried to find solace in religion. He died at Mont-de-Marsan in France on February 12, 1933.

The mélodie comes to full glory with Gabriel Fauré. He was a French Romantic, but with a difference. In his music he spoke with a subdued voice, touched only lightly by emotion. His was a quiet restraint that whispered gentle confidences. Fauré was averse to making music interpret texts literally; he preferred subtle nuances to realism. He was in his element in serene, contemplative expression within beautifully balanced but comparatively modest structures.

The son of a schoolmaster, he was born in Pamiers, France, on May 12, 1845. As a child he learned by himself the rudiments of organ playing, which made such an impression on Louis Niedermeyer, a distinguished music educator, that in 1855 he enrolled the boy into his school (the famous École Niedermeyer) without charging him anything either for lessons or for room and board. Under the protective wing of a teacher who was to become a profound influence on his musical development—Camille Saint-Saëns—Fauré wrote a good deal of music while attending the école. Before 1865 he published *Three Romances* for piano and wrote many songs to poems by Gautier, Hugo, Baudelaire, and others. Two of these songs are representative of his best efforts. "Après un rêve" ("After a Dream") tells of a young man's dream that he is being brought to heaven's gate with his beloved; having had a glimpse of celestial beauties, he awakens to the sadness of life. The exquisitely spun, wide-ranged melody on a subtle harmonic base has such pervading charm that this has remained one of Fauré's best-loved songs. "Lydia," a tribute to a lovely girl, permits Fauré to indulge in a kind of musical pun. Bearing in mind the title of his song, Fauré passes in his melody from an F-major tonality to the old-time Lydian mode.

He was a brilliant pupil at the école, gathering prizes in piano, organ, harmony, and composition by the time he was graduated in 1865. He then became the organist at a church in Rennes, Brittany, where he stayed four years. There another of his early songs became his first to get public performance: "Le Papillon et la fleur ("The Butterfly and the Flower"), featured by the noted singer Marie Miolan-Carvalho at her concert in Rennes in 1868.

Fauré wrote no songs between 1865 and 1880. But in that time he did produce notable compositions in other areas, which brought him into the limelight. During part of this period he served as organist and choirmaster at the Madeleine Church in Paris.

In 1883, Fauré married Marie Frémiet, daughter of a sculptor. Two years later, Fauré's father died. This tragedy spurred him on to write a Requiem, for solo voices, chorus, and orchestra. By the time it was performed, in 1888, Fauré's mother had also passed away, so that this concert served as a memorial for both his parents.

Fauré's Requiem differs from other works in this form in its slender structure, intimate tone, and subdued style. What speaks most often in this music is the tranquillity death brings rather than its torment. The first of seven sections pronounces a soft plea for eternal rest, while, in the concluding part, rest is assured when the dead are ushered to paradise to be received by angels and martyrs.

Fauré returned to the song form in or about 1880 with three numbers collected in op. 18, the best of which is "Nell," poem by Leconte de Lisle. Two exquisite songs followed between 1883 and 1884: "Le Secret" ("The Secret") and "Les Roses d'Ispahan" ("Roses of Isfahan"). The year of 1887 was a momentous one for Fauré as a song composer, for it was then that, for the first time, he set to music a poem by Paul Verlaine, "Clair de lune" ("Moonlight"), which must not be confused with one of Debussy's best-known piano pieces. Henceforth some of Fauré's greatest songs used poems by Verlaine. Verlaine was a Symbolist poet, writing in a style that made its appeal through the senses. The Symbolists were concerned with the sound of their words as a means of expression. These poets tried to convey the essence of a poetic experience not directly with ideas but through symbols and metaphors. They did not try to develop a narrative, or to preach a moral lesson, or to express overwhelming emotions. The Symbolists explored the shifting states of the human psyche while trying to suggest the mystery of human existence. Verlaine was one of the leading voices of this Symbolist movement, and Gabriel Fauré was the first significant composer to devise elusive, moody, evocative kind of melodies suitable for Verlaine's words.

In 1890, Fauré wrote *Cinq mélodies,* op. 58, music for five poems by Verlaine. The union of Verlaine's poems and Fauré's music scales heights in the song cycle *La Bonne chanson (The Beautiful Song),* op. 61, nine songs completed between 1891 and 1892. In his *La Bonne chanson,* Verlaine had written not nine poems but twenty-one. At that time he was in love with the sixteen-year-old girl who later became his wife. Never before or afterward had he known or was he to know the happiness that was his during this romance. This rapture glows in each of his poems. Fauré caught and fixed Verlaine's ecstatic moods in melodies that reflect every shade of emotion experienced by the poet, from excitement to serene happiness, and from love to fear. In this cycle Fauré achieves unity by quoting melodic ideas from the earlier songs in the last one, "L'Hiver a cessé" ("Winter Has Passed"). This song ends with a love motive found in the opening number, "Une Sainte en son auréole" ("A Saint with Her Halo"). So beautifully intertwined are words and music and music and words that many musicologists look upon *La Bonne chanson* as the best song cycle in French music.

Fauré continued to write songs virtually up to the end of his life. His last song cycle, *L'Horizon chimérique* (*Illusory Horizon*), op. 118, came just two years before his death. Here, as well as in the cycle *La Chanson d'Ève* (*Song of Eve*), op. 95, which had preceded it between 1907 and 1910, Fauré remains master of the song form. Now his style has become simpler, more economical, and more personal; the structure is more rarefied, the expression more elusive, the harmonies bolder. *La Chanson d'Ève* is made up of ten pantheistic songs about the reactions of Eve, the first woman, to the newly created world around her. *L'Horizon chimérique* comprises four songs of the sea. Fauré, now an old man, and completely deaf—totally removed from the maelstrom of his former activities as organist, teacher, and director of the Paris Conservatory—saw in the sea a symbol of the great beyond toward which he was heading. These songs are filled for the most part with a touching pathos.

Fauré passed on to that great beyond on November 4, 1924, in Paris.

The first prominent composer of Italian art songs was late in coming. He, too, was a son of Romanticism.

Before then, Italian composers preferred to concentrate their vocal writing on operas. The handful of nonoperatic songs surviving from the seventeenth century on are really opera arias masquerading as villanellas (songs in the style of Italian street songs), canzonettas, or cantatas. The best vocal-display music written in the nineteenth century is found in the operas of Vincenzo Bellini (1801–35), Gaetano Donizetti (1797–1848), and Gioacchino Rossini (1792–1868), all three of whom were masters of the bel canto style ("bel canto" being an elegant kind of vocal music stressing beauty of sound and brilliant virtuosity).

One of the first Italians recognizing the basic truth that the art song was a medium far different in style from the opera aria was Sir Francesco Paolo Tosti. He was born in Ortona on April 9, 1846. When he was twelve he entered a conservatory in Naples to study violin and composition. He remained there eleven years. He then returned to his native city to recover from a serious and prolonged illness. It was then that he first tried his hand at writing songs. Those he submitted for publication were rejected—most unwisely, it now appears, since two of them subsequently enjoyed considerable vogue: "Non m'ama più" and "Lamento d'amore."

For a number of years Tosti endured such extreme poverty that his diet often consisted of little else but oranges and stale bread. His inability to get ahead as a composer compelled him to make a change of scene. He went to Rome, where he gave a song recital featuring some of his own music. The concert was enthusiastically received. Princess Margherita of Savoy, who was in that audience, forthwith hired him as her singing teacher.

Tosti now began to make significant headway as a composer. Two of his songs were published by the powerful house of Ricordi. After Princess Margherita became queen of Italy in 1878, she appointed Tosti keeper of the musical archives at the royal palace. Meanwhile, in 1875, Tosti had begun making annual trips to England, where he gathered considerable accolades both for his singing and for his songs.

In 1880 Tosti took up permanent residence in London, becoming a teacher of singing to the royal family. During the next five years he completed the songs that brought him international renown. Some were to Italian texts, such as "Amore," "Aprile," "Mattinata," and "Vorrei morire," some to French. Others had English words, including "Goodbye," "Mother," "That Day," and "At Vespers." The Italian warmth of his lyricism, and its strong sentimental appeal, made these songs instantaneous and permanent successes. By 1885 Tosti had realized such an enormous fame throughout Europe that his publishers, Ricordi, paid him a retainer of $500 a week to write just one song a month.

Tosti now became a frequent and welcome visitor to the palaces of royalty, including those of Queen Victoria, a favorite of the rich, powerful, and highborn not only for his talent and fame but also because he was a man of unusual wit and charm. In 1894 he was appointed to the faculty of the Royal Academy of Music in London; in 1906 he was honored by the British government with the title of Commander of the Victorian Order; and in 1908 he became Sir Francesco when he was knighted by King Edward VII.

As a British subject upon whom honors had been showered by the government, Tosti became a target for attack in Italy, where it was felt he had exchanged his Italian heritage and nationality for success in a foreign land. *119*

This was the heaviest cross Tosti had to bear when his fame and fortune were at their peak. But his ties to England had by now become too strong to be broken.

Then an illness in 1913, and the fear that he did not have much longer to live, sent him back to his homeland. He spent his last three years in Rome, where he died on December 2, 1916.

Since Giuseppe Verdi (1813–1901) was the foremost opera composer Italy produced, his most rewarding writing for the voice is found in the glorious arias, duets, ensemble numbers, and choruses of his many stage masterworks. He was the creator of only a handful of compositions intended for the concert hall instead of the opera house. With the exception of two works for chorus, none bears the hallmark of his genius. But these two choral compositions well deserve to carry the hallowed name of Verdi, for nothing so inspired or exalted had been written in Italy for chorus since the age of the Baroque. Both of these choral works by Verdi came after most of his operas had been written, when his creative and technical powers were at their fullest. They are the Requiem Mass (sometimes called the *Manzoni Requiem*) and the *Quattro pezzi sacri* (*Four Sacred Pieces*).

His apprenticeship as composer took place with the writing of some instrumental music, a handful of romantic songs, and a choral cantata—none of which was particularly notable. This was between 1832 and 1835 when he lived in Milan and received an intensive musical training from Vincenzo Lavigna. Only then did he turn to the stage. His first opera, produced in 1839, was a fair success, but the second in 1840 was a failure. It took Verdi only about a year and a half to recover from the disaster sustained by his second opera and to write a new one. But with *Nabucco*, in 1842, he achieved a triumph that made his a familiar name. From then on, his operas came thick and fast, the luster of his fame and the magnitude of his fortunes growing all the while. Among his most celebrated operas are *Ernani* (1844), *Rigoletto* (1851), *Il Trovatore* (1853), *La Traviata* (1853), *La Forza del destino* (1862), *Aida* (1871), *Otello* (1887), and *Falstaff* (1893).

Between the writing of *Aida* and *Otello,* Verdi went into a sixteen-year retirement from the stage. For a long time it seemed that he would never again write another opera. Instead, he did a string quartet in 1873, the Requiem Mass in 1874, a five-part chorus in 1880—lean pickings, indeed, when we compare them with the fertile crop of music that had preceded them! But this leanness comes more from quantity than quality, since at least the Requiem Mass is a masterwork of the caliber of his greatest operas.

The Requiem is the most important nontheatrical work Verdi wrote. He wrote it in loving and grief-stricken memory of his friend and compatriot Alessandro Manzoni, a distinguished novelist, poet, and patriot. After Manzoni died in 1873, Verdi proposed to the city authorities of Milan that he write a large religious work in honor of the writer for the first anniversary of Manzoni's death. When Verdi received an enthusiastic approval, he threw himself unsparingly into a project which, as he said, was a "tribute to the respectful affection and the expression of my sorrow." He finished the score in time to have it played in Milan on the first anniversary, May 22, 1874. Verdi himself conducted.

Verdi had experienced many a triumph for his operas before 1874, but few to equal that enjoyed by the Requiem. Audiences and critics outdid themselves in expressions of enthusiasm. Verdi was invited to conduct a second performance of the Requiem at La Scala, where a silver crown was presented to him on a silken cushion, symbolic of his regal position in Italian music. At subsequent presentations at La Scala, sections of the work had to be repeated to satisfy the thunder of acclaim. Similar outbursts greeted this work wherever it was given in Italy, and later throughout Europe when in 1875 Verdi conducted it on a tour. In Italy the music was in such popular demand that, in some cities, unauthorized presentations were given by splinter groups until Verdi put a stop to this practice. In Bologna, for example, four pianos were used as accompaniment in place of an orchestra; in Ferrara, the local military band was recruited.

Though a requiem is essentially a religious composition, and though Verdi's Requiem received its world premiere in a Milanese church (San Marco), this music is more fitting for the concert hall than for a house of worship. As a man of the theater, Verdi was guided by his dramatic instincts to produce stirring music, as in the "Dies Irae" and the "Rex tremendae," which sweep forward toward power and grandeur. With broad strokes Verdi portrays the terrors of Judgment Day and sings praises to the glory of God. But Verdi was also a supreme master of melody. Time and again he spins a delicate web of the most touching lyricism: the "Recordare," the final section of "Libera me," and the "Agnus Dei."

Falstaff, in 1893, was Verdi's last opera, but it was not his last composition. His farewell to music came with four liturgical compositions collectively entitled *Quattro pezzi sacri.* The first was "Ave Maria," the next two, "Stabat Mater" and "Laudi alla vergine Maria," the latter to a text by Dante; the last, "Te Deum." The "Ave Maria" and the "Laudi" were for unaccompanied four-part chorus; the "Stabat Mater" was for chorus and orchestra; the "Te Deum," for double chorus and orchestra.

Structurally, the "Te Deum" was the most ambitious of the four choral pieces; musically, it was the most grandiose. In comparison to its three companions, it is like a cathedral placed beside churches. Without abandoning religiosity, this music has a power and a glory not encountered in the other three "pieces." There are pages in the "Te Deum"—just as there are in the Requiem—to arouse wonder. Among these are the glorious Sanctus, the funereal unison passage "Dignare, Domine," and the closing "In Te, Domine, speravi."

The "Te Deum" had a deep personal meaning for Verdi. He once asked that this score be buried with him. Verdi was not a religious man. Why did this religious piece mean so much to him? The conjecture is that he wrote it for his beloved wife, Giuseppina, who all her life had been a pious Catholic and who was deathly sick when Verdi first planned this composition. Fearing that Giuseppina did not have long to live, Verdi wrote liturgical music of great religious fervor to honor her religious convictions. Giuseppina died in 1897, about a year after Verdi had committed his last notes to paper. From then on, he considered this music as his memorial to his wife.

His will to live and create died with his wife. He went into a physical decline at his home at the Grand Hotel in Milan. His sight and hearing were failing him. His limbs, as he lamented in a letter, "no longer obey me." He died in his hotel suite on January 27, 1901, six days after suffering a paralytic stroke.

a simple ceremony in the village's only church, it was carried to the composer's final resting place, a small chapel in the villa that had been his home for so many years.

On April 25, 1926, *Turandot*, the opera Puccini never finished, was given its first performance at La Scala, with Toscanini conducting. Following the composer's death, Franco Alfano, a diligent if undistinguished musician, was given the task of completing the opera, based on the thirty-six pages of notes that Puccini had left behind. On the evening of the première, Toscanini stopped the performance after the death of Liù. Choked with emotion, he turned to the audience and quietly announced that it was at this point that the composer had left his opera unfinished. For a few long moments, the audience was silent. The silence was broken by a shout of "Viva Puccini" from the balcony, which was followed by one of the most moving ovations in the history of La Scala.

Puccini left no successor; his death meant the end of a glorious era of Italian opera. His music is as alive today as it was when it was first written, and his critics, who predicted that his unprecedented success was ephemeral, have been proven wrong by the immense pleasure his works have continued to give to music lovers wherever opera is heard. It would be wrong to place him among the greatest of composers, but it is also unfair to minimize his considerable gifts. Perhaps the most fitting epitaph would be the words of Ernest Newman, who wrote:

> No artist, of course, ever achieves such popularity, and such enduring popularity, among art lovers of all kinds without there being excellent reasons for it. Puccini's genius is a very limited one, but he has always made the very most of it. His operas are to some extent a mere bundle of tricks: but no one else has ever performed the same tricks nearly as well.

Last page from "Puccini" by Howard Greenfeld (1980), an excellent book.

A Gallery of Singers

Jenny Lind, Swedish soprano, made her debut at the Stockholm Opera in 1838 in Der Freischütz *and gave concerts in many parts of the world, finally settling in England, where she taught at the Royal College of Music. Her voice was bright, strong, and pure, with fine breath control and impressive skill in coloratura singing.*

Ernestine Schumann-Heink, Austrian (later American) contralto,
made her debut as Azucena at the Dresden Court Opera in October, 1878.
Mme Schumann-Heink, one of the outstanding lieder interpreters
of her time, had a rich, powerful voice of even quality and great range.

Elisabeth Schumann in 1938. Mme Schumann, a German (later American) soprano, had a high, delicate voice of unusual purity that suited her especially for Mozartean operatic roles. Richard Strauss was so pleased with her interpretation of his songs that he made a recital tour of the United States with her.

*Elisabeth Rethberg, German (later American) soprano,
began her career with the Dresden Opera.
She had a high, clear liquid voice of singular brightness.*

Beniamino Gigli, Italian tenor, made his operatic debut in
La Gioconda *at Rovigo in 1914. Possessed of a voice of great natural*
beauty, he further enhanced his singing with unusual technical skills.

Paul Robeson, American bass-baritone, after studying at Rutgers University and the Columbia University Law School and establishing himself as a noted actor, began his singing career, specializing in spirituals but soon expanding his repertory into other varieties of song.

Marian Anderson, American contralto, studied in the United States but first established her concert career in Europe. Her voice is of remarkable range with an unusually rich middle register.

Elisabeth Schwarzkopf, German soprano, studied in Berlin and from early in her career concentrated on the recital art as well as opera. Her singing, featuring especially the lieder of Wolf and Strauss, is marked by intelligence of interpretation and perfection of intonation.

Janet Baker, English mezzo soprano,
has a rich, full voice that she uses
with outstanding interpretive skill in
a wide-ranging song repertory.

A performance of Bach's
Passion According to Saint Matthew
by the Musica Sacra of New York,
conducted by Richard Westenburg, in 1974.

*Christa Ludwig, German soprano, singing at a
recording session in Vienna. Mme Ludwig uses her unusually
pure voice with interpretive mastery.*

Dietrich Fischer-Dieskau,
German baritone and eminent lieder singer.

7

Late Romanticism

Johannes Brahms, Hugo Wolf,

Gustav Mahler, Richard Strauss

In the Romantic music of the second half of the nineteenth century, Johannes Brahms and Richard Wagner towered like two Alpine peaks. They were the two, above all others, to whom the composers of that period looked for inspiration and guidance. Brahms favored absolute music, while Wagner represented the ultimate development up to his time of literalness in programmatic writing. Brahms never wrote an opera, Wagner wrote little else. Brahms tended to look backward in time by sometimes writing contrapuntally, by favoring such classical forms as the concerto, the symphony, the sonata form, and even such older Baroque structures as the orchestral serenade, the concerto grosso, and the passacaglia. Wagner faced the future. In promoting music drama that was a synthesis of many arts, Wagner had to devise new harmonic and instrumental resources, a new style of vocal delivery and orchestral performance, and a new concept of tonality, to bring his vision to life. To Wagnerians, Brahms was a reactionary, since he was never an innovator and was happy with the *status quo* in music. To Brahms-ites, Wagner represented, both in theory and practice, a destruction of tradition. Each—Brahms and Wagner—had his coterie of passionate admirers who vigorously repudiated the opposing cult. The musical world of the late nineteenth century, then, was split into two warring factions. With the nearsighted vision of those pursuing a single dogma, these factions failed to realize that Brahms and Wagner complemented each other rather than standing in opposition to one another. Brahms and Wagner themselves recognized this truth. They neither encouraged nor themselves engaged in battles fought in their names. In fact, they respected each other's genius. The one time they met face to face—at Penzing, near Vienna, on February 6, 1864—they were most cordial to one another.

Brahms has become so famous for his orchestral, chamber, and piano music that it is easy to disregard the importance of his vocal compositions. Brahms had learned to admire the voice and its artistic capabilities from personal experience: as a piano accompanist to two distinguished lieder singers (Julius Stockhausen and Amalie Joachim), as conductor of a women's chorus in Hamburg between 1859 and 1863, and for one year after that as the director of a chorus, the Singakademie, in Vienna. Indeed, it was with a choral work—*A German Requiem*—and not with an instrumental one that Brahms first gained public recognition.

Born in poverty and misery in a drab waterfront apartment in Hamburg, Germany, on May 7, 1833, Brahms began composing when he was still a child. Since he had not yet learned to put music down on paper, he had to invent his own system of notation. At the age of ten he began taking piano lessons from a distinguished teacher in Hamburg, Eduard Marxsen. Brahms soon helped to support his family by playing the piano in disreputable saloons on Hamburg's waterfront, and later on by writing hack music, published under pseudonyms. But there was no question of the seriousness of his purpose as a musician. He worked long and hard at the piano and turned into an impressive young virtuoso. He also developed his compositional skill by writing a piano scherzo in 1851 and, by 1853, completing several ambitious piano works (including his first three sonatas), together with eighteen songs, which were subsequently issued in three volumes, op. 3, 6, and 7. One of the songs in the first volume—"Liebestreu" ("True Love")—betrays facets of the later mature Brahms in the way a dreamlike melody is combined with cogent declamatory phrases. This song is strophic (a structure to which Brahms was partial) and consists of a dialogue between mother and daughter. The mother exhorts her daughter to renounce love, since it can bring her only grief. The love-stricken girl, in vivid imagery, defiantly insists that her love is as indestructible as the wind.

136   When he tied up a bundle of his songs and piano music into a package

and dispatched it to Robert Schumann for criticism, Brahms could hardly have guessed how vital a role this great composer would occupy in his own life. But if he harbored such hopes, they were certainly crushed when this package was returned—unopened. Yet it was not long before Schumann—and his wife, Clara—became a decisive turning point in Brahms's life and career. After Brahms had toured Germany in 1853 as the piano accompanist for the Hungarian violinist Eduard Reményi, Brahms paid an uninvited call at the Schumann home in Düsseldorf. He played for Schumann some of his piano works and sang for him some of his own songs. "My dear Clara," Schumann called out from the drawing room, "come quickly. You must hear this!" They listened. With their sure musical intuition, they knew they were in the presence of genius—a fact publicly acknowledged by Schumann in his famous article on the young and unknown Brahms in the *Neue Zeitschrift für Musik* on October 28, 1853. Through Schumann, too, Brahms acquired a publisher who, between 1853 and 1854, released Brahms's first volumes of piano music and songs.

The friendship between the Schumanns and Brahms deepened quickly from that meeting on. Brahms proved a source of strength and solace to Clara Schumann and her children when Robert Schumann was confined to a mental institution in 1854, and also after his death there in 1856. For a time Brahms took up residence in an apartment over one occupied by Clara Schumann and her children in Düsseldorf to provide such help and comfort as he could. Brahms began to regard Clara's children as his own—he looked after them, played with them, tried to give them paternal guidance.

For the Schumann children, Brahms made arrangements of German folk songs (*Volkslieder*) for voice and piano between 1857 and 1858. These songs were published anonymously under the title of *Children's Folk Songs* (*Volkskinderlieder*). In this volume, as well as in his settings of twenty-eight German folk songs in 1858, Brahms reveals his preoccupation with German folk music. He had made an intensive study of this field and had found it to be a bountiful source of wonderful melodies for adaptation or imitation. Many of his later songs were influenced by the *Volkslied* in their strophic structure, their unpretentious projection of a simple mood or emotion, their emphasis on melody, and their pervading charm. It is as if we were listening to old German folk songs whenever we are brought into contact with the gentle loveliness of such Brahms songs as "Der Schmied" ("The Smith"), with its suggestion of the hammer blows of the smith in the accompaniment; that perennial favorite "Wiegenlied" ("Cradle Song"), which more than one mother throughout the world has sung as a lullaby to her child; "Sonntag" ("Sunday"); "O komme,

holde Sommernacht'' (''Come, O Holy Summer Night''); ''Agnes'';
and ''Feldeinsamkeit'' (''Solitude in Summer Fields'') which speaks so
eloquently of nature's beauties.

But his interest in the folk song was not altogether confined to North
Germany. Many other of Brahms's four hundred or so songs are modeled
after the folk songs of Austria, Hungary, and Bohemia (Czechoslovakia);
and still others were inspired by poems of antiquity. In the last category
we must place two gems: ''Die Mainacht'' (''May Night'') and ''Sap-
phische Ode'' (''Sapphic Ode''). On the other hand, the *Liebeslieder*
waltzes (*Songs of Love*), op. 52, and the *Neue Liebeslieder* (*New Songs of
Love*), op. 65—both of them for vocal quartet and piano duet—are
thoroughly Viennese. Once, in presenting his autograph to the stepdaugh-
ter of Johann Strauss II, Vienna's noted waltz king, Brahms scribbled
above his own signature a few measures of the Strauss waltz *By the Beautiful Blue Danube,* adding the comment ''Unfortunately—not by me.'' If
imitation be the highest form of flattery, then Brahms gave Johann Strauss
an even higher compliment in the *Liebeslieder* waltzes, since throughout
this music we find the lilt, pulse, and buoyancy of Johann Strauss at his
best.

That gentle, poetic personality for whom Schumann concocted the
name of ''Eusebius'' can be detected in those Brahms songs mentioned
above which are derived from *Volkslieder* and from Austrian folk songs
and dances. But in other Brahms songs we find the fiery nature to which
Schumann assigned the name of ''Florestan.'' There is passion in ''Lie-
besglut'' (''Love's Ardor'') and in ''Meine Liebe ist grün'' (''My Love Is
Green''), and there is high drama in ''Am Sonntag Morgen'' (''On Sunday
Morning''). The *Zigeuenerlieder* (*Gypsy Songs*), op. 103, for vocal quartet
and piano on texts from Hungarian folk songs, have the sensuousness of
true gypsy music.

Brahms wrote many memorable love songs reflecting his dual Euse-
bius-Florestan creative personality. Sometimes he speaks with tenderness,
and sometimes with flaming fervor. One brings to mind such love songs as
''Wie bist du, meine Königin?'' (''Where Are You, My Queen of
Hearts?''); ''Botschaft'' (''Message''); ''Minnelied III'' (''Love Song'');
''Alte Liebe'' (''Old Love''); ''Vergebliches Ständchen'' (''Fruitless Sere-
nade''); ''Bei dir sind mein' Gedanken'' (''My Thoughts Are with You'');
''Von ewiger Liebe'' (''Of Eternal Love''); and ''Mein Mädel hat einen
Rosenmund'' (''My Girl Has Rosy Lips''), a setting of a German folk
song. The nightingale also chirps a love message in ''Der Tod, das ist die

kühle Nacht'' ("Death Is Like the Cool Night''), an apostrophe to the beauty and tranquillity of night.

Brahms wrote many of his love songs now with one woman in heart and mind and now with another. Though he remained a bachelor, he loved many women with depth of feeling. Women were attracted to him, though he was short and squat and hardly romantic in appearance, because he was highly personable and stimulating. Here is how J. V. Widmann described Brahms when the composer was in his early thirties, a description that serves equally well for his later years. "His whole appearance was . . . steeped in force. The broad, leonine breast, the Herculean shoulders, the powerful head, which he often tossed back with an energetic movement . . . the thoughtful, fine brow, radiant as though with wondrous fire from between the lashes, revealed an artistic personality which seemed to be charged to the very fingertips with the magnetism of genius. There was also something confidently triumphant in his face, the radiant serenity of a mind happy in the exercise of his art.''

In late youth, Brahms had been in love with Agathe von Siebold, daughter of a professor. She reciprocated. But when marriage seemed imminent, Brahms fled precipitously from this romance and sublimated his passions by writing music for and about Agathe. "Chains I cannot wear!'' he exclaimed. After that, there were other women in his life. There was the beautiful singer Luise Dustmann. There was his pupil Elisabeth von Stockhausen, whom he turned over to another teacher when he realized how much she had come to mean to him. There was another Viennese singer, Ottilie Hauer, about whom he once remarked wryly that he would surely have made a fool of himself over her "if, as luck would have it, someone had not snatched her up at Christmas.'' There was, ever and always, Clara Schumann, with whom he was emotionally involved throughout his life. He also harbored a secret passion for Clara's daughter, Julie, who was so many years younger than he. Why he avoided marriage remains an unanswered question, since time and again he bemoaned the fact that a man without wife and children was doomed to loneliness, and he often spoke sadly about his celibacy. This mystery grows deeper when we remember how much Clara Schumann and Brahms meant to one another over a period of many years.

There was one woman whom he cherished and adored above all others—his mother. It was his all-encompassing love for her that motivated him into writing the work that first threw the limelight of recognition upon him: *A German Requiem,* op. 45, for soprano and baritone   *139* soloists, chorus, and orchestra. The ambition to write a requiem first stirred within him in 1856 when Schumann died in the asylum and Brahms aspired to write an important work to his memory. He made some sketches, then laid the plan aside for other projects, including his first piano concerto. Then in 1865 Brahms was stricken by perhaps the greatest tragedy of his life, his mother's death. Once again he began thinking of writing a requiem, this time as a memorial to his mother. By 1866 he completed six of its seven sections; two years after that, the requiem was finished.

It is called *A German Requiem* (*Ein deutsches Requiem*) because, unlike traditional requiems, it does not use a Latin text from the Catholic liturgy but a German one taken from the Lutheran Bible. In character and emotional content it differs from most other famous requiems. It is primarily concerned not with the dead but with the living. It speaks of resignation and hope, intended as a comfort for those who have lost loved ones. Whatever sorrow Brahms experienced at the death of two people who meant so much to him—his mother and Schumann—does not invade this loftily conceived music.

It opens with a short orchestral introduction that leads into a serene chorus, ''Blessed Are They That Mourn.'' There is strength and courage, as well as an affirmation of the human spirit, in the marchlike tread of the second section, ''All Flesh Is As the Grass.'' In the third part, the baritone plaintively appeals to God for guidance (''Lord Make Me to Know Mine End'') while the contemplative character of the fourth part (''How Lovely Is Thy Dwelling Place'') makes way in the fifth to the comforting strains of ''Ye Now Are Sorrowful,'' sung by the soprano and chorus. The sixth part, ''Here on Earth We Have No Continuing City''—for baritone and chorus—prophesies the coming of the Resurrection and ends with a fugal hymn of praise to God. The requiem concludes on a note of sublimity with ''Blessed Are the Dead,'' toward the end of which the main theme of the opening section is quietly repeated.

When the requiem was first heard—in Vienna on December 1, 1867—only three parts were given. The public reacted negatively, possibly because the performance was far from acceptable, and possibly because taken out of context the three sections lacked artistic validity. But when all but one part (the fifth, which Brahms had not yet written) was given in Bremen on April 10, 1868, the success was monumental. As one member in that audience, Albert Dietrich, wrote: ''The effect . . . was simply overwhelming and it at once became clear to the audience that *A German Requiem* ranks among the loftiest music ever given to the world.'' Triumphant, too, was the performance of the complete requiem, in Leipzig on February 18, 1869.

But the sweetness of his first success was soon touched with bitterness—a setback in Brahms's love life. By 1869 Julie Schumann, whom Brahms had known from her childhood, had grown into a lovely young lady of twenty-four. He fell in love with her, although he was twelve years older than she. Whenever they were in the same room, he would throw at her furtive glances full of tenderness. It is unlikely that either Julie or her mother, Clara, were in the least aware of Brahms's feelings, since he was highly secretive; it is also more than probable that this ''romance'' existed only in Brahms's imagination. One day, in 1869, Julie quietly confided to Brahms she had just become engaged to a count. His dreams of an idyllic life with Julie suddenly destroyed, Brahms became so grief-stricken that, overnight, he changed in appearance and in spirit.

There was only one way to escape from despair, by writing music. While suffering rejection from Julie, Brahms came upon Goethe's poem *Harzreise im Winter,* a somber set of verses about loneliness. This poem struck a responsive chord in Brahms. He selected three of the verses to set for alto voice, male chorus, and orchestra, calling the composition *Rhapsodie (Rhapsody)*, op. 53 (1869). The chill of loneliness shudders through the pages of the first two verses, sung by alto with orchestral accompaniment. But apparently Brahms successfully freed himself from melancholia, for in the last verse a male chorus lifts the music out of its somber depths. A burst of sunlight dispels the earlier gloom, as the spirit of a proud man is victorious over desolation.

In Vienna—where Brahms had established permanent residence and where, for several years, he conducted its leading choral organization, the Singakademie—he completed two major works for chorus between 1870 and 1871: the *Schicksalslied (Song of Fate)*, op. 54, and the *Triumphlied (Song of Triumph)*, op. 55. The first used a poem by Hölderlin dealing with the conflict between life and death, the ephemeral and the eternal. The other commemorated the recent victory of the German army in the Franco-Prussian War, its texts derived from the nineteenth chapter of the Book of Revelation. Brahms dedicated the *Triumphlied* to Wilhelm I, the German emperor, but he actually wrote it with Prince Bismarck in mind, because he admired him almost to the point of adulation.

Brahms fulfilled his destiny as the greatest symphonist since Beethoven by writing four symphonies, the first in 1876, and the other three between 1877 and 1885. He further advanced his status as a leading proponent of absolute music with other masterworks for orchestra, chamber-music combinations, and the piano. His fame kept pace with the continual growth of his artistic stature. In 1879 he received an honorary doctorate from Breslau University in Germany. In 1886 the German government made him Knight of the Prussian Order of Merit and elected him a member of the Berlin Academy of Arts. In 1889, the city of his birth, Hamburg, presented him with the freedom of the city, and the emperor of Austria conferred on him the exalted honor of the Order of Leopold.

For all his identification with instrumental music, Brahms did not abandon the voice, which remained a particularly grateful medium of self-expression. Between 1880 and 1882 came two more distinguished choral works. Both touch on death. *Nänie,* op. 82, has much of the calm and resignation encountered in *A German Requiem. Gesang der Parzen (Song of Fates)*, op. 89, with text by Goethe, is filled with torment. Thus these two compositions are complementary to each other.

He never stopped writing songs—wonderful songs—many of which have already been mentioned. One group of four songs appeared just one year before his death, and over them hovers its ominous shadow: the *Vier ernste Gesänge (Four Serious Songs)*, op. 121 (1896). They are serious indeed—in each instance the projection of a tragic mood. The words come out of the Bible: two from Ecclesiastes, one from the Apocrypha, and one from the First Epistle to the Corinthians. The first three songs grimly contrast the ideal world as conceived by the highest principles of Christianity with the far less ideal world as it really exists. In the last song, hope for the world comes through faith and charity. It is almost as if in these, his last songs, Brahms was giving a final evaluation of life as he saw it—and was repelled. "O death, how bitter you are to a man who has lived remembering his possessions, who has lived without care and has enjoyed prosperity." When Brahms wrote the music for lines such as these, was he speaking for himself? He had known as high an esteem as could be meted out to a composer. There had been no lapse to his creativity or productivity. Death, then, had become for him a threat—a threat that was translated into reality in Vienna at eight-thirty in the morning of April 3, 1897.

On one of the rare occasions when Wagner strayed from the musical stage to write concert music, he wrote a group of five songs for voice and piano, the *Fünf Gedichte von Mathilde Wesendonck,* now frequently referred to as the *Five Wesendonck Songs.* The "Mathilde Wesendonck" in the German title was the wife of a wealthy merchant who, in 1857, became Wagner's patron and invited him to occupy a little garden house, The Asyl, on his estate near Zürich, Switzerland. Wagner and Mathilde

became lovers. In 1857 and 1858 Wagner wrote music for five poems by
Mathilde. On her birthday on December 23, 1857, he had "Träume" ("Dreams"), one of the songs, sung under her window.

While residing at The Asyl, Wagner was deep in the writing of his mighty music drama of love and death *Tristan and Isolde*. Two of the songs in the Wesendonck set were described by the composer as "studies for *Tristan and Isolde*," because he used thematic material from his music drama. In "Träume" the melody comes out of the second-act love duet, while in "Im Treibhaus" ("In the Greenhouse"), two motives connected with Tristan are used. Neither song is sensuous or dramatic but, rather, moody and atmospheric. Less often heard, though no less appealing, are the three other songs: "Der Engel" ("The Angel"), "Stehe still" ("Be Still"), and "Schmerzen" ("Pain").

Strange to say, in his lieder Hugo Wolf proved to be far more Wagnerian than Wagner himself had been in his own songs. Hugo Wolf worshiped Wagner with an almost religious fervor. He heard his first Wagnerian opera (*Tannhäuser*) when he was fifteen—then a first-year student at the Vienna Conservatory. The experience proved overwhelming. Since at that time Wagner was visiting Vienna, Wolf stood outside Wagner's hotel for hours at a stretch several successive days in the hope of catching a glimpse of the master. Failing, he prevailed upon the hotel manager to arrange a face-to-face meeting. Wagner looked through the manuscript of a song by young Wolf and told him, "I cannot give you an opinion since I have too little time." Then, taking into account the composer's youth, he added, "When I was your age and composing music, no one could tell whether I should ever do anything great. When you are older and when you have composed bigger works, and by chance I return to Vienna, you will show me what you have done. But this is of no use now. I cannot give you an opinion yet."

This was Wolf's sole meeting with Wagner. From that time onward he became one of the most dedicated believers in the Wagnerian cult. When, in 1881, Wolf left Vienna to take on a job as assistant conductor in Salzburg, he arrived with a bundle of clothes under one arm and a bust of Wagner under the other. Two years later Wagner died. Upon hearing the news, Wolf went to the piano (as one of his friends related) "without a word, without any notice of us . . . and played the funeral music from *Götterdämmerung*. Then he shut down the piano lid and went—silently as he came. In the evening he reappeared in a subdued and deeply sorrowful mood. 'I have wept like a child,' he told me."

Hugo Wolf.

Gustav Mahler.

The Vienna Musikverein, in 1870.

Richard Strauss.

His adoration of Wagner crept into his own music when Wolf began to write lieder. So thoroughly did he assimilate Wagner's style that Wolf has come to be known as "the Wagner of the lied." Unfortunately, since Wolf's maturely conceived songs were written after Wagner's death, Wolf never had the opportunity of proving to the master how faithful a disciple he had become!

Wolf's was a life of struggle, sorrow, turbulence, and, in the end, disaster. Born in Windisch-Graz, Austria, on March 13, 1860, he received his first music lessons from his father. Talented in music, but thoroughly lackadaisical in his academic education in elementary and high schools, Wolf seemed marked for a musical career. But he had to overcome the opposition of a strong-willed father to a profession that brought nothing but poverty and hardships. Young Hugo won out in 1875 when he received parental permission to enter the Vienna Conservatory. Strange to say, he was no better a student there than he had previously been in academic schools. He was bored with routine music study. He abhorred perfunctory exercises. He chafed restlessly under the discipline of conservatory rules. He was forever at odds with his teachers. Once he was falsely accused of having written a scurrilous letter to the director of the conservatory. Actually, this was the handiwork of a mischievous fellow student who signed Wolf's name to the document. In vain did Wolf plead his innocence, for his past unruly behavior made the director skeptical. Wolf was summarily dismissed from the conservatory. His formal music education was over.

An intensified period of autodidactic music study followed. Wolf memorized the scores of his musical gods: Gluck, Mozart, Beethoven, and Wagner. He spent hours poring over textbooks on theory and composition to fill in the yawning gaps in his musical training. For poetry he displayed a similar passion. He read the German Romantics voraciously, committing to memory poems by Goethe, Heine, Mörike, Kleist, and others. When he read one of his favorite poets, "his hands trembled . . . his eyes lit up, and he appeared transfigured," one of his friends revealed, "as if at the sight of higher, brighter regions, the gates of which had suddenly sprung open. He gasped for air." To poetry, as to music, he responded with vehemence. A beautiful line enchanted him, while a poor one almost brought on physical disorder.

He was poor, most of the time penniless. He gave music lessons, but because of his explosive nature he never kept any one pupil long. Since he never averaged more than eighteen dollars a month, he would not allow himself more than a single meal a day. But most of the time he earned

nothing and was saved from starvation by his friends, who came to his help with loans (which he could never hope to repay) or gifts. However oppressive was the sting of poverty, his spirit remained high. When he had a book of poetry in hand, when he was studying the music of Beethoven or Wagner, when he was developing his technique in composition, when he was scribbling music to verses by Goethe and Heine, he was unassailable. "Restlessly," he wrote, "I am driven to improve my weak talents, to extend my horizon, to endow my thoughts, my actions, my feelings with as ripe an expression as possible."

He was very much the bohemian, unfitted for the ordinary ways of living. He loved freedom above all, and the life of a music teacher galled him. And he would never compromise with his ideals. In 1881 he found a job as an assistant conductor in Salzburg, Austria. He lasted only a few months because he had no respect for the music he was required to rehearse. Back in Vienna, he was given a miserly salary to write music criticism for a Viennese journal from 1884 to 1887. Too fiercely honest not to speak his mind openly at all times, he accumulated enemies among those whom he criticized severely. His hostility to Brahms turned some of Vienna's most powerful musicians against him. They saw to it that his attempts to get his music played led only to a dead end. Pressure by the Brahms faction led two leading Viennese chamber-music groups to turn down his Quartet in D minor. In 1885 Wolf wrote a symphonic poem, *Penthesilea,* which he thought had been accepted by Hans Richter, conductor of the Vienna Philharmonic. But Richter, a dedicated Brahms-ite, was merely interested in humiliating Wolf. After playing through the tone poem at a rehearsal, he told his musicians acidly, "The only reason I rehearsed this work today was because I was interested in finding out what sort of music is written by a composer who dares denounce our master Brahms."

Wolf's father died in 1887. For the first time Hugo Wolf felt unmoored. He had failed to prove himself as a musician. His father's warnings about the hardships of a composer's life had proved valid. Now that his father was dead, Wolf could never do anything to justify himself and his ambitions to him. For a moment, revulsion of feeling shook him. Then he gave up his job as music critic to work more feverishly than ever on songs. A kind of frenzy seized him, and at times, as he composed, he was almost in delirium. Sometimes he wept as he fashioned melodies to poems that stirred him. By the end of 1887 he had completed over fifty songs. That same year his first two volumes of lieder were published through subscription by his friends—six songs in each volume to poems by Rückert, Hebbel, Mörike, Goethe, and others.

And now it was as if he had a demon in him, driving him on to write one song after another. In 1888–89 he finished fifty-three songs to poems by Mörike, thirteen to poems by Eichendorff, the first twenty-six songs of his *Spanisches Liederbuch* (*Spanish Songbook*) to poems by Heyse and Geibel, and fifty songs to poems by Goethe. The last batch took him less than four months to write. By the end of 1890 he had done the remaining eighteen songs for the *Spanish Songbook,* the six songs in *Alte Weisen* (*Old Melodies*) to poems by Keller, and the first seven songs of the first volume of the *Italienisches Liederbuch* (*Italian Songbook*). This amazing fertility was matched by his confidence in his greatness. "Am I the one who has been called—am I of the elect?" he inquired. Then he provided his own answer. "I have just written a new song for the gods—divine, wonderful!" The next day he added, "What I wrote this morning is a million times better still." And after that he said, "What I now write . . . I write for posterity. . . . There has been nothing like them [the songs] since Schubert and Schumann."

He was right, of course—even more than he himself knew. There was nothing like these Wolf songs since Schubert and Schumann, and there are songs here that not even those masters could have matched in felicitousness of word setting, in the dramatic power of his declamations, in the spaciousness and breadth of his accompaniments, in the originality of his intervallic structure, harmony, and modulations.

Between 1887 and 1891 Wolf had re-created the lied. Though as a songwriter he was descended from Schubert and Schumann, he would never have been able to uncover those newer regions of the art song we find in his music were it not for Wagner. The idiom in which he spoke, like that of Wagner, looked forward, not backward.

In the hands of Schubert and Schumann the lied had sought for an ever closer approximation of tone to word. Wolf carried on this aspiration, striving more and more intensively to fuse melody and word so that the song sometimes became almost something spoken rather than sung. Melody was blended with declamation. Words and music became a single entity. We listen to songs like "Verborgenheit" ("Withdrawal") or the ballad "Der Feuerreiter" ("The Fire Rider") in the Mörike set; to "Nachtzauber" ("Night Magic") or "Das Ständchen" ("The Serenade") in the Eichendorff group; to "Anakreons Grab" ("Anacreon's Grave") or the ballad "Prometheus," both settings of poems by Goethe; or, in the *Spanish Songbook,* to "In dem Schatten meiner Locken" ("In the Shadow of My Tresses"); and in the *Italian Songbook,* to "Auch kleine Dinge" ("Little Things"), "Heb' auf dein blondes Haupt" ("Lift Up Your Fair

Head''), and ''Und willst du deinen Liebsten sterben sehen'' (''Would You See Your Lover Die?''). We listen to these songs and we become conscious how in through-composition every line, every phrase, every word of the poem becomes alive and individualized through its musical content.

Only an acute sensibility, a nervous mechanism responsive in every cell, could have extracted from every poem its essence the way Wolf did. Only a poet who had drunk in the suggestions of the Wagnerian tradition, and had fully understood the Wagnerian dream of marrying word to tone, could have brought to the poems the newer melodic life. No one listening to these songs can escape the feeling that here Wagner's star has shone with benign influence.

Then in 1891 the seemingly measureless reservoir of Hugo Wolf's inspiration ran dry. Wrestle as he would with poems, melodies to satisfy him simply would not come. He was parched of musical ideas. What he put down on paper seemed arid and desiccated. He was convinced that he had written himself out for good. ''What a fearful lot it is for an artist not to have anything new to say,'' he lamented. ''I have given up the idea of composing. Heaven knows how things will finish. Pray for my poor soul!''

Just as mysteriously as it had deserted him, his inspiration suddenly became revivified. On November 29, 1891, he wrote ''Dass doch gemalt all' deine Reize wären'' (''If Only a Picture Were Painted of All Your Charms'') for the first volume of the *Italian Songbook,* upon which he had stopped work one year earlier. Then his one-time enthusiasm and energy burst like a flood. Between December 2 and 23 he put on paper fourteen numbers for the first volume of the *Italian Songbook,* often producing a song a day, or in one case, two songs.

But this proved just a temporary revival of his former strength. Once again his inspiration dried up. This time he remained creatively silent for three years. This was a time of such harrowing mental distress that at times he thought he was going mad. ''If you can give me back my inspiration,'' he wrote pathetically to a friend, ''wake the familiar spirit asleep within me, I will call you a god and raise altars to your name.'' He rediscovered his creativity by temporarily abandoning songs and working upon an opera, *Der Corregidor,* which he finished in 1895. The Vienna Royal Opera would not consider it, so he sent it to Mannheim, where it was produced on June 7, 1896, and was a dismal failure. The opera went into temporary discard, but as far as Wolf was concerned, its writing had not been a total loss. The spark within him was once again ignited. In 1896 he completed a second volume of the *Italian Songbook,* numbering twenty-four songs, all masterpieces. For the moment his dreary memories became less oppressive. Only the present mattered, and it looked bright. There were concerts of his music now that might be called successful. There were new friends, many of them highly esteemed musicians, who understood him and bore with his volcano-like passion for the sake of his genius. And, in 1897, there was even the anticipation of fame with the formation of a Hugo Wolf Society to promote his songs.

But his disappointment in the fate of his opera eventually proved lethal. He tried writing a second opera, but could work only by fits and starts. He was afflicted with tortured dreams and strange delusions. On September 7, 1897, he wandered aimlessly at three o'clock in the morning mumbling to himself. The friends whom he sought out failed at first to guess that he was losing his mind. They had seen him distraught before more than once. On September 19 he spoke of himself as the director of the Vienna Royal Opera and raved in anger at his "subordinates." In the evening, he sat down at the piano to play a part of Wagner's *The Mastersingers*. His memory failed him, and he exploded into hysteria.

He was taken to a sanatorium from which he was released four months later. It seemed that he was at least partially cured, for he made a renewed effort to work on his second opera. But musical thoughts would not come. Despair led him to try to commit suicide. Failing to destroy himself, he decided to remove himself completely from the society of men and music. He asked to be confined to a mental institution, where he lived his last years in solitude. Outside, his fame was growing. But the pale, thin little man with the blazing eyes was past understanding. Paralysis had crippled his body and speech, and his mind had become so twisted that he no longer knew who he was. He died in that mental institution of peripneumonia on February 22, 1903.

The ghost of Wagner also haunts the music of Gustav Mahler (1860–1911). This is as true of his symphonies, for which he is most famous, as of his vocal music. In either medium he was always conscious of melody. The "song" was uppermost in his mind even when he wrote for instruments. But he was the spiritual heir not of Schubert—that crowning genius of "song"—but of Wagner. Following Wagner's lead, Mahler was given to grandiose pronouncements. A man of exceptional intellectual endowments, Mahler concerned himself in his music with philosophic or metaphysical problems, with the mysteries of life and death, with pantheism, and at times even with paganism. A poet, thinker, dreamer, and idealist, he spoke of life and love, of joy and desolation, of conflict and serenity, not only in personal but also in universal terms. The great task he set for himself was to transmute his continuous intellectual and moral searches and struggles into musical terms, to embody a mystical sense of some transcendent truth in music. "When I conceive a large musical work," he once wrote, "I always arrive at a point where I am compelled to draw upon the 'word' as the bearer of musical ideas." He was partial to the voice and dependent on the "word" even in four of his nine completed symphonies, written against a background of his ceaseless intellectual probings. The Symphony no. 2, the *Resurrection* (1894), which is sometimes described as "a tonal allegory of the life of man," calls for a soprano, alto, and mixed chorus in its final two movements, where verses from *Des Knaben Wunderhorn* (a collection of German folk songs) and by Klopstock are used. The Symphony no. 3 (1896), which mirrors the composer's pantheism, engages a solo contralto, women's chorus, and boys' chorus—the contralto singing words from Nietzsche's *Thus Spake Zarathustra* in the fourth movement, and the women's and boys' choruses chanting verses from *Des Knaben Wunderhorn* in the fifth. *Des Knaben Wunderhorn* again contributes the "word" in the Symphony no. 4 (1901), in the closing movement, a child's description of paradise, sung by a soprano. And in the Symphony no. 8 (1907) the words of a medieval Latin hymn, "Veni, Creator Spiritus," and the closing scene of Goethe's *Faust* are presented by eight solo voices, two mixed choruses, and a boys' chorus. Such giant forces are enlisted in this epical work that it has come to be known as "the symphony of a thousand."

Mahler was, to be sure, even more deeply concerned with both the voice and the "word" in his vocal music. He wrote his first symphony in 1888. But long before that, in 1880, he began producing vocal music. His first composition within a large structure was *Das klagende Lied* (*The Song of Lamentation*), for solo voices, chorus, and orchestra (1880–1900). Mahler's first series of songs for voice and piano was the *Lieder und Gesänge aus der Jugendzeit* (*Songs from Youth*), fourteen songs, nine with texts from *Des Knaben Wunderhorn*. *Des Knaben Wunderhorn* yet again provided him with texts for a dozen songs in the *Lieder aus "Des Knaben Wunderhorn"* (*Songs from "The Youth's Magic Horn"*), both for voice and piano and for voice and orchestra (1888). In the words of these old German folk songs Mahler found echoes of his own inner yearnings and intellectual quests.

Between the two settings of *Des Knaben Wunderhorn* Mahler wrote the

Lieder eines fahrenden Gesellen (*Songs of a Wayfarer*), for voice and orchestra (1883–85). A frustrated love affair with a singer prompted him to write four poems about the sorrow of love and the consolation the beauty of nature brings to the rejected lover. Having put such thoughts down in verses, Mahler conceived appropriate music for them.

Two of his later song cycles belong with his greatest symphonies as his supreme achievements. One was the *Kindertotenlieder* (*Songs on the Death of Children*), five songs for voice and orchestra with texts by Friedrich Rückert written as elegies for the death of this poet's children. Mahler completed the cycle in 1904. In his music he tried to explore the mystery of death as well as to voice grief at the death of children. "The songs," once wrote Bruno Walter, the famous conductor and an ardent admirer and interpreter of Mahler's music, "contain perhaps the most sublime achievements of his orchestral ability and are exemplary for the ideally shaded sound relations between singing voice and orchestra." But, adds Bruno Walter, "common to all . . . is their song style. Even the most highly dramatic expression never led him to overstep the boundaries of song."

Mahler soon repented writing *Kindertotenlieder,* but not for aesthetic reasons. In 1906 his little daughter died of a combination of scarlet fever and diphtheria. The loss shattered him. He succumbed to the superstitious belief that his daughter died only because he had written elegies for dead children, that thus he was personally responsible for his daughter's death. This guilt feeling followed him to his grave. Soon after the death of his daughter, Mahler suffered a heart attack, a condition probably aggravated by his inner torment.

Das Lied von der Erde (*The Song of the Earth*) is a song cycle for tenor, contralto, and orchestra (1907–10), but Mahler often referred to it as a "symphony." It is, however, never numbered with his nine completed symphonies and his tenth unfinished one. The six songs, offered alternately by the tenor and the contralto, are based on Chinese poems. So funereal is some of this music that the composition has been interpreted by some Mahler authorities as the composer's farewell to the world. The pessimism of this music finds few parallels among Mahler's works. This is the voice of one who, having pondered the problems of life, can find no solution; one who has looked at the face of suffering and was well acquainted with tragedy. "And will my burning tears never be dried?" he asks in the second song, "Der Einsame in Herbst" ("Autumn Loneliness"). The closing song is called "The Farewell"; in it the poet longs to bid farewell to a friend since he knows his own end is near. Suffering as he was from a serious heart condition, Mahler, too, knew his end could not be far off.

The Chinese texts, then, were like Mahler's own personal statements, and this is why *Das Lied von der Erde* is his most personal composition.

Perhaps his feeling of impending doom brought a passion-laden force to Mahler's writing. Working on *Das Lied von der Erde,* Mahler looked inward. In his late symphonies he may have been driven by the Faustian urge to express the inexpressible, by a passion to embrace the meaning of a universe in its entirety. But in *Das Lied von der Erde* Mahler, at the close of his life, was forced back on himself, driven to express the tragedies that had beset him as a composer and conductor, as a father, and as an idealist.

Some of the greatest lieder of Richard Strauss (1864–1949) appeared early in his career, and virtually during the same years that Hugo Wolf and Mahler were productive. In Strauss's vocal music, as in that of Wolf and Mahler, Wagner was a vital presence.

But before he became a commanding figure in the pro-Wagner forces, Strauss had stood solidly in the camp of Brahms's followers. Strauss's father, a famous horn player in Munich, Germany (where Richard was born), was an ardent admirer of Brahms and a bitter opponent of Wagner; and the same held true for Strauss's music teachers. Young Richard adopted their standards. He, too, was vitriolic in his denunciation of Wagner, whose works he began hearing when he was fourteen. About Wagner's *Siegfried* young Strauss wrote: "I was bored out of mind. It was a gruesome boredom, so horrible I cannot describe it! Really awful!" He regarded *Lohengrin* as "terribly sweet and sickly" and the harmonies of *Tristan and Isolde* as "tiring as a steady diet of lobster mayonnaise." He prophesied that "you may be certain that ten years from now not a soul will know who Richard Wagner is."

Brahms, on the other hand, was his model for emulation. Being exceptionally precocious, Strauss began composing when he was still a boy. He was sixteen when a concert artist presented a few of his songs in a recital in Munich (Strauss's first appearance in public as composer). These first songs were so derivative that Strauss never had them published. The voice here is that of Brahms. The voice of Brahms is also heard in Strauss's more ambitious compositions of his apprentice years—chamber music, concertos, and orchestral music.

There is also a good deal of Brahms in Strauss's first published volume of lieder, op. 10, issued in 1883 when Strauss was nineteen. In the long arch of the melodies, in the volatile moods and the vernal freshness of the lyricism, we hear the echoes of Brahms's songs. But for all their deriva- *155* tiveness, these songs carry the hallmark of greatness. Some of them are still in circulation, particularly "Allerseelen" ("All Souls' Day"), "Die Nacht" ("The Night"), and "Zueignung" ("Dedication").

Strauss's shiftover from Brahms to Wagner was a gradual process. Soon after his highly unfavorable first reaction to *Tristan and Isolde* he acquired a copy of the score and studied it at the piano. Apparently something in the work struck his interest, for he attended another performance of this music drama that made him sit up and take notice that here was something new and important. Before long he attended his first hearing of *Die Walküre,* which drew him closer into the Wagner orbit. In 1882 he went to Bayreuth, where he heard *Parsifal* for the first time, during the year in which its world premiere took place. His esteem for Wagner mounted. But old values are not easily discarded, and new ones not readily adopted. It took several more years before Strauss reached that moment of truth when he realized that his destiny as a composer lay not in the direction of Brahms but in that of Wagner.

This took place in 1885, when Strauss was the assistant conductor to Hans von Bülow with the Meiningen Orchestra. Von Bülow had conducted the world premieres of *Tristan and Isolde* and *The Mastersingers* in Munich. He was in awe at the majesty of Wagner's genius and always did whatever he could to propagandize Wagner's music. It was inevitable, then, that in their personal associations von Bülow should try to infect Strauss with his own fiery enthusiasm.

But a still more powerful force in sweeping Strauss toward Wagner was Alexander Ritter, a violinist in the Meiningen Orchestra. He was second to none in his adoration of that master, whose niece he had married. Ritter was some thirty years older than Strauss, a man of trenchant intellect and supreme egotism. He did not converse, he lectured. He did not offer opinions, he dictated them as if from an oracle. Whatever Wagner had said or done or written represented to him the ultimate truth. For him Wagner's theories were the apotheosis of art. "All that is still ideal and worth preserving in the German spirit," Ritter once wrote, "lives in this one head [Wagner's]." As for Brahms: "One has to study Brahms carefully until one notices that there's nothing in it."

Being Ritter's friend meant being subjected to a continual barrage of his penchants and prejudices, his enthusiasms and his ideas. Young Strauss was overwhelmed by them. He freely confessed that Ritter's impact was that of a "stormwind." Strauss explained further: "He urged me on to the development of the poetic, the expressive in music, as exemplified in the works of Liszt, Berlioz, and Wagner." But Wagner, most of all.

Because of Ritter's counsel and urging, Strauss adopted the structure of the tone poem to carry into orchestral music Wagnerian theories and methods. In this form (which Liszt had formerly developed) Strauss achieved international renown between 1887 and 1898 with such masterworks as *Don Juan, Till Eulenspiegel's Merry Pranks, Death and Transfiguration, A Hero's Life, Thus Spake Zarathustra,* and *Don Quixote.* During this period his greatest songs were written, and through all of them strides the giant figure of Wagner. Typical of these songs is "Morgen" ("Tomorrow"), in 1894. The poem describes a lover contemplating the morrow when he can once again be with his beloved. He thinks how he will walk with her down a sun-drenched path to contemplate the deep blue waters. A sixteen-measure piano introduction is like an orchestral prelude. Dramatic, and Wagnerian, is the way in which, two measures before the ending of this instrumental opening, the voice enters with a brief declamatory line: "And tomorrow the sun will shine again." Effective also is the way the piano and voice now become inextricably enmeshed. After the piano spins out a brief new melodic thought, the voice returns with the melody and concludes with a last-line declamation. The five-measure epilogue in the piano is an extension of the first two measures of the song.

In songs completed between 1886 and 1900 Strauss became one of the greatest composers the lied has known. His song masterpieces of this period are "Ständchen" ("Serenade"), "Cäcilie" ("Cecile"), "Ruhe, meine Seele" ("Be Peaceful, My Soul"), "Traum durch die Dämmerung" ("Dream in Twilight"), "Befreit" ("Release"), "Wiegenlied" ("Cradle Song"), and "Freundliche Vision" ("Friendly Vision").

After 1900 Strauss also proved himself to be a genius in opera, composing *Salome* (1905), *Elektra* (1908), and *Der Rosenkavalier* (1910), among many other works for the stage. He continued during this period to write songs as well as orchestral compositions.

For more than a quarter of a century, however, Strauss neglected the song form, composing very few songs after 1919. He turned again to songs in 1948 with the *Vier letzte Lieder* (*Four Last Songs*), for voice and orchestra, his last pieces of music. When he worked on these songs Strauss knew that death was not far off. To bid farewell to life he selected three poems by Hermann Hesse and one by Joseph Eichendorff. Three of the four songs are elegiac in both words and music. "September" equates the fall of the summer leaves and the withering of flowers at the approach of autumn with the passing of life. In "Beim Schlafengehen" ("Time to Sleep"), Strauss yearns for the rest and peace sleep brings. This thought is further projected in the last song, "Im Abendrot" ("At Dusk"). The closing words of "At Dusk" pose the question "Is this really death?" In the quiet phrases following this query Strauss lifts a theme from *Death and Transfiguration,* his orchestral tone poem of 1889. This interpolation represents Strauss's farewell both to music and to life. One year of total creative silence preceded his death, which took place at Garmisch-Partenkirchen in Germany on September 8, 1949.

Floodtide of Nationalism

Modest Mussorgsky, Peter Ilitch Tchaikovsky,

Sergei Rachmaninoff, Antonín Dvořák,

Edvard Grieg, Jean Sibelius,

Béla Bartók, Zoltán Kodály,

Enrique Granados, Manuel de Falla

Many art songs in different countries in the nineteenth and early twentieth centuries had their source in the sentiments, orientations, and techniques of folk music.

Folk songs are the work not of any single composer, as is the case with the art song, but are handed down orally from one generation to the next, usually undergoing change in the process. They are music that is indigenous to its country, or to a region of that country. Folk songs are usually simple in idiom. They have an immediate emotional appeal and thus are readily singable and easily remembered. They are strophic in structure, and the melodic line is usually neatly divided into even phrases. In character and feeling they mirror a country's personality.

The aroused nationalism that swept like a floodtide over Europe in the nineteenth century drove many Romantic composers to write music whose melodies were modeled after those of folk songs. Consequently, many art songs of the Romantic era are deeply rooted in the earth of folk music.

Nationalism first became an element in Romantic music in Russia, with the works of Mikhail Glinka (1804–57), the first Russian to gain acceptance outside the borders of his own country, and the first Russian to whose music we still listen. When Glinka was twenty-six he traveled in Western Europe, where he was attacked by homesickness. This feeling generated in him the ambition to write music in a Russian style. (Before Glinka, Russian composers slavishly imitated Western European music.) Glinka not only went to Russian backgrounds, history, and poetry for his subject matter. He also shaped his music after the physiognomy of Russian folk songs and dances. With two operas—*A Life for the Tsar* (1836) and *Russlan and Ludmilla* (1842)—and in such songs as "Doubt," "The Lark," "Midnight Review," and "The Northern Star," he laid the foundations of musical nationalism in general, and Russian musical nationalism in particular. Many other songs by Glinka were settings of poems by Alexander Pushkin, Russia's greatest poet and dramatist: for example, "Remember the Moment" and "Do Not Sing, My Beauty." After Glinka, many Russian composers followed his example by dipping into the rich resources of Pushkin's literary genius for national compositions large and small, instrumental and dramatic as well as vocal.

Glinka was the beacon lighting the road upon which subsequent Russian nationalists would travel. Just about a decade after Glinka's death, Mili Balakirev (1837–1910) became the founding father and the guiding force of a group of five Russian composers completely dedicated to nationalism. They have since come to be known as "the Russian Five" or "the Mighty Five." Besides Balakirev, this group included Alexander Borodin (1833–87), César Cui (1835–1918), Modest Mussorgsky (1839–81), and Nikolai Rimsky-Korsakov (1844–1908). All of them were convinced that the only way a Russian composer could free himself from Western musical influences was to become thoroughly Russian in subject and materials. They also felt that the way to do this was to draw copiously from Russian geography, history, backgrounds, and culture, and by quoting or imitating Russian folk songs and church music. All of these five composers wrote songs to texts of major Russian poets. Between 1858 and 1865 Balakirev wrote twenty songs, to poems by Lermontov, Pushkin, and others. Cui's "The Statue of Tsarskoë Selo" was a setting of Pushkin's poem. Two of the most successful songs by Rimsky-Korsakov used texts by Tolstoi and Koltsov respectively: "It Is Not the Wind" and the highly popular "The Rose and the Nightingale."

The foremost composer of this group was Modest Mussorgsky. The son of a prosperous landowner, he was (in spite of early manifestations of a pronounced talent for music) trained for a military life. In 1856 he became an officer of the Imperial Guards in Saint Petersburg. He had not abandoned music, however. While serving as an officer he worked on an opera. Then, around 1857, he met Balakirev, who taught him musical theory, of which Mussorgsky knew little. His enthusiasm for music now swelled to such proportions that, in 1858, he resigned from military service to devote himself exclusively to the art. By 1860 he had one of his orchestral pieces played in public in Saint Petersburg. In 1865 he allied himself with Balakirev, Borodin, Cui, and Rimsky-Korsakov to promote musical nationalism.

But Mussorgsky had a goal all his own. He consciously aimed to seek musical truth that did not glorify, idealize, or sentimentalize life but reflected it authentically. If life was crude and ugly, then the only music capable of interpreting it had to be aurally disagreeable. To paint life in music in the raw (so to speak), Mussorgsky did not hesitate to use discords, awkward modulations, unconventional rhythmic patterns, unexpected chord progressions—and with them, a new kind of lyricism to which he gave the name of "the melody of life," which was modeled after the inflections of speech. "If I have succeeded in rendering the straightforward expression of thoughts and feelings as it takes place in ordinary speech, and if my rendering is artistic and musicianly, then the deed is done," he wrote.

Mussorgsky's songs, above and beyond their indebtedness to Russian folk sources, had an identity of their own. Beauty as such was not Mussorgsky's aim. Had he not said that "the quest for artistic beauty for its own sake is . . . art in its dotage"? In his songs he aspired to capture the sounds, rhythms, and feelings of his texts, be they comic, tragic, morbid, or satirical. His four most often heard individual songs are striking examples of felicitous word setting and musical realism: the frenetic "Hopak," which captures the wild gaiety and abandon of that Russian dance; the atmospheric "Night" with its bleak recitative-like melody; the haunting "Forgotten," sometimes also called "Ballade"; and the nonsensical "Song of the Flea" to Goethe's celebrated poem. In the less familiar "Darling Savishna," to his own words, Mussorgsky gives a half-comic, half-tragic picture of an unhappy fool making a declaration of love. In the song cycle *The Nursery,* he catches the shades and nuances of the mumblings of a child's speech. In the opening song of this cycle, "With Nurse," Mussorgsky changes the meter twenty-seven times (within a fifty-three-measure song) to follow the ever-changing inflections of the child as it hounds the nurse with a barrage of questions. At the end of the fourth song, "With the Doll," there are continual pauses interrupting the flow of the melody to suggest that the mother is slowly tiptoeing out of the nursery as the child is falling asleep.

To appreciate fully the pessimism that pervades Mussorgsky's two greatest song cycles (and two of the finest in Russian song literature)—*Sunless* and *Songs and Dances of Death*—we must know something of the state of Mussorgsky's life and spirit at the time he wrote this music and what had happened to him in the preceding years.

When the Russian serfs were liberated in 1861, the Mussorgsky family lost its fortune. From then on, poverty dogged Mussorgsky's footsteps. He had to support himself, from 1863 until a year before his death, by working as a clerk for a niggardly salary in government offices. His jobs were dull and routine, and he performed them badly. He was embittered that so much of his time was consumed by the trivialities of a desk job when he hungered to write music. The decline in his life was accelerated in 1865 by the death of his mother, to whom he had always been singularly attached. He now began losing control of himself. To escape from the boredom of his government post, and from the depressions to which he now frequently succumbed, he took to drink. By 1873 he had lost all self-respect. He was now a chronic alcoholic who lived like a beggar. He was slovenly and dirty in his appearance. He avoided his former friends and colleagues, to associate with disreputable people. Often he became involved in ugly fights; often he was ejected from his shabby rooms for nonpayment of his rent; and often he went on binges of intoxication that left him senseless. That he could compose at all under such harrowing conditions is surprising; that he should have composed such masterpieces as his folk opera *Boris Godunov* and his two song cycles (among other works) is almost beyond belief.

With this unpleasant image of Mussorgsky before us—an image captured by the painter Repin in a portrait drawn during Mussorgsky's last days—we can begin to understand the utter desolation permeating both *Sunless* and *Songs and Dances of Death,* which were written in the 1870s. Mussorgsky here speaks from the depths of his despair and degradation. The six songs of *Sunless* are filled with stark melodies and discordant harmonies. What binds the six songs into a unity is the feeling of despair in each. But in *Songs and Dances of Death* the common denominator is death. In the first song, "Lullaby," a child dies in the arms of its mother. In "Serenade" Death sings a funereal chant to a girl. Death dances with a drunken peasant who has lost his way in a snowstorm in "Trepak." And in "The Field Marshal" Death is riding across a moonlit battlefield. In the contemplation of death in these four episodes Mussorgsky speaks with the tragic accents of one who has come to realize that in death alone lies his ultimate salvation.

Truman Daniel to move to Chicago

Margaret Truman Daniel, shown in 1980, plans to write her next murder mystery here.

Margaret Truman Daniel, the only child of the late President **Harry S. Truman**, is selling her longtime apartment on New York's Park Avenue and moving to Chicago to live and work on the latest addition to her series of murder mysteries, her son said Monday.

Daniel has lived at her Park Avenue address since 1956, when she used the proceeds from her first book to buy the home.

Now at 83 and a widow, she needs to downsize from her enormous New York apartment, said her son, **Clifton Truman Daniel**, director of public relations for Truman College in Chicago.

She will likely live with him and his family on the city's North Side, he said.

Though she hasn't visited Chicago in years, her son said his mother has pleasant memories of the city.

She recalls tromping up the wrong way on the old-fashioned wooden escalators at Carson Pirie Scott on State Street, he said.

She was a 20-year-old history major in 1944 when she was on hand for her father's nomination as vice president at the Democratic National Convention in Chicago. And she lunched at the Pump Room with **Irv Kupcinet**, when he squired her about town on her father's directive, while she waited for a connecting flight to Los Angeles to film a TV show, her son said.

When Truman was a year into his presidency, Daniel completed her degree at George Washington University, then spent years as a concert singer and TV show guest.

When a performance by Daniel was panned by a Washington music critic in 1950, Truman famously dashed off a letter on White House stationery: "It seems to me that you are a frustrated old man who wishes he could have been successful. When you write such poppycock ... it shows conclusively that you're off the beam. ... Some day I hope to meet you. When that happens you'll need a new nose, a lot of beefsteak for black eyes, and perhaps a supporter below."

—*Alexa Aguilar*

re airport. The carrier, which
hat will depart before 6 a.m.

uled 772 departures nationwide before 6 a.m., more than double the 381 flights it offered a year earlier, according to data provided by Connecticut-based Back Aviation.

At O'Hare, United's earliest flight leaves at 6 a.m. But the airline has increased the number of departures scheduled for that time to 234 for the month of June, up from 157 a year ago.

Some business travelers say they would jump at flights that leave even earlier.

"I will do it for two reasons: for business productivity and

to 15 additional cities out of Chicago that they previously would have missed, Medina said United will test this new flight time during June and make it permanent if customers warm to it, she said. United also is reducing the number of flights it offers during the peak morning periods, which coincide with rush-hour times on the roads while increasing the number of flights leaving after 9 a.m., according to the Back Aviation data. But skeptics question whether United will find sufficient numbers of passengers willing to fly outside popular flying times, particularly early birds wanting to make predawn departures.

"Good luck," said aviation analyst Robert Mann, president of R.W. Mann & Co., a consulting firm based in Port Washington, N.Y.

Mann noted that most major carriers haven't offered many ultraearly morning flights since the Sept. 11, 2001, terrorist attacks, when airlines drastically reduced the number of scheduled flights.

"The first and last flights were prized by business travelers, who disappeared after 9/11," he said. "Unless you can get people to pay extra money for those flights, it's not worth it."

But United, which is courting business travelers, may have found a lucrative niche, especially since it deals with far greater numbers of connecting passengers than Southwest does, Hurwitz noted.

But whether there are a sufficient number of early-bird travelers to support a major strategic shift isn't yet clear. Chen of Strategos says he wouldn't get up at 3:30 a.m. to make a business flight but knows others who would do so.

"Some of my colleagues would definitely take the night at home and get up, no matter

No composer influenced Peter Ilitch Tchaikovsky (1840–93) more than Glinka. And no composer influenced Sergei Rachmaninoff (1873–1943) more than Tchaikovsky. Both composers were cut from the same cloth. They were hypersensitive to the point of neuroticism. Their nerves were continually exposed so that any contact with an adverse agency made them quiver with pain. They went through life burdened with sadness that kept growing within them like a cancer. Since both were Romanticists who openly expressed their feelings through music, their best songs vibrate in the winds of their chronic melancholia.

Above and beyond his innate emotional imbalance, Tchaikovsky had, indeed, a heavy cross to bear: his crushing frustrations in love. The woman whom he adored above all others—his mother—died of cholera when he was only fourteen. He never quite recovered from that shock; whenever he thought of her, even late in his life, his eyes would fill with tears. A singer, Désirée Artôt, with whom he thought he was in love when he was twenty-nine, jilted him to marry a Spanish baritone. The girl he married in 1877 he did not love at all. Antonina Miliukova was a high-strung music student who had fallen on her knees before him to confess she worshiped him. In Tchaikovsky's own words, "some mysterious force" led him to propose to her. He married in haste, and repented not in leisure but also in haste. His first few weeks with his bride were so nerve-racking that he tried to commit suicide, and would probably have suffered a nervous breakdown had he not fled from home to travel about in Europe. He never again returned to Antonina. Then hardly had he recovered from this trauma when he entered upon his strange love affair with Nadezhda Filaretovna von Meck, which lasted thirteen years, during which time he never once saw her face to face but carried on his romance through a prolific exchange of letters. When, in the end, Mme von Meck decided to break off this curious affair, Tchaikovsky reacted with an anguish as if the most intimate kind of relationship had been suddenly terminated.

But a still-deeper wound burned within Tchaikovsky than his failure to fulfill himself with a woman. He suffered from his homosexual tendencies, about which he confessed in letters and his diary. A profound sense of guilt continually overwhelmed him, together with the gnawing fear that others might learn of his terrible secret. This may very well have been the reason why he entered upon matrimony so precipitously: to provide a cloak of concealment for his aberration. His condition was probably the reason Mme von Meck had set down the rule that they could communicate with one another only through letters and never in personal meetings.

Tchaikovsky's frustrations, disappointments, and morbidity fill the *163* measures of his first published set of songs, op. 6 (1869), in which he included "None but the Lonely Heart," words by Goethe. Here pathos reaches a moving climax with the phrases "how I suffer" and "my bosom bursts." Balakirev thought so little of this song that he convinced the singer to whom Tchaikovsky had dedicated it to delete it from her program on the grounds that it was not sufficiently Russian in character. This is the same accusation that each of the members of the Russian Five continually hurled at all of Tchaikovsky's music: it was much too Western European and too little Russian. Yet, since Tchaikovsky's death, the world has come to look upon Tchaikovsky as one of the most Russian of all that country's composers, and upon "None but the Lonely Heart" as one of his most characteristic songs. Yet other of his songs are thoroughly Russian, most significantly "A Legend," which sounds like a folk tune and the melody of which was used by Anton Arenski (1861–1906) as a theme for variations in his String Quartet no. 2, and later rewritten for string orchestra as *Variations on a Theme by Tchaikovsky*. Other Tchaikovsky songs, while less folklike, remain identifiably Russian: "I Bless You, Forests" and "Gypsy's Song," for example.

Melancholia also followed Rachmaninoff through his life like some omnipresent shadow. Early in his career, when he was twenty-four, he suffered a nervous breakdown after his First Symphony had been a fiasco. An extended period of treatment at the hands of a physician specializing in autosuggestion was required before Rachmaninoff recovered from his psychopathic fears and nervous disorders. He emerged from this dark period into the shining sunlight of success with the triumphant premiere of his Piano Concerto no. 2, in 1901. After that, successes kept mounting for him, not only as a composer but also as a conductor and as a world-renowned piano virtuoso. However, he was not to free himself of his chronic sadness and feeling of loneliness. These were aggravated after 1917 when he left Russia forever, since he opposed the forces of revolution that had created a social and political upheaval in his country. Henceforth he was an exile, first in Switzerland, then in the United States. He never adjusted himself to a strange new language, new culture, and new way of life. Homesickness for a land to which he could not return became a disease. Its sorrow, together with Rachmaninoff's chilling loneliness and yearnings, throbs in his greatest music.

Rachmaninoff early revealed a natural gift for songwriting. In 1893 he published a group of songs, op. 4, which includes two exquisite miniatures: "In the Silent Night" and "O Cease Thy Singing" (the latter sometimes also known as "The Songs of Grusia"). Three years later he wrote the lovely "Floods of Spring." His gift at spinning a long and sensitive melody over a sophisticated accompaniment is as prominent here as is the pronounced Russian identity of the music. These songs have become repertory numbers with recitalists, with later songs such as "Lilacs," "Before My Window," "To the Children," "Christ Is Risen," and "Daisies."

Two of Rachmaninoff's songs are unusual. In "Fate," his melody is based on the famous theme from the first movement of Beethoven's Fifth Symphony. "Vocalise" has no words whatsoever. A "vocalise" is an exercise for the voice. Upon the pretense of producing one, Rachmaninoff creates a soaring melody whose text consists merely of a single vowel. So effective is this number that it has been transcribed for orchestra, for the piano, and for various solo instruments and piano.

In many different lands outside Russia, composers were impelled to become avowed nationalists through their pride in their country's heritage. In all such instances, folk music played a decisive role.

When Austria granted Bohemia (now part of Czechoslovakia) a measure of political autonomy in the 1860s, the spirit of nationalism was ignited in the hearts of Bohemians. A national theater was founded in 1862 to encourage the writing of Bohemian operas on native subjects with music of a folk character. In the vanguard of this cultural movement stood Bedřich Smetana (1824–84), composer of Bohemia's most famous folk opera, *The Bartered Bride* (1866–70). But Smetana's ardent nationalism expressed itself more eloquently in operas and orchestral and piano music than in songs, the earliest of which (1846) are in a Germanic style. A notable exception is his set of five *Evening Songs* (1879) with words by the Bohemian poet V. Hálek.

The songs of Antonín Dvořák (1841–1904) are far more distinguished and familiar than those of Smetana. Dvořák played the viola in the orchestra of the Bohemian opera house of which Smetana was director. Thus he came under the older man's influence and was inspired by him to become involved in Bohemian nationalism. It was a national work that helped carry Dvořák out of the humble career and obscurity in which he had thus far been languishing. Between 1875 and 1877 he set twenty-four Moravian folk poems for two voices, some of these duets expropriating the rhythms and styles of such native Bohemian dance forms as the furiant and the polka. He submitted a number of these duets in an annual competition conducted by the Austrian State Commission, winning the first prize of $250. One of the judges of the Austrian State Commission was the great Jo-

Sergei Rachmaninoff.

Béla Bartók.

Zoltán Kodály.

Manuel de Falla.

hannes Brahms, who was so taken with these duets that he recommended them to his own publisher, Simrock. "If you play them through," Brahms wrote to Simrock, "you will enjoy them as much as I have done. . . . Decidedly he is a very talented man. Besides he is poor. Please take this into consideration." Simrock did. He published thirteen of these duets in a collection entitled *Moravian Duets,* (op. 32). In addition, he commissioned Dvořák to write the work that made him a household name—the still-popular *Slavonic Dances,* op. 46, for piano duet, and also for orchestra (1878).

In 1875 one of Dvořák's children died when she was only two days old. Dvořák's grief sent him a few months later into the writing of his first major religious work, the *Stabat Mater,* completing the sketches in May of 1876. He put the work aside to concentrate on other compositions. Then in 1877 the death of two more of his children—an eleven-month-old daughter and a three-and-a-half-year-old son—left him and his wife childless. Once again he tried sublimating his sorrow in the writing of religious music by returning to his sketches of the *Stabat Mater.* He completed the entire work by mid-November of that year. The significance of the *Stabat Mater,* op. 58—for solo voices, chorus, and orchestra—goes beyond the fact that this is Dvořák's first large work as a mature composer, and his first major religious composition. Historically, this *Stabat Mater* assumed importance because it is the first such work in modern Bohemian music, the cornerstone on which later Bohemian religious choral music rests. Both at its premiere in Prague in 1880, and in its introduction in England in 1883, it was a triumph. It had to be repeated in England under Dvořák's own direction the following season.

The most touching parts of the *Stabat Mater* are those in which Dvořák's sorrow found an outlet: in the lamentation "Quis est homo" for vocal quartet, and in the anguished quartet with chorus "Quando corpus." These are some of the dark pages of this score. But lighter ones are also present to provide a contrast, as the "Fac, ut ardeat" and the closing "Paridisi gloria," which leads into an "Amen" of Handelian grandeur.

Thirteen years after this *Stabat Mater,* Dvořák completed another grandiose religious choral work, the Requiem, op. 89 (1890). For some strange reason, this masterwork long lay in neglect following its initial success at the Birmingham Festival in England on October 9, 1891. It was performed with orchestra for the first time in sixty years in New York in 1964, when it was hailed as one of Dvořák's supreme achievements. Dvořák integrated this work by using a leading motive (a tender two-measure phrase) presented in the strings at the beginning, then recurring throughout the score.

To Dvořák's biographer Paul Stefan this Requiem "is one of the most beautiful, original and worthwhile settings of the Mass for the dead."

Dvořák wrote about fifty songs. Most often remembered is "Songs My Mother Taught Me," the fourth number in *Gypsy Songs,* op. 55 (1880). This cycle comprises seven songs from Bohemian poems by Adolf Heyduk. In the first two songs—"My Songs Tell of My Love" and "Hark, How My Triangle"—Dvořák employs rhythms of Bohemian folk dances. In "Songs My Mother Taught Me" and "Silent Woods," he captured the gentleness and languor of Bohemian folk songs.

The first stirrings of national pride in Edvard Grieg (1843–1907) came when he was twenty years old, in Germany. He had been born in Bergen, Norway, on June 15, 1843. Having been trained in music at the Leipzig Conservatory, from which he was graduated in 1862, he was now a young composer whose music echoed that of the German Romantic composers. After graduation, Grieg went to Copenhagen. There he became a close friend of another Norwegian-born musician, Rikard Nordraak. Nordraak was a Norwegian patriot, the composer of Norway's national anthem. He introduced Grieg to the sweet, rustic beauties of Norwegian folk songs and dances. He was also eloquently persuasive in convincing Grieg that a composer had to reach toward national sources to achieve a personal identity. Awakened to his destiny as a composer, Grieg now embraced musical nationalism. One of the first pieces of music he wrote that was derived from Norwegian folk music was his greatest art song, "Jeg elsker dig" ("I Love You"), with words by Hans Christian Andersen; it is sung most frequently in a German translation as "Ich liebe dich." Grieg wrote it in Copenhagen in 1864 for his cousin Nina Hagerup, to whom he was betrothed secretly because her parents looked with disfavor on their romance. This song is the third of a group of four, all entitled *The Heart's Melodies,* op. 5. The tenderness that yields to ardor in "I Love You" betrays Grieg's rapturous feelings for his beloved, who became his wife in 1867.

Almost as popular as "I Love You" among Grieg's vocal compositions is "Solveig's Song." This is one of the numbers Grieg wrote as incidental music for a production of Henrik Ibsen's poetical drama *Peer Gynt,* mounted in Christiana (now Oslo) in 1876. Grieg gathered the best parts of this incidental music into two suites for orchestra, the first of which is a classic. The second suite ends with "Solveig's Song," arranged for orchestra. In its original version it was sung with orchestral accompaniment in a vision scene concluding the fourth act. This is one of the rare instances in which Grieg borrowed his melody from a Norwegian folk song.

In his other songs Grieg generally preferred inventing his own melodies. Grieg wrote in all about one hundred and fifty songs. Some were to German texts, as was his first song publication, op. 2 (1862), in which the poems were by Heine and Chamisso, and the *Six German Songs,* op. 48 (1889) to poems by Goethe, among others. In the latter group, "A Dream" is particularly favored by singers.

Generally speaking, Grieg's best song efforts were to Norwegian texts, many of them by Ibsen; here is revealed the heart and soul of Grieg's country. The most famous of these songs are "A Swan," "With a Waterlily," "A Bird Song," "The Wounded Heart," "Spring," "To Norway," "While I Wait," and "Eros." "The Wounded Heart" and "Spring" were transcribed by Grieg for string orchestra and renamed *Two Elegiac Melodies,* op. 34 (1880). "To Norway" belongs to a cycle of five songs carrying the collective title of *Norway,* op. 58. Another distinguished song cycle is *Haugtussa,* op. 67.

Other composers in other countries drew creative sustenance from the folk music of their respective lands. There is a bleakness and austerity to the folk music of Finland that filters through so much of the music of Jean Sibelius (1865–1957). Sibelius's nationalism was part and parcel of a movement in Finland to free itself from domination by Russia. Robbed of their freedom, Finnish patriots banded together secretly to liberate their country from foreign tyranny. This struggle generated a pride in and love for their country that affected Sibelius deeply and drove him to write music inspired by Finnish legends and modeled after Finnish folk music. His familiar tone poem *Finlandia* (1899) is one such work, and so are many of his other tone poems and symphonies. His songs are given less frequently than his orchestral compositions, because Sibelius was at his best working on large canvases with bold brushstrokes. Yet a few of his songs are characteristic of a style that has the somber feeling of a Finnish forest and the gray, brooding quality of a wintry Finnish sky: songs like "Black Roses," "The Kiss," "The Tryst," "In the Fields a Maiden Sings," and "The Tree."

Béla Bartók (1881–1945) and Zoltán Kodály (1882–1967) were the two leading nationalist composers in Hungary. Before they became nationalists, both had written music in a German Romantic style—Bartók in the vein of Liszt and Richard Strauss, and Kodály in that of Brahms. Bartók was the first of these two to be made forcefully aware of Hungarian folk music. In 1904, while vacationing in a remote region of Hungary, he heard a peasant girl sing a strange tune indigenous to that place. This led him to suspect that other parts of Hungary might also have fascinating folk songs and dance tunes of their own. In 1905 he embarked upon a hunt for such music throughout Hungary in the company of his friend and colleague Zoltán Kodály. They discovered a rich repository of folk music unknown outside its own restricted area. In 1906 they issued *Twenty Hungarian Folksongs* arranged for voice and piano. From then on, Bartók and Kodály were indefatigable in their travels in Hungary and neighboring countries in search of folk music. Through their arrangements and publications they brought to the light of recognition several thousand folk tunes. All this music was far different from that which the world had long accepted as authentically Hungarian. When Liszt wrote his *Hungarian Rhapsodies* and Brahms his *Hungarian Dances,* they were using the sentimental, sinuous, meretricious melodies of gypsies in the belief that these were truly representative of Hungary. But the researches of Bartók and Kodály proved that *real* Hungarian music was a far different product. It was austere, exotic in its use of old modes, and at times crudely constructed. It did not concern itself with beguiling melodies but with a strong declamatory line, irregular rhythms and meters, and abrupt accentuations.

In their own compositions both Bartók and Kodály were profoundly affected by the style and idioms of the native Hungarian music they had discovered. Bartók himself put it this way: "The outcome of these studies was a decisive influence on my work, because it freed me from the tyrannical use of major and minor keys. The greater part of the collected treasure, and the more valuable part, was in old ecclesiastical or old Greek modes, or based on the more primitive scales, and the melodies were full of the most free and varied rhythmic phrases and changes of tempi. . . . It became clear to me that the old modes, which had been forgotten in our music, had lost nothing of their vigor. Their new employment made new rhythmic combinations possible.''

Bartók and Kodály were thus led away from the methods of the German Romantics toward a new style. But each was influenced by Hungarian folk music in his own way. Bartók realized a severe and complex style that was dynamic in its brute force. Kodály, on the other hand, softened the hardness of the melodic line and simplified the complexity of rhythmic and metric structures, to permit a more ingratiating and lyrical approach.

Though both Bartók and Kodály wrote songs in the style of Hungarian folk tunes, their most significant contribution to vocal music lay in their adaptations of Hungarian folk songs and dances, and in their choral compositions. In two important choral works—each representative of its composer at his best—the difference between these two Hungarian nationalists becomes apparent. Bartók's *Cantata profana,* for tenor, baritone, double mixed chorus, and orchestra (1930), is patterned after Rumanian peasant songs. The text also has ethnic sources, being based on an old Rumanian folksong about nine sons who are transformed into stags. In searching for his lost sons, the father comes upon the stags and begs them to come back home with him, only to be told that they prefer to live the rest of their lives as stags in the quiet forests. Bartók's music is intricately conceived, emphasizing virile forces rather than lyrical expression. The melodic line is declamatory, the tonality is free, the accents are abrupt and shifting, and the rhythmic patterns change continually.

Kodály's *magnum opus* in choral music is the *Psalmus Hungaricus* (1923). It is filled with lyrical beauty and deep sentiment. Kodály was commissioned to write it by the Hungarian government in commemoration of the fiftieth anniversary of the union of the towns of Buda and Pest into Budapest. Befitting such an occasion, Kodály chose a sixteenth-century text (which had been adapted from the Fifty-fifth Psalm) bemoaning the fate of Hungary at the hands of its cruel oppressor, Turkey. Kodály's *Psalmus Hungaricus,* after an introduction, opens elegiacally with a refrain chanted by altos and basses that reappears throughout the work: "Sad was King David, dismal and downcast." This chant is taken over by a unison chorus, which interrupts a plea to God (sung by the tenor) to take cognizance of the misery of the Hungarian people. An eloquent orchestral episode precedes another affecting passage for tenor. The work ends rhapsodically as the chorus sings the praises of God who, in His infinite mercy and wisdom, will destroy the enemy of Hungary.

Art songs with instrumental accompaniment appeared in Spain in the sixteenth century, the work of Luis Milán (c. 1500–after 1561) and Alonso de Mudarra (years of birth and death not known) among others. For the next three centuries, however, the art song languished. Most of the solo vocal music of that period came out of the theater, mainly from zarzuelas, which were the Spanish equivalent of American musical comedy or operetta. Not until the twentieth century did the Spanish art song become revitalized, even as did other forms of Spanish music as well. This came about through the monumental researches of a great Spanish musical scholar, Felipe Pedrell (1841–1922). His studies helped to lift out of obscurity a wealth of forgotten Spanish folk and dance music, and his influence among his contemporaries was largely responsible for bringing about an awareness that an important Spanish musical art could be realized through the exploitation of folk material. Musical nationalism now took hold in Spain, and in this development (in which Spain assumed a place of importance in music it had not known for centuries) the art song prospered.

One of these national composers writing art songs that had their roots in Spanish folk music was Enrique Granados (1867–1916). As a nationalist composer, Granados distinguished himself for his *Goyescas,* which is both a suite of piano pieces (1912) and an opera (1915). It was to attend the world premiere of his opera *Goyescas* at the Metropolitan Opera in New York on January 26, 1916, that Granados paid his first and only visit to the United States. It proved a fatal trip. En route back to Spain, the ship on which he was sailing from Folkestone, England, to Dieppe, France, was torpedoed by a German submarine, this being the time of World War I. Granados was one of the victims.

Whether writing *Goyescas* as a piano suite or as an opera, Granados was influenced by the paintings and tapestries of the distinguished Spanish artist Goya, and by Goya's re-creation of eighteenth-century Madrid in his art works. The Madrid of Goya's times plays an important role in Granados's art songs as well. Granados wrote a dozen songs, all to texts by Fernando Periquet. These were not called "songs" but "tonadillas written in the old style." The word *tonadilla* was derived from *tonada,* meaning a ballad tune from old Castile; and tonadillas became popular in Madrid theaters in the nineteenth century. To Granados, a tonadilla represented a romantic song associated with eighteenth-century Madrid evoking the images of "majas" and "majos" that Goya immortalized in many of his paintings—a "maja" and "majo" being an ostentatiously dressed young lady and man of that period. Thus, among Granados's songs we find "La Maja de Goya" ("The Maja of Goya"), "El Majo discreto" ("The Discreet Majo"), "El Majo timido" ("The Timid Majo"), and "El Majo olvidado" ("The Forgetful Majo"). The best of his songs are the three in a triptych collectively entitled "La Maja dolorosa" ("The Grieving Maja"). In this triptych a young Spanish lady recalls in anguish, the passion and the exultation of the past joys she had known with a lover now dead.

As a young man, Manuel de Falla (1876–1946) was a student of Felipe Pedrell at the Madrid Conservatory. At that time Falla was preparing to become a virtuoso pianist, having received highest honors in piano playing at the conservatory. But Pedrell redirected him to composition and interested him in using his music to interpret Spanish backgrounds and subjects while employing techniques, methods, and styles of Spanish folk music. "It is to the lessons of Pedrell and to the powerful stimulation exercised on me by his works that I owe my artistic life," Falla later confessed. In works such as *La Vida breve* (*Life Is Short*), an opera composed in 1905; *El Amor brujo* (*Wedded by Witchcraft*), a ballet completed in 1915; and *Noches en los Jardines de España* (*Nights in the Gardens of Spain*), impressions for piano and orchestra (1915), Falla's fame as a Spanish nationalist composer became worldwide and his important position in twentieth-century music was confirmed.

Falla's major vocal composition is the *Siete Canciones populares españolas* or *Seven Spanish Popular Songs* (1914). Here Falla took his melodies from the folk songs of various parts of Spain. "El Paño moruno" ("The Moorish Shawl") comes from Andalusia, as do "Nana" (a lullaby), "Canción" ("Song") and "Polo." "Asturiana" comes out of Asturias in northern Spain, "Seguidilla murciana" from the province of Murcia, and "Jota" from the province of Aragon. But these songs are not adaptations by any means. Such a wealth of harmonic and rhythmic invention is found in Falla's piano accompaniments, and so completely does Falla re-create the melodies in his own creative image, that these seven songs become, in Falla's hands, original compositions rather than transcriptions. In the languor, sensuality, and that low-voiced throb which is known as *cante hondo* ("deep song") of the melodies, in the rhythms that often remind us of the clicking of castanets, and in the piano accompaniment that at times suggests the plucking of the strings of a guitar, this is music that evokes for us tonally the colorful, exotic world of Spain.

Joaquín Turina (1882–1949) is another twentieth-century Spanish nationalist who brings us in his songs the magic world of Andalusia, most particularly in *Canto a Sevilla,* or *Song to Seville* (1926). This is a cycle of four songs to words by José Muñoz San Román: "Semana Santa" ("Holy Week"), "Las fuentecitas del Parque" ("The Little Fountains of the Park"), "El Fantasma" ("The Phantom"), and "La Giralda" (the giralda being the famous belltower of the Seville Cathedral). "In totality," wrote the American music critic Irving Kolodin, "they comprise a kind of rapturous adulation of a city."

Among the other notable song composers of Spain, perhaps the most distinctive and original is Federico Mompou (1893–   ). He is a Catalonian born in Barcelona, who spent many of his years in Paris, and who visited the United States in 1970. Mompou wrote twenty songs for voice and piano to Catalan, Spanish, and French texts. The Catalan songs include five to poems by José Janés, grouped under the single title of *Combat del Somni;* they were written between 1942 and 1951. Two of Mompou's Spanish songs used poems by Juan Ramón Jiménez, winner of the

Nobel Prize for literature. They are "Pastoral" and "Llueve sobre el rio" ("It Is Raining on the River"), both written in 1945. Some of Mompou's songs, like those of Falla discussed earlier, are re-creations of authentic folk tunes, among which are found the cycle of six called *Comptines*.

Voices of France

Claude Debussy, Maurice Ravel,
Francis Poulenc, Arthur Honegger

Before he discovered a musical world of his own, that of Impressionism, Achille-Claude Debussy (1862–1918) had been touched by the spell of Wagner. He first became acquainted with Wagner's music while he was a student at the Paris Conservatory. But not until 1885 in Rome, when he studied the Wagner scores more thoroughly, did he succumb completely to the spell of Wagner. Since, from his boyhood on, Debussy had been impatient with the musical establishment of his time and dreamed of a music freed of conventions and rules, he found Wagner's unconventional harmonic, melodic, and tonal language to be "the music of the future." Debussy's enthusiasm for Wagner mounted after visits to Bayreuth in 1888 and in 1889, when he heard *The Mastersingers, Parsifal,* and *Tristan and Isolde.* But the fascination of the music eventually palled. Debussy reacted against Wagner's superstructures, big sonorities, sensuousness of counterpoint, and social and philosophic concepts. As a Frenchman, Debussy felt that musical eloquence lay in understatement, and not in Wagner's overstatements; in refinement, restraint, and delicacy, and not in the thunderbolts hurled by Wagner's orchestra and singers; in transparency of structure, clarity of thought, and economy of means, and not in the com-

plicated harmonic and contrapuntal network spun by Wagner in his elabo-
rately conceived formats. Debussy's mission now was to become *"un musicien français"*—"a French musician"—in opposition to the Teutonic Wagner.

Not until he came into personal contact with the French Impressionist painters (headed by Manet, Degas, and Renoir) did Debussy come upon the means with which to realize himself as a "French" composer. The Impressionist painters were not interested in ideas as much as in conveying the impression they gained by direct observation of the subject. Their work was characterized by subtle suggestions and nuances, nebulous effects achieved through deft use of color and light. Seeing their canvases and listening to their discussions, Debussy realized how to achieve his own identity in music: by transferring the concepts, theories, and methods of the Impressionist painters to musical composition. In doing this he represented the first major revolt against the cult of Wagner. He also created a cult of his own: Impressionism.

Before he sharpened the tools with which to shape his Impressionist art, Debussy had written vocal music whose sensitivity and whispered beauty anticipate his later mature style. His first compositions were written while he attended the Paris Conservatory. They were songs to French texts in which he already demonstrated his responsiveness to French poetry and his ability to adapt his melodic line to the contours, accents, and inflections of the French language. "Beau soir" ("Beautiful Evening"), written about 1876, has a fragile beauty and an air of mystery often encountered in Debussy's later masterpieces.

The Symbolist poet Paul Verlaine and Debussy's first major love affair were the two forces helping him to develop his highly individualized manner of writing mélodies. This was even before he had become an Impressionist. In 1880 Debussy read Verlaine for the first time and forthwith responded to Verlaine's appeal to the senses and his concern for the sounds of words. This was also the time when, having fallen in love, he sought an outlet for his emotions. The woman on whom Debussy lavished his affections was Mme Vasnier, a voice student whom Debussy sometimes accompanied on the piano. She was older than Debussy, and married to an architect. The Vasniers frequently invited Debussy to their home at Ville d'Avray (not far from Paris). Debussy's reaction was to fall madly in love with his hostess. Apparently the Vasniers were fond of Debussy, and apparently, too, Mme Vasnier was flattered by the young man's obvious infatuation. Over a period of several years Debussy spent a good deal of time at the Vasnier household—composing music there, playing the piano, reading their books, playing cards, and always moping and mooning. He would become surly if another visitor were present, since he wanted all of Mme Vasnier's attention for himself. Often he would be moody and easily offended. But, just as quickly, he would spring back into the best of humor through a tender look, or a gentle word, or a considerate act by the woman of his heart.

Between 1880 and 1884 Debussy wrote several songs for Mme Vasnier, including the still-honored ''Mandoline'' and ''Pantomime,'' both to poems by Verlaine. These, and other songs to poems by Verlaine, Alfred de Musset, and Stéphane Mallarmé among others, were Debussy's avowal of love. In dedicating these songs to Mme Vasnier, who became the first to sing them, Debussy wrote: ''To Mme Vasnier. These songs which she alone has made live and which will lose their enchanting grace if they are never again to come from her singing lips. The eternally grateful author.''

In 1884—after having attended the Paris Conservatory for eleven years, where he had been a brilliant, albeit frequently rebellious, student— Debussy received the coveted Prix de Rome. The prize entitled him to spend three years at the Villa Medici in Rome, devoting himself to study and to the writing of music. From time to time he was required to send back compositions to the conservatory. The last one Debussy submitted was a lyric poem for women's voices, solo soprano, and orchestra: *La Demoiselle élue* (*The Blessed Damozel*), to a poem by Dante Gabriel Rossetti. The authorities in Paris criticized it for its ''vagueness'' of expression and form and for its unusual harmonies, and did not allow it to be performed. *La Demoiselle élue* had to wait five years to be heard, when it won public and critical favor for its sensitive beauty. It has often been heard since then.

Debussy did not complete the prescribed three-year residence at the Villa Medici. He hated Italy, he was irritated at the high-handed and unsympathetic way in which his compositions were being received by the academicians in Paris, and he was pining for Mme Vasnier. He was back in Paris in 1887. It was now that his associations with the avant-garde French painters transformed him into an Impressionist composer.

His initial music as an Impressionist composer appeared in 1888, with six songs to Verlaine's poems collectively entitled *Ariettes oubliées* (*Forgotten Ariettas*), the most exquisite of which was the song ''Il Pleure dans mon coeur'' (''Tears Fall in My Heart''). His Impressionist style unfolded further in the first set of *Fêtes galantes* (*Gallant Feasts*), three songs to poems by Verlaine (1892), the most celebrated being ''Clair de lune'' (''Moonlight''), which must not be confused with the extremely popular piano piece of the same name, also by Debussy. With Debussy's String Quartet in G minor (1893) and the orchestral work *Prélude à l'après-midi d'un faune* (*The Afternoon of a Faun*) in 1894, Impressionism became the most significant and influential new force in music since the time of Wagner.

The masterworks now kept coming—music for orchestra, for the piano, for the stage, and for the voice. In the last category we find the *Chansons de Bilitis,* poems by Pierre Louÿs (1897), the second set of *Fêtes galantes,* again to poems by Verlaine (1904), *Trois Ballades de François Villon* (*Three Ballads of François Villon*), later also orchestrated, and the *Trois Poèmes de Stéphane Mallarmé* (*Three Poems of Stéphane Mallarmé*) in 1913. Debussy's last song was "Noël des enfants qui n'ont plus de maisons" ("Christmas of Children Who No Longer Have a Home"), in 1915, for which he wrote both the poem and the music and which he also transcribed for children's chorus. When he wrote it he was suffering from cancer, which finally took his life just about three years later.

In 1907 (by which time Debussy had become recognized as the foremost composer in France) a scandal exploded in musical Paris. In the eye of the hurricane stood a composer who had been influenced by Debussy into becoming an Impressionist. He was Maurice Ravel (1875–1937).

Ravel was by no means an unknown quantity when, in 1907, one of his works aroused in Paris a storm of conflicting opinions and accusations. At the Paris Conservatory, which he had attended from 1889 to 1904, he had been an outstanding student, though on four occasions he was turned down for the Prix de Rome. Even as a student he captured fame with two piano pieces: the *Pavane pour une Infante défunte* (*Pavane for a Dead Infanta*), in 1899, and *Jeux d'eau* (*Fountain*) in 1901. In 1904 the premiere of three "poems" for voice and orchestra, *Shéhérazade,* had drawn attention to his exceptional gift for evoking the color and mystery of the Eastern world in Western music. His string quartet, introduced later the same year, was hailed as a masterwork by influential French critics. And in 1905 he made front-page news when an important segment of musical Paris raised a hue and cry because Ravel had been turned down for the Prix de Rome three times, and in 1905, for what would have been his fourth attempt, was not even allowed to compete.

He was, then, more or less of a musical celebrity when on January 12, 1907, there took place the premiere of his *Histoires naturelles* (*Natural History*), a cycle of five songs for voice and piano to a prose text by Jules

Renard. Some critics attacked Ravel for being an imitator of Debussy, one of whom came right out and called him a plagiarist. Other critics, equally prominent, came to his defense by insisting that, far from being an imitator, Ravel had a style and personality all his own, even though he was an Impressionist; that his Impressionism had a far different character from that of Debussy; that it opened up fruitful new areas untouched by Debussy. The battle of printed and spoken words was vitriolic. But when the clamor died down, the forces supporting Ravel proved victorious. From this time on, the accusation that Ravel was an echo of Debussy was put to permanent rest.

It is surely strange that of all of Ravel's works up to 1907 it should have been *Histoires naturelles* that inspired this bitter controversy, since this is a composition we would never associate with Debussy. Renard's text speaks mockingly of a peacock, a guinea hen, a swan, a cricket, and a kingfisher. For the ironic, at times even impudent, lines, Ravel wrote fittingly satiric music with many of the melodies almost assuming the informal character of a conversation to an accompaniment generously spiced with piquant harmonies. Rarely was Debussy capable of such levities.

Ravel's staunch supporters of 1907 were, of course, right, as he would prove decisively time and again in subsequent compositions. He was no shadow of Debussy. His writing was more muscular than Debussy's; he did not make the whole-tone scale the spine of his melodic and harmonic language; he had a greater sense of classical symmetry and balance of structure than Debussy; and his creative lyre had more strings than that of Debussy. As an Impressionist, Ravel could be atmospheric and evocative in his tone painting. But he was also outstanding as a wit and satirist. And he skillfully adapted his Impressionist style for foreign or esoteric folk music, which Debussy never did. Fascinated by a collection of Greek songs shown him by a French critic, Ravel edited five melodies to which he provided his own distinctive accompaniments in *Cinq mélodies populaires grecques* (*Five Popular Greek Melodies*) in 1905. He did the same service for popular and folk songs of Spain, France, and Italy, and for the religious and folk music of the Jews (though Ravel was not himself a Jew) in *Quatre chants populaires* (*Four Popular Songs*), in 1910, and in *Deux mélodies hebraïques* (*Two Hebrew Melodies*), in 1914. A dozen years later, Ravel evoked the spirit of an exotic land in *Chansons madécasses* (*Madagascan Songs*) for voice, flute, cello, and piano. But to whatever foreign or exotic land or people Ravel's imagination might take him, the aristocratic elegance of his structure and style remains recognizably Ravelian.

The Musicians of the Orchestra, *an Impressionist painting by Edgar Degas. In art and in music, the Impressionist movement represented an abrupt break with the past and an attempt to achieve fresh artistic expression through a new use of colors and tones.*

Claude Debussy.

Paul Verlaine, French Symbolist poet,
many of whose poems were set to music by Debussy.

Francis Poulenc.

Guillaume Apollinaire, French poet and critic whose poems were set to music by Poulenc. Drawing by Picasso.

Arthur Honegger.

Jean Cocteau, French poet and dramatist,
who wrote the text for Poulenc's Cocardes.

Paul Claudel, French poet and dramatist, who wrote the text for Honegger's Jeanne d'Arc au bûcher *and* La Danse des morts.

More French in manner is one of Ravel's best-known songs, the "Ronsard à son âme" ("Ronsard to His Soul") of 1924. Here he used lines from the French Renaissance poet Pierre de Ronsard in which he addresses the "much-loved occupant of my body" that is descending "into the realm of the departed." The poem closes with the request that his sleep not be disturbed. Ravel's music maintains a quiet classic beauty by avoiding almost any change in dynamics throughout the song. The polyphonic age of the Renaissance is recalled in the piano accompaniment through the use of consecutive intervals of the fifth to simulate the organum technique of early polyphony.

Ravel's last composition was a song cycle for baritone and orchestra (or piano) to poems by Paul Morand: *Don Quichotte à Dulcinée* (*Don Quixote to Dulcinea*) in 1932. It was intended for a motion picture, but it was not used because of disagreements between the motion-picture producer and the composer on the type of songs suitable for the production. Ravel then released the three songs as a concert work. Here, as in many an earlier masterwork, Ravel betrayed his love for Spain and its people, backgrounds, and folk music, and also his uncanny ability to simulate Spanish musical styles. In the first song, "Chanson romanesque" ("Romanesque Song"), Don Quixote offers to lay down his life for his lady love if she so desires. "Chanson épique" ("Epic Song") is Don Quixote's soulful prayer to Saint Michael and Saint George. The cycle ends with "Chanson à boire" ("Drinking Song"), a rousing number in the style of the lively Aragonese dance the jota.

Soon after completing the *Don Quichotte* songs, Ravel was in a taxi accident that was responsible for brain damage that later revealed itself. He had to be operated upon on December 19, 1937. A few hours after the operation, Ravel opened his eyes, called for his brother, and then fell into a sleep from which he was never again to awaken.

Francis Poulenc was not only the principal composer of vocal music since Debussy and Ravel. He was also one of the most richly endowed and productive composers of art songs in the twentieth century. Though he was never an Impressionist—his style was eclectic—he was as thoroughly French as Debussy or Ravel.

Born in Paris on January 7, 1899, to a wealthy and cultured family, Poulenc began to study the piano with his mother when he was five. His real awakening to music, as he subsequently confessed, came some years later when he heard a composition by Debussy for the first time. He felt as if he had discovered a new world. Now motivated into becoming a professional musician, he studied the piano industriously with Ricardo Viñes while absorbing experiences in early-twentieth-century music by going to concerts and studying published music. Stravinsky, as well as Debussy, became his idol. But he did not ignore the music of the past. He became infatuated with the songs of Franz Schubert, a volume of which he found in a music store. This fascination laid the groundwork for his later activity as a writer of songs.

His first bid for attention came on December 11, 1917, with the premiere in Paris of his *Rapsodie nègre* (*Negro Rhapsody*) for baritone, piano, flute, clarinet, and string quartet. At that time a vogue for all things Negro seized Paris. To make fun of this fad, some nonsensical poems were published credited to a Liberian. Actually this work was a hoax. Poulenc was so amused by this volume that he wrote music for one of these poems, "Honoloulou." Poulenc's music was satirical, and the delicious nonsense of this bizarre composition delighted critics and audiences.

After serving in the French army during World War I, Poulenc continued to write music. Two of his compositions, in 1919, were song cycles, each witty or sardonic. *Le Bestiaire* (*The Bestiary*), for medium voice, flute, clarinet, bassoon, and string quartet, caricatured six animals, insects, and fish in verses by Guillaume Apollinaire: a dromedary, goat, grasshopper, dolphin, crawfish, and carp. *Cocardes* (*The Cockades*), for voice, violin, cornet, trombone, bass drum, and triangle, was an ironic takeoff on three popular songs. The poems (by Jean Cocteau) were just a series of words strung together rhythmically, hopping around, as Poulenc said, "like birds from tree to tree." As Poulenc's music hopped along with the words, the cycle became a mischievous musical escapade.

On April 5, 1919, a group of young French composers calling themselves the "Nouveaux Jeunes" ("the New Young People") gave a concert in Paris. The program included works by Poulenc, together with compositions by Darius Milhaud (1892–1974), Arthur Honegger (1892–1955), Georges Auric (1899–   ), Louis Durey (1888–   ) and Germaine Tailleferre (1892–   ). In reviewing this concert, the Parisian critic Henri Collet headed his article "Les Cinq Russes, les Six Français, et Satie" ("The Russian Five, the French Six, and Satie"). A year later, when a volume of piano pieces by the six young French composers was published, Collet reviewed it and once again referred to this group as "the French Six." The name stuck, permanently replacing "Nouveaux Jeunes," even though the six composers had little in common stylistically and were not happy to have their names linked together as if they were a cohesive little group with similar ideals. But for a number of years each of these composers was invariably identified throughout the musical world as a "member" of the French Six.

However much their paths diverged, one avenue was at one time or another traveled upon by all six composers—a road paved with levity. And levity was to be the soul of Poulenc's wit in a few ballets and some instrumental compositions that enjoyed popularity in the 1920s and the early 1930s.

In August of 1935, Poulenc appeared as piano accompanist for a French singer, Pierre Bernac, in a recital held at a private garden party in Salzburg, Austria, during the festival season. This association with Bernac—which continued for many years and resulted in concerts throughout Europe and America—reawakened Poulenc's interest in art songs, which had once been stirred by the lieder of Schubert. Late in 1935, Poulenc wrote the music for five poems by Paul Eluard. Two years later, once again to Eluard's poems, Poulenc was the author of his first song masterpiece, a song cycle *Tel jour, telle nuit* (*What a Day, What a Night*) comprising nine tragic songs.

Between 1937 and 1956 Poulenc completed about a hundred songs, many to surrealist poems by Eluard, Apollinaire, and Max Jacob. Tender lyricism, poetic moods, subtle emotion, and a thorough command of the song form placed Poulenc with the aristocratic composers of art songs in twentieth-century France. His treasures include the cycles *Miroirs brûlantes* (*Scorching Mirrors*) in 1938, to poems by Eluard; *Banalités* (*Banalities*) in 1940, to poems by Apollinaire; and *Deux poèmes* (*Two Poems*) in 1943, to words by Louis Aragon. "Tu vois le feu du soir" ("You See the Fire of Evening") in *Miroirs brûlantes,* "Sanglots" ("Sobs") in *Banalités,* and "C" in *Deux poèmes* are among the greatest songs Poulenc ever wrote and, by the same token, among the finest in the twentieth-century repertory.

Poulenc's song output petered out after he wrote "Dernière poème" ("Last Poem") in 1956. One song in 1958, and another in 1960, and then he refused to write any more for voice and piano. He explained: "Today poets do not write in a manner that inspires me to song. . . . To write more would be to force myself in a direction in which I really have nothing more to say."

A tragic event in 1936 became an important influence in giving direction to Poulenc's career as a choral composer. One of Poulenc's friends, a gifted composer, Pierre-Octave Ferroud, was decapitated in a gruesome automobile accident. The horrible news reached Poulenc just as he was about to visit the shrine of Rocamadour, which held a statue of the Virgin Mary carved from black wood. The death of his beloved friend and the visit to this shrine led Poulenc to write a composition for women's (or children's) voices and organ, *Litanies à la vierge noire* (*Litanies for the Black Virgin*), using as his text a recitation he had heard at the sanctuary. This was Poulenc's first important religious composition. He had been born to devout Catholic parents and in his boyhood he had received religious training. After the death of his father in 1917, he started to lose his deep religious feelings until he became totally irreligious. But the tragedy of his friend's accident and his own visit to the shrine awakened his religious convictions that apparently had been slumbering within him for so many years. From then on, until life's end, he was a dedicated Catholic, who was repeatedly impelled to give voice to his religious feelings in music.

In 1937 he produced the Mass in G major for unaccompanied chorus, in memory of his father. This was choral music uniting religious fervor with beatific serenity. Other equally moving religious works followed, including cantatas, motets, prayers, *Stabat Mater* (1950), *Ave Verum* (1952), and *Gloria* (1960). Of these, the *Stabat Mater,* for soprano, chorus, and orchestra, has been acclaimed most widely in Europe and America. Written in memory of a then recently deceased painter, the *Stabat Mater* is a work in twelve contrasting sections that move from a gentle opening to a heart-rending pathos. It encircles, as Poulenc's biographer Henri Hell wrote, "the whole range of religious experience from grace to drama and majesty."

One of Poulenc's most poignant choral works is political rather than religious, the *Figure humaine* (*The Face of Man*), a cantata for unaccompanied double mixed chorus, written in 1943, during the occupation of Paris by the Nazis in World War II. Eluard's text describes the suffering of the French at the hands of their ruthless conquerors. It then goes on to proclaim a hymn to freedom. The words and music of this cantata were secretly printed and distributed under the unsuspecting eyes of the Nazis. But a performance had to wait for France's liberation. When the war was nearing its end the score was flown to London, where it was performed by the chorus of the BBC in January of 1945. After that it was finally given in free Paris. Most of the music is touchingly simple in its emotional appeal. In one part Poulenc interpolated one of the songs from his cycle *Tel jour, telle nuit:* "Une herbe pauvre" ("A Poor Herb") accompanied by murmuring voices. A climax in the cantata is achieved with a fugal section involving both choruses, rising to a resounding peak with the words "the decay had a heart." Silence follows, finally broken by the majestic strains of the closing hymn to liberty.

But it was with religious music that Poulenc sounded the closing chords of his career: with a wonderful six-part *Gloria* for soprano solo, chorus, and orchestra commissioned by the Koussevitzky Music Foundation and introduced by the Boston Symphony on January 20, 1961, and with a devout vocal and orchestral composition, *Sept répons des ténèbres* (*The Seven Responses of Darkness*) written for the opening season of the New York Philharmonic orchestra at its new auditorium at the Lincoln Center for the Performing Arts and introduced there posthumously on April 11, 1963.

Poulenc's death came suddenly. Only two evenings before his death he seemed hale and cheerful at a ballet performance at the Opéra-Comique in Paris. His heart stopped beating, without warning, in his apartment overlooking the Luxembourg Gardens in Paris on January 30, 1963.

The son of Swiss parents, Arthur Honegger was born in the French seaport Le Havre on March 10, 1892. From 1910 to 1912 he attended the conservatory in the Swiss city of Zürich, from which his parents had come. In 1912 he was enrolled in the Paris Conservatory. There he wrote *Quatre poèmes,* four songs for voice and piano, which were performed in Paris in 1916. One of them was "Prière" ("Prayer"), which Honegger himself always considered one of the best songs he ever wrote. Several of his instrumental compositions were heard in Paris between 1917 and 1918.

Recognition came shortly after his name had been linked with those of five other young composers as the French Six. It came with a major choral work for narrator, solo voices, chorus, and orchestra—the oratorio *Le Roi David* (*King David*). In 1921, the year of its composition, it was staged with costumes and scenery in Switzerland. Honegger then revised and reorchestrated it for concert performance. It returned to Switzerland in 1923 to receive a resounding acclaim, an acclaim that followed it with presentations in Paris that same year, New York in 1925, and Rome in 1926.

The text by René Morax tells the story of the biblical David from his days as shepherd, through his victory over Goliath, to his rise as king and prophet, up until the time of his death. In twenty-seven sections, gathered into three major units, Honegger's score is a cloth of many colors. It is partly Baroque, with reminders of Bach or Handel in some of its powerful polyphonic choruses. It is partly Romantic, especially in several folklike melodies of disarming simplicity and poignant beauty. It is partly esoteric, when it adopts the intervallic structure of Hebrew music. And it is partly modern in its occasional use of discordant harmonies. But whatever style or idiom is employed, the music conveys religious ardor through psalms, songs of penitence, a Jewish song of mourning, and a closing Alleluia.

Honegger's chef d'oeuvre in choral music is *Jeanne d'Arc au bûcher* (*Joan of Arc at the Stake*) in 1935, text by Paul Claudel. This, too, is an oratorio, which was first performed in a concert version and later was given with costumes, scenery, and staging. Since then the oratorio version has won universal acceptance in concert halls, though frequently given with some discreet stage and lighting effects and modest costuming to enhance the dramatic interest.

Throughout the composition, Joan of Arc (exclusively a speaking part) is fastened to a stake where she is to be burned as a witch. Near her is Frère Dominique (also a speaking part). They exchange a series of flashbacks in which Joan's life, the summons of supernatural voices for her to liberate France, her victories on the battlefield that led to the crowning of Charles VII, her trial at the hands of the English as a heretic, and her condemnation to burn at the stake are reviewed. From time to time the text digresses to criticize the low state of morals and ethics in France in Joan's time. Symbolism helps to point up ignorance, avarice, malice, and corruption. Animals represent the bestiality of man; and a game of cards, the intrigues of the state in peace and war. All this is in sharp contrast to the courage, nobility, and self-sacrifice of Joan, who faces death with head high, since she sees it not as defeat but as triumph. "Now I feel God rising triumphant," she exclaims just before the flames devour her, to which the chorus responds: "Greater love hath no man than this—to give his life for those he loves."

Honegger uses the spoken word, recitatives, melodies, choruses, choral readings, and orchestral music, all of which he blends masterfully into an integrated score rich with spiritual values, vivid in its pictorialism, and stirringly theatrical.

Paul Claudel also prepared for Honegger the text of another dramatic oratorio, *La Danse des morts* (*The Dance of the Dead*), for narrator, solo voices, chorus, and orchestra (1938). Claudel's point of departure was images of death on woodcuts by Holbein the Younger that he had seen in Basel, Switzerland. With these images in mind, he prepared a text combining words from the Old Testament with his own mystical thoughts.

Words and music were written at a time when the thought of death was
uppermost in the minds of Europeans, since the threat of a cataclysmic war

hovered ominously on the horizon. World War II exploded in Europe only a year or so after the oratorio was completed, and its world premiere took place in Switzerland just about six months after the outbreak of hostilities.

Death stalks through Honegger's music like some gray ghost, beginning with the nineteen-measure outburst of anguish in the orchestra with which the work opens, and continuing with a macabre march with which the dead are awakened to form a mighty army. The rhythms of a French folk song ("Sur le pont d'Avignon") and a Revolutionary song "La Carmagnole") provide the material for an orgiastic dance into which the strains of a "Dies Irae" intrude grimly. But later there comes the at times ecstatic and at times mystical music announcing the prophecy of the Resurrection, the return of the people of Israel to the Promised Land, and the Revelation of the Lord.

During World War II, Honegger was a member of the underground French Resistance when Paris was occupied by the Nazis. Those searing times served to sharpen further the edge of Honegger's creativity. His first important symphony, the second, for string orchestra (1941), speaks of the desolation and despair of the war years. Hope for peace, and the liberation of France, led Honegger to write a new choral work, *Chant de libération* (*Song of Liberation*), with a text by Bernard Zimmer. It was written while Paris was still occupied, and in words and music it aspired to give hope and assurance to the stricken French that their land would once again be free. Its world premiere took place in Paris on October 22, 1944, in celebration of the recent liberation of France.

Honegger's best works after that were his symphonies, of which he wrote five in all, the last in 1950. In 1947 he came to the United States to give a master class in composition at the Berkshire Music Center at Tanglewood in Massachusetts. This was his second visit, his first having come in 1929 when he toured America as a guest conductor of several major orchestras in performances of his music. He never did complete his teaching assignment at Tanglewood, since he was stricken by a heart attack. He returned to Paris, where, depleted though his strength was, he worked on several compositions, including his last symphony. His death in Paris on November 27, 1955, was the consequence of another heart attack.

High Priest of Musical Expressionism

Arnold Schoenberg

A new trend in twentieth-century music was set into motion in the early 1920s: musical Expressionism, a rebellion against the excesses of Wagnerian Romanticism and the preciousness and delicacies of Debussy's Impressionism. The Expressionist composer, taking his cue from Expressionist painters, sought for inspiration in his inner experience. He tried to free his art of any outside influences. He used the technique of abstraction, showing a concern for design rather than subject matter, reducing materials to elementals. The Expressionist composer made a fetish of brevity, concentration, compression. His music was directed more to the intellect than to the heart. The musical practices of the past were abandoned. With the Expressionist, dissonance replaced consonance; one-time slavery to basic tonalities gave way to the absence of any consistent tonality (atonality); a stark, severe, brutal kind of melodic line displaced lyricism; structures were made so pliable in allowing the musical thought to flow without restriction that they almost seemed formless.

The initial architect of musical Expressionism was Arnold Schoenberg (1874–1951). As a young man, in his native city of Vienna, he too had been a true believer in Wagner. In his first composition still today performed he speaks in the musical language of Wagner: *Verklärte Nacht* (*Transfigured Night*), a tone poem written in 1899 as a sextet but transcribed by the composer in 1917 for chamber orchestra, the version that made it famous.

More Wagnerian still is the *Gurre-Lieder* (*Songs of Gurre*), a huge cantata begun around 1900, most of which was finished by 1901 (though the orchestration and the final chorus were delayed for another decade). This work has the dimensions of a Wagnerian music drama. It is so long that it makes a complete program by itself. It enlists the services of a huge mixed chorus, three male choruses, a narrator, five solo voices, and an orchestra of 140 instrumentalists. Schoenberg had to have special music paper manufactured to get all his notes down on paper. (The usual music manuscript paper contained from a dozen to twenty staves on a page, whereas the *Gurre-Lieder* required forty-eight!) In style as well as size this work is Wagnerian. It utilizes chromatics extensively and indulges in Wagnerian sensuous sweeps of melody and a complex contrapuntal fabric of intertwining themes.

The text—by the Danish poet Jens Peter Jacobsen—is made up of nineteen poems relating the tragic story of King Waldemar IV and Princess Tove in Denmark during the Middle Ages. There are three parts. In the first, the king presents Tove with the gift of a castle. After a passionate love episode, a bird describes how Tove was murdered by the queen, Waldemar's wife ("Song of the Wood Dove"). In the second part, the king bitterly denounces God, whom he blames for Tove's death. The third part departs from the narrative to become descriptive or atmospheric. It opens with a nocturnal ride by Death and ends with the description of the rising sun in the magnificent chorus "Behold, the Sun!"

In 1906 Schoenberg came to the conclusion that he had exhausted the possibilities of Wagnerian Romanticism. In fact, the overstatements and emotional extravagance of Romanticism had begun to repel him. He now had a compelling need to seek greater objectivity and austerity. He also became convinced that the laws thus far governing the writing of music had become obsolete. And so he abandoned the accepted rules of harmony and lyricism to produce new sounds. At the same time, he liberated tonality from what he described as the "tyranny of the key center." In other words, a piece of music no longer had to be faithful to a basic tonality but could move with anarchistic freedom from one key to another without modulation. The final movement of Schoenberg's String Quartet no. 2, op. 10 (1908) is the first piece of music ever written atonally; and it is here that we find the real beginnings of Schoenberg as an Expressionist.

Schoenberg charted yet another new course for music with *Pierrot
Lunaire* (*Pierrot of the Moon*), op. 21 (1912). This was an atonal song
cycle for speaking voice, piano, flute (alternating with piccolo), clarinet
(alternating with bass clarinet), violin (alternating with viola), and cello.
The text for the speaking voice is twenty-one decadent poems by Albert
Giraud, which the poet labeled as "three-times-seven [that is, twenty-one]
melodramas." The thought contained in each poem is vaguely expressed,
while the images are nebulously drawn. Many of the poems are concerned
with the moon: how its light shimmers on the waves of the sea, like wine
we can drink with our eyes; how it is like pale blossoms of white roses;
how it is sick or black. Pierrot glides through the lines of other poems as
"a silent dandy" by a fountain, or as a thief, or as a man who performs a
blasphemous mass. Some of the poems have about them a surrealistic feeling. One tells of Pierrot stealing the ducal rubies, symbols of the bloody
drops of past fame; in another Pierrot imagines himself decapitated by the
crescent of a moon, which he thinks is a Turkish sword; in a third, he
bores a hole into a skull into which he stuffs Turkish tobacco, and then
uses it as a pipe with which to smoke.

For the speaking voice declaiming the poems against a discordant,
atonal accompaniment, Schoenberg devised a radically new kind of lyricism for which the terms *Sprechstimme* or *Sprechgesang* ("song-speech")
have been coined. Song-speech is declamation in which the voice soars
and plunges to indicated pitches and rhythm, gliding from one note to the
next. The speaking voice seems to have a life of its own, and the accompanying instruments another, with each seeming to move in its own direction. In fact, Schoenberg had no intention of capturing in his music any of
the extramusical connotations of the poems the way German and Austrian
composers of lieder had been accustomed to do. At times he makes a conscious effort to negate the text: for example, one of the poems speaks
about a viola, but the accompanying music is for the cello.

No wonder, then, that Schoenberg's contemporaries were at turns puz-
zled and infuriated by this outlandish music. When *Pierrot Lunaire* was introduced in Berlin on October 16, 1912, the audience went into an uproar
of dissent, which expressed itself in outraged shouts, hissing, and guffaws.
Schoenberg's followers engaged the dissenters in fist fights. The critics
raged and fumed. One of America's most venerated critics, James Gibbons
Huneker, later described this work as music of "depravity, ugliness, of
base egoism, of hatred and contempt, of cruelty." Huneker then added:
"If such music-making is ever to become accepted, then I long for Death
the releaser."

But the violent attacks of critics, fellow musicians, and enemies failed to deter Schoenberg from his self-appointed destiny to free music from the bonds of the past. His writing after *Pierrot Lunaire* became increasingly iconoclastic, increasingly difficult to assimilate at first hearing, as he penetrated ever more deeply into musical abstraction.

Then, in the early 1920s, Schoenberg felt that in his quest for full freedom of expression he was hovering on the edge of total anarchy. He now sensed the need for some system with which to discipline his thinking. The older systems were useless, he felt. He therefore went on to develop, perfect, and master a new one: dodecaphony, popularly known as the twelve-tone system. He did not invent it; that credit should probably go to one of his little-known Viennese contemporaries, Joseph M. Hauer, who was experimenting with twelve-tone music even before Schoenberg. But it was Schoenberg who realized its full creative possibilities.

It is not necessary here to go into a detailed explanation of what the twelve-tone system is, since only a fraction of Schoenberg's compositions in that style are for the voice. A few basic explanations, however, are in order. Before beginning work on a composition, Schoenberg arranged the twelve tones of the diatonic scale into a "melodic" pattern, or row, in which no tone is repeated until the other eleven have been utilized. The row is the core of the composition, which is constructed from any of the forty-eight patterns or formations to which a row can be subjected, or from restatements of the row itself. A composition, then, is conceived from basic formulas as coldly calculated and inflexible as a mathematical formula.

Though writing in the twelve-tone system is a cerebral process, it is possible to bring to its writing human values and emotional responses— however much the Expressionist composer tries to avoid them. For a long time, however, Schoenberg's own personality was divorced from the instrumental works conceived in the twelve-tone system. But late in his life he began to fill his music with subjective feelings, humanizing his music and making it more palatable for the general sophisticated music public. This change came about through an upheaval in his personal life brought on by the rise of the Nazi regime in Germany in 1933.

The ruthless dictatorship of the new order in Nazi Germany, which soon controlled every facet of German life and thought—combined with an organized program to "purify" the German race by annihilating the Jewish population—broke down the walls of insularity which Schoenberg had built around himself as a protection from a world so hostile to his music. Though an Austrian (and though Austria at that time had not yet been

Arnold Schoenberg.

A portrait of Arnold Schoenberg by Oskar Kokoschka, a leading Expressionist painter who significantly influenced the composer. Expressionist painters, using strong lines and figure distortion, strove to explore the subconscious world rather than to record external realities in the conventional way of the past. This artistic objective was shared by Expressionist composers.

· UNIVERSAL-EDITION ·

№ 3651

ARNOLD SCHÖNBERG

ZWEI GESÄNGE

OP. 1

No. 2

ABSCHIED

BARITON UND KLAVIER

*The title page and first page of an early edition
of Schoenberg's* Abschied.

Abschied.

(Karl Frh. von Levetzow.)

Arnold Schönberg, Op. 1. № 2.

Gesang.

Aus den Trümmern ei - ner ho - hen Schön - heit lass mich

bau - en ei - nen tie - fen Schmerz. Wei - nen lass mich aus den

tief - sten Schmerzen ei - ne Thrä - ne, wie nur Män - ner wei - nen.

Und dann geh!

seized by the Nazis), Schoenberg decided to leave Europe for good in the fall of 1933 to become an American. He made another momentous decision. He had been born a Jew but was converted to Catholicism. The doctrine of the Nazis toward the Jewish people impelled Schoenberg to rejoin the Jewish religion. On his way to America, he stopped off in Paris to go through the formal ritual of returning to the faith of his birth. Once in the United States, he established permanent residence in Los Angeles, Anglicized his name to Schoenberg (it had previously been spelled Schönberg), and became an American citizen.

The impact of his experiences was felt in some of the twelve-tone compositions completed in the United States—but most particularly in three vocal works. Schoenberg for the first time identified himself with his religion in the *Kol Nidre,* op. 39, for narrator, chorus, and orchestra (1938). The "Kol Nidre" is a Hebrew prayer for the holiest of all Hebraic holidays: Yom Kippur (Day of Atonement), when the worshiper atones for sins committed the preceding year. Making his own musical setting for a prayer so awesome to every Jew was perhaps one way for Schoenberg to make atonement for his having at one time deserted his religion. The twelve-tone system, for all the restrictions it imposed upon human feelings, and the Sprechstimme, for all its austerity, no longer were sterile of emotions.

This proved true once again in *Ode to Napoleon,* op. 41, for narrator, piano, and string quartet (later revised for string orchestra, in place of the quartet). By 1942, when the work was completed, the free world had become involved in the life-and-death struggle of World War II. Byron's poem "Ode to Napoleon" moved Schoenberg to use it for a composition in which, for the first time, he could express his own political ideology. In Byron's poem, Napoleon was the symbol of tyranny, and George Washington, of democracy. These symbols were translated by Schoenberg into musical terms within the formats of twelve-tonalism. Melodic intervals are recruited to portray Napoleon, the autocrat, and the freedom-loving democrat Washington. In speaking of tyranny and freedom, Schoenberg achieves a new expressiveness, particularly in the closing page, a stirring tribute to Washington.

No less personal to Schoenberg was the writing of the brief cantata, *A Survivor from Warsaw,* op. 46, for narrator, men's chorus, and orchestra, in 1947, four years before his death. Here Schoenberg prepared his own text in English. His theme was the heroic stand of the Jews in the ghetto of Warsaw during World War II, against a blistering attack by Nazi tanks and machine guns. With only the most primitive, improvised weapons, these

Jews held the bastions of their ghetto not for a single day, not for a week, but for over a month. By then almost everybody within the walls had been killed. A few managed to escape through an underground passage. Another handful was captured when the Nazis finally penetrated the stronghold.

It is a profoundly tragic work. An exclamation in the orchestra and the sounding of a note of despair in the cello lead to the opening lines of the text: "I cannot remember everything. . . . I only remember the grandiose moment when they all started to sing, as if prearranged, the old prayer they had neglected for so many years—the forgotten creed!" To an illustrative accompaniment, based on a twelve-tone row, the narrator then describes what transpired within the ghetto on the day the surrender took place; how the Nazi officer shrieked at the surviving Jews that they would soon be dispatched to gas chambers; and how unexpectedly, now one voice and now another, and after that several others still, joined together to sing that most sacred of all Hebrew prayers: "Hear, O Israel, the Lord Our God, the Lord Is One." This prayer, presented so movingly, is the overpowering climax of the composition, and with it the cantata comes to its dramatic conclusion.

II

Renaissance of English Music

Sir Edward Elgar, Ralph Vaughan Williams,
Sir William Walton, Benjamin Britten

From the death of Henry Purcell in 1695 until the dawn of the twentieth century, English music produced only a scattered handful of native-born composers still remembered (and then usually only in the history books) and but a meager and impoverished repertory of compositions still being heard (mainly vocal). It is no wonder, then, that the English music public lavished such adulation on Handel in the early eighteenth century, and on Mendelssohn in the nineteenth, both of whom were of German birth. Who among English composers of these centuries could offer competition? William Boyce, Thomas Arne, Thomas Attwood in the eighteenth century? Sir Henry Bishop, Michael William Balfe, Sir Charles Hubert Parry, Sir Charles Villiers Stanford in the nineteenth? Hardly! Their names and works have long lost their one-time appeal. From these two centuries a few solitary items have managed to avoid the oblivion that engulfed so much of English music. Some of Boyce's symphonies and church music . . . Balfe's opera *The Bohemian Girl* (1843), from which comes the famous air "I dreamt that I dwelt in marble halls" . . . songs such as "Under the Greenwood Tree" by Thomas Arne to Shakespeare; or "The Lass with the Delicate Air," by Arne's illegitimate son, Michael; Sir Henry Bishop's

"Home Sweet Home," which is not a concert song at all but an air from an opera, *Clari* (1823), the words by an American, John Howard Payne; and Bishop's "Lo, Here the Gentle Lark," which is a concert song . . . The operettas of Sir William Gilbert and Sir Arthur Sullivan have, of course, their own place on the musical stage. Sullivan was also the composer of the familiar hymn "Onward! Christian Soldiers."

A few virtually forgotten composers, a scattered number of compositions—this is the heritage of English music from the time of Purcell to the closing of the nineteenth century. These two centuries in England, then, represent fallow soil as far as music is concerned until Sir Edward Elgar (1857–1934) came to make it once again abundantly fruitful.

It hardly seemed at first as if Elgar was the man capable of recouping England's past musical glories. After his music study ended in 1879, he became a jack-of-all musical trades in Worcester, England (near the town of Broadheath where he was born), but a master of none. He led a band for the County Lunatic Asylum; he appeared as a violinist; he wrote functional music for various occasions; he officiated as church organist; he gave music lessons to private pupils. What he did, he did competently enough, but there was nothing to indicate in any of these efforts that he was destined for world fame. Then, in 1889, he married one of his pupils, Caroline Alice Roberts, the daughter of a major-general. She was a high-minded, strong-willed, and ambitious girl who was convinced that Elgar was capable of greatness as a composer. It was she who persuaded him not to scatter his energies so recklessly but to concentrate entirely on composition.

He first attracted attention with several ambitious and talented choral works, successfully performed at festivals in Worcester and Leeds between 1893 and 1898. His fame was further enhanced in 1899 with the writing of the *Variations on an Original Theme,* for orchestra, op. 36 (better known as the *Enigma Variations*) and a song cycle, *Sea Pictures,* for solo voice and orchestra, op. 37. With the oratorio *The Dream of Gerontius,* op. 38 (1900) he became an English institution; and such he remained as long as he lived.

The Dream of Gerontius is the most distinguished oratorio by an English composer—only a few degrees lower in popularity in England than Handel's *Messiah* and Mendelssohn's *Elijah*. It is a setting of Cardinal Newman's poem of the same name, which presents the doctrine of Purgatory as expounded by the Catholic Church. The oratorio opens as the dying Gerontius, in a trance, sees the mysteries of the unseen world. His Guardian Angel then prepares him for the experience of appearing at the throne *209* of the ultimate Judge, the Omnipotent. After the Angel of the Agony pleads for the salvation of Gerontius's soul, it is brought to the Holy Presence, which delivers it back to the arms of the Guardian Angel. In the end this angel chants a tender song of farewell to Gerontius.

Elgar's structure is not in the tradition of Handel's oratorios—that is, a succession of recitatives, arias, choruses, and ensemble numbers—but maintains a continuous fluidity with one part of the oratorio flowing into the next. The score spills over with Romantic music, sometimes of surpassing beauty and nobility, much of it in a Wagnerian style. Because it was both structurally and stylistically so different from a *Messiah* or an *Elijah, The Dream of Gerontius* was a failure when first heard at the Birmingham Festival in 1900. But one year later, in Germany, it was hailed as a masterpiece—the first time such a thing had happened in Germany to the work of an English composer. Subsequent performances in England helped audiences to appreciate the vivid imagery, the poetry, and the deeply imbedded mysticism of this music.

After that, Elgar wrote a good deal of choral music, including two oratorios (*The Apostles* and *The Kingdom*), as well as hymns, anthems, and other pieces. But he never again wrote a choral work to match the eloquence of *The Dream of Gerontius,* and his later choral compositions are rarely given. His vocal music includes several delightful songs for voice and piano, such as "Is She Not Passing Fair?" and "Like to the Damask Rose," and "Shepherd's Song," all of which was early Elgar, some preceding *The Dream of Gerontius* and some contemporary with it.

Elgar's most famous song was not conceived for the voice. The melody of "Land of Hope and Glory" first appeared in *Pomp and Circumstance* in D major, for orchestra, op. 39 no. 1 (1901). Later the same year, Elgar was commissioned to write a composition for the coronation of King Edward VII, official recognition that by now Elgar was regarded as his country's leading composer. For this occasion he prepared the *Coronation Ode,* for solo voices, chorus, and orchestra, op. 44 (1901), in which he adapted his majestic melody from *Pomp and Circumstance* to a patriotic poem, "Land of Hope and Glory." The premiere of Elgar's *Ode* was planned for June 30, 1902, but had to be postponed because the king was then too ill to attend the performance. It was never used for the purpose for which it had been intended. Now it is remembered exclusively for the stirring patriotic song that is almost as popular in Britain as its national anthem.

By the time Elgar died, he had received the highest honors a grateful country could confer on a composer who had brought his country back to the world community of great music: knighthood in 1904; appointment as Master of the King's Musick in 1924; and a baronetcy in 1931.

After Elgar died in 1934, his place at the head of English music was assumed by Ralph Vaughan Williams (1872–1958). Vaughan Williams was a nationalistic composer. Beginning with 1904, when he joined the Folk Song Society in England, he did intensive research in the folk music of various regions of England. He uncovered a rich lode of musical diamonds (carols, madrigals, folk songs, and dance tunes) with which the musical world at large first became acquainted through his skillful adaptations and valuable publications. In his own compositions, Vaughan Williams sometimes quoted and elaborated upon these folk tunes. But his more usual practice was to absorb the basic characteristics of the English folk song into his own writing: its modality, its serenity, the clear texture of its polyphony, its introspection. This represented assimilation rather than imitation. Through assimilation, Vaughan Williams's music became thoroughly English. As that eminent English musicologist Ernest Newman wrote, nowhere in music do we get "the brooding beauty of the quiet English countryside" as we find in so many of Vaughan Williams's compositions, or "an expression that has no rival anywhere in the music of what thoughtful Englishmen regard as one of the most precious possessions of their race, the vein of mellow mysticism that runs through so much of our heritage of poetry and prose."

Vaughan Williams first achieved his maturity as composer only after he had perfected his own style, incorporating the identifiable stylistic traits of English folk songs. But even before this had happened, he showed himself to be in possession of a gift for beguiling melodies, together with a skill in writing for the voice. As early as 1901, he wrote a fetching song for voice and piano, "Linden Lea." Between then and 1907 he produced the song cycle *The House of Life* (to six sonnets by Dante Gabriel Rossetti), and two sets of *Songs of Travel,* to poems by Robert Louis Stevenson. "Silent Noon" from *The House of Life* and "The Roadside Fire" from the first set of *Songs of Travel* are of special interest.

A more important song cycle finds Vaughan Williams reaching creative maturity: *On Wenlock Edge* (1909), a cycle of six songs for tenor, string quartet, and piano to poems by A. E. Housman, written not long after Vaughan Williams had completed a short period of study with Maurice Ravel in Paris. The spontaneity and the emotional restraint that characterize old English folk music can be found in this cycle. From this point on, the nationalistic style of Vaughan Williams developed rapidly:

first in the *Fantasia on a Theme by Thomas Tallis,* for string quartet and double orchestra (1910)—still a strong favorite with music lovers everywhere—and the *Fantasia on Christmas Carols,* for baritone solo, chorus, and orchestra (1912).

In the *Fantasia on Christmas Carols* Vaughan Williams quotes and develops four carols from three different parts of England: "The Truth Sent from Above" and "There Is a Fountain" from Herefordshire; "Come All You Worthy Gentlemen" from Somerset; and "On Christmas Night" from Sussex. In addition, he interpolates brief snatches of other English carols, including the familiar "The First Nowell" and "The Wassail Bough." What is of special interest in this composition is the varied way in which Vaughan Williams uses the chorus. Sometimes the chorus sings the words and music in the conventional manner; sometimes it sings the syllable *ah* with half-closed lips; sometimes it chants with completely closed lips; and sometimes it produces a humming tone.

A prolific composer throughout his life, Vaughan Williams contributed a good deal of vocal music, together with symphonies, concertos, and chamber and solo instrumental compositions. These have placed him with the foremost composers of the twentieth century. In vocal music he is most often heard at concerts through his adaptations of old English music, and most particularly through the music of the Tudor period. Who today does not know and love "Greensleeves," for example? "Greensleeves" dates from the sixteenth century and is mentioned in Shakespeare's *The Merry Wives of Windsor.* In the seventeenth century it became the party song of the Cavaliers in England. But not until Vaughan Williams adapted and published it did it gain extensive circulation—to such a point that, in 1957, its melody became a popular song hit in the United States. Besides making his felicitous setting for voice and piano, Vaughan Williams used "Greensleeves" in other compositions: in an orchestral fantasia and in his opera *Sir John in Love.*

In addition to his English folk-song adaptations, Vaughan Williams wrote many songs and choral works that find him at his creative best. His repertory of songs for voice and piano was enriched by *Three Poems* to words by Walt Whitman (in or about 1925) and *Four Poems* to verses by Fredegond Shove (1922), the last containing two of the finest songs he ever wrote, "The New Ghost" and "Water Mill." In 1954 Vaughan Williams published a group of nine songs to poems by A. E. Housman that he had actually written a quarter of a century earlier; these are also the cream of his vocal crop.

Jenny Lind singing in a performance of Mendelssohn's oratorio
Elijah *at Exeter Hall in London in 1855.*

Ralph Vaughan Williams.

William Walton.

Benjamin Britten.

Abundant, too, are his various works for chorus: part-songs, church music, hymns, and major compositions enlisting soloists and orchestra as well as chorus. *Sancta Civitas* (1923–25), to a text taken from the Book of Revelation based on the vision of Saint John, is a huge oratorio for solo voices, chorus, a "semi-chorus," and orchestra. The mysticism that creeps into so many of Vaughan Williams's other works pervades this lofty music. Its ending, a song of praise to God in contrapuntal style, is one of the most awesome pieces of music by this composer.

The *Five Tudor Portraits,* for contralto, baritone, chorus, and orchestra (1936), is another major vocal work, even though it has not yet received the recognition it deserves. Its choral writing is masterful, its melodies are hauntingly beautiful, its spirit is vigorous as the music gives voice to faith, optimism, and happiness. The *Serenade to Music,* for sixteen solo voices and orchestra (1938), is better known. It was written to honor the English conductor Sir Henry J. Wood on the fiftieth anniversary of his debut with the baton. Vaughan Williams used sixteen solo voices at Sir Henry's request, since the conductor wanted to feature at his anniversary concert the sixteen singers most often identified with his career. For his text, Vaughan Williams chose lines from Shakespeare's *A Merchant of Venice,* beginning with that of Lorenzo: "How sweet the moonlight sleeps upon this bank." The composition begins with a gentle chorale for all the solo voices, after which it goes on to concentrate now on one solo voice and then on another.

The *Fantasia on the Old 104th Psalm,* for chorus, piano, and orchestra (1949) is described by the composer as a "fantasia quasi variazione"—that is, a fantasia as if it were variations. This indicates that the usual variation technique is not adhered to but only suggested. There are three sections, each introduced by a cadenza for solo piano, and each based freely on the psalm melody that is first heard fully in the piano.

In commenting on Vaughan Williams's vocal music it is important to remember that two of his nine symphonies employ choral forces so extensively that it is possible to think of them as choral compositions. Vaughan Williams's first symphony was *A Sea Symphony* (1905–10), to a text by Walt Whitman, scored for soprano, baritone, mixed chorus, and orchestra. In using a sea voyage as a symbol for the travel of a soul to unknown regions, Vaughan Williams makes considerable use of voices, beginning with the chorus "Behold the Sea Itself" and ending with the eloquent section for solo voices "O My Brave Soul, O Further Sail" to which the chorus provides a solemn echo.

About forty-odd years—and six symphonies—later, Vaughan Williams wrote the *Sinfonia antartica,* for soprano, women's chorus, and orchestra. This is a picture of the struggle of man *vis à vis* natural forces in the icy Antarctic regions. Both the solo soprano and the chorus sing without any text whatsoever. However, before each of the first four movements (Prelude, Scherzo, Landscape, and Intermezzo) brief quotes from Shelley, Coleridge, John Donne, and Psalm 104 are printed to provide a clue to the intent of the music, while the Epilogue is preceded by three lines from a journal by the explorer Captain Robert Scott, in which he details his ill-fated expedition to the South Pole in 1910–12.

English vocal music continued to prosper at the hands of several eminent composers. Sir William Walton (1902–   ) was in his early twenties when he first came to the attention of the music public with a highly provocative and unconventional composition called *Façade.* This is a setting of twenty-one nonsense poems by Edith Sitwell for a "reciting voice" originally accompanied by seven instruments but later on rewritten for full orchestra. These Sitwell poems were appealing for their sounds rather than meaning, for their assonance rather than ideas. As the poet herself explained, her aim was to achieve "a new kind of beauty as well as gaiety." Entering into the jocund spirit of these verses, Walton provided a tuneful, spirited, and popular-styled musical background in which parody, burlesque, and caricature were important elements. Words and music combined to make a mockery of pomposity or pretentiousness. When *Façade* was first given, in London in 1923, it caused shock, dismay, and anger— and only occasionally amusement. But in an enlarged, revised version in 1926 it proved an unqualified success.

Walton graduated from the levities of *Façade* to the dignity and sobriety of *Belshazzar's Feast* (1931), an oratorio in epic mold for baritone, chorus, and orchestra. With it, Walton's fame was permanently solidified. No English oratorio since Elgar's *The Dream of Gerontius* so captured the enthusiasm of the music world as this one did, following its premiere at the Leeds Festival in England on October 10, 1931.

Osbert Sitwell (brother of Edith) was the author of a text, which found its source in the Book of Daniel in the Bible. Belshazzar was the last of the kings of Babylon. During an orgiastic feast he is warned of coming doom by handwriting on the wall, which is interpreted for him by the prophet Daniel. To Handelian grandeur Walton contributes a style dramatized through the use of such twentieth-century idioms as dissonance and polytonal effects.

The work falls into three parts. The first begins with the prophecy of Isaiah concerning the fate of Babylon and the Jewish captives. Their sad plight is underlined in a chorus, "By the Waters of Babylon." In the second part, Babylon is vividly described. The third part tells about the writing on the wall during the great feast in which Belshazzar is a participant. The fall of Babylon and the death of Belshazzar are hailed in a stirring chorus of thanksgiving by the Jews. The oratorio ends with a resounding "Alleluia."

Walton has never been a prolific composer; by the same token, his activity in vocal music has been limited. One other choral work deserves mention: *Te Deum,* commissioned by the British government for the coronation of Queen Elizabeth II. It was introduced during the festivities in London, on June 2, 1953, two years after Walton had been knighted.

The versatility of Benjamin Britten (1913–   ) has been matched only by his prodigious gifts. He has employed every medium, enriching them with compositions that have made him one of the most widely performed and recorded composers of this century. His vocal music has been both rich and varied. Here, as in other media, Britten is an eclectic composer who chooses whatever style or idiom best suits his subject. He is always in complete control of his musical language. He is particularly successful whenever he writes music for texts. This is the reason why he has become one of the foremost opera composers of our time, and why his vocal music holds such a high place of honor among his masterworks.

His first major addition to song literature was *Les Illuminations* (*Illuminations*), op. 18 (1939), a cycle for high voice and string orchestra to ten decadent poems by the French Symbolist Rimbaud. Britten wrote this work in the United States. He had come just to attend the American premiere of one of his orchestral compositions. What had been planned as a brief visit turned out to be a three-year stay. Europe plunged into the maelstrom of World War II while Britten was in New York. An avowed pacifist, Britten refused to be a participant in the war and consequently decided to remain in the then still-neutral United States.

In this country he continued to produce vocal music, even while working on other forms of composition, including a first opera, *Paul Bunyan.* In 1942 came two choral works—*Hymn to Saint Cecilia* and *A Ceremony of Carols.* The latter, scored for a boys' chorus and solo harp, begins with a Procession in which choristers file up the church aisle singing about Christ's birth. Nine carols follow. In a closing Recession, the choristers march out of the church singing. The chant "Hodie Christus natus est," which opens and closes *A Ceremony of Carols,* is of medieval origin, but the rest of the music is original with Britten. The work as a whole is distinctively Britten in its poetic content. The medievalism of the plainchant is neatly combined with the spice of modern idioms as the treble voices receive an individualized accompaniment from the solo harp.

In 1942 Britten returned to England. By that time his country and people were enmeshed in a Titanic struggle for survival from the relentless air attacks by the Nazi *Luftwaffe.* Britten felt impelled to bring such help to his countrymen as he could, but without bearing arms. Officially exempted from military duty, because his pacifist convictions were respected, Britten enlisted his music in the war effort by giving concerts in hospitals, bombproof shelters, and army camps. Despite these taxing assignments, he managed to do considerable composing. It was at this time that he labored upon the opera that brought him world fame, *Peter Grimes* (1945). Other major works included *Serenade,* op. 31 (1943), for tenor solo, horn, and string orchestra. This is a charming setting of several English poems by Tennyson, Blake, Ben Jonson, Keats, and others on the subject of night, its varying pictures, and the different thoughts and moods it inspires. The work begins and ends with a horn solo (at the end of the composition it is played offstage)—the two polar points between the evocative beauty of the songs.

Britten added considerably to the luster of his fame with the *Spring Symphony,* op. 44 (1949), a large choral work for soprano, contralto, tenor, mixed chorus, boys' chorus, and orchestra. From the deep well of English poetry about the vernal season, Britten selected fourteen poems by Spenser, Nashe, Milton, Herrick, Auden, Blake, and Beaumont and Fletcher, among others. He dressed the verses with music simulating old-time madrigals, but without sacrificing modernity of expression or style.

Britten's *magnum opus* for chorus—possibly one of his greatest compositions in any form—is *A War Requiem,* op. 66 (1962), for soprano, tenor, baritone, mixed chorus, boys' chorus, and orchestra. This is as compelling and as bitter an indictment of war as can be found in all music. Britten adopted a unique method. Between each of the Latin sections of the traditional requiem mass (''Requiem aeternam,'' ''Dies Irae,'' ''Offertorium,'' ''Sanctus,'' ''Agnus Dei,'' and ''Libera me'') Britten interpolated antiwar poems by Wilfred Owen. Owen, recipient of the Military Cross for bravery during World War I, was killed in action just one week before the Armistice. Though he fought bravely until his untimely death, Owen was violently opposed to war. He used poetry as a trumpet for his antiwar sentiments. On Britten—the lifelong pacifist—these poems had a particularly forceful impact.

The following lines by Owen appear on the title page of Britten's score: "My subject is War, and the pity of War. The poetry is in the pity. All a poet can do is warn." *A War Requiem*—both in Owen's poems and Britten's music—is a mighty expression not only of pity but also of anguish, horror, and at times outright despair.

It begins with the "Requiem aeternam" with which every requiem mass opens. Tolling bells accompany the singing of the chorus. Then the tenor appears with these bitter lines by Owen: "What passing bells for these who die as cattle? Only the monstrous anger of the guns." From then on, each part of the requiem text is followed by lines from Owen's antiwar poems. Within the closing "Libera me," an Owen poem speaks of the death of two soldiers who are enemies to each other. The two soldiers say quietly, "Let us sleep now." Then, reverting to the missal text, the chorus sings a final benediction for the war dead.

The juxtaposition of sections of the requiem mass in Latin with Owen's English poems is not the sole innovation here. Original, too, is the way Britten deploys his musical forces. He uses three performing groups, to each of which he assigns a different mission. The performance of the Latin sections of the traditional mass falls to the full chorus, the soprano solo, and the orchestra. In contrast to their rich sound textures, the soft sweet voices of a boys' chorus are also recruited for parts of the requiem text. For the antiwar sentiments of the Owen poems, which are set to declamations, a solo tenor, solo baritone, and a small chamber orchestra are enlisted.

Britten once again used a Latin text to expound his pacifist dogma, this time without English-language interpolations, in his *Cantata Misericordium,* op. 69 (1963), for tenor, baritone, mixed chorus, and small string orchestra. He wrote it to help celebrate the centenary of the International Red Cross. The Latin text dramatizes the parable of the Good Samaritan as told in Saint Luke's Gospel. The best musical pages are those that, through lyricism of great tenderness, portray the compassion of the Samaritan ("Ah, di boni!") and the choral admonishment to the people to emulate his noble example ("Vade et tu fac similiter"). In this admonishment, with which the cantata ends, we can almost hear Britten himself pleading with his listeners to follow him in his vision of brotherhood, and of mutual understanding among fellowmen, through which the dream of permanent universal peace can finally become a reality.

"I Hear America Singing"

William Billings, Charles Ives,
Samuel Barber, Ned Rorem, Leonard Bernstein

The first music in the New World was vocal, and America's first serious composer, William Billings, was exclusively a composer for the voice. His psalms, hymns, and secular tunes are mostly in four-part harmony and mark the beginnings of American-made music.

Fate had not been kind to him. He was born in Boston on October 7, 1746, with one eye, a withered arm, and legs of uneven length. His father died when Billings was fourteen, compelling the boy to shift for himself as best he could. Lacking proper home upbringing and guidance during those formative years, he developed boorish manners, a slovenly appearance, and a disdain for cleanliness that remained fixed with him all his life. Added to his deformities, these made him a truly pitiable spectacle to behold.

At fourteen he became an apprentice to a tanner. Even then his mind was fully on music, although the sole instruction he had received was some elementary lessons in singing from a local choirmaster. As a tanner's apprentice he spent hours studying rules of composition from a "musical grammar" and would scribble melodies of his own with chalk on leather hides and on the walls of his shop. He soon came to the brave decision to try to make music his profession—brave because nobody in the colonies then earned a living solely through music. He left the tannery and soon thereafter set up business as a teacher of singing in Boston, hanging a sign outside his home with which professional music in the New World comes into existence. It read simply: "Billings—Music." He also began composing in earnest. In 1770 he published his first volume of compositions, *The New England Psalm Singer*. Partly because he had been poorly trained in the rules of harmony and counterpoint—but mainly because he instinctively felt the need of arriving at a more robust and virile kind of music than those stately hymns and psalms which the colonists had brought with them from England—his music had a vigor and brusqueness not to be found in any other heard then in New England. Billings's second volume, and his most famous one, appeared in 1778, two years after America's independence. He called it *The Singing Master's Assistant,* though it is most often referred to as *Billings Best*—and with it music in America established its own independence. In later years Billings issued several more volumes. His writing remained to the end uncouth almost to the point of being primitive. He continually broke the rules of harmony and counterpoint and sometimes of consonance as well—sometimes consciously. But he did achieve a style that in its independence and strength was the first authentic voice of the rugged New World: "I Am the Rose of Sharon," "David's Lamentation," "The Lord Is Risen," "Be Glad Then America," "The Bird," "Kittery," "When Jesus Wept," and "Chester."

"Chester," which started out as a religious hymn tune in *Billings Best,* was destined to become America's first great war song. An ardently dedicated revolutionist—friend of Samuel Adams and Paul Revere—Billings used his music as a weapon in the struggle for independence. He prepared new martial lyrics for his hymn tunes in an effort to strengthen the fighting morale of the colonists, with songs such as "Lamentation Over Boston," "Independence," "Columbia," and "Chester." "Chester" was the most famous. It was sung so widely by colonists in army camps and on the field of battle that it has come to be known as the American "Marseillaise."

Billings was an original. Into his psalms and hymns he interpolated realistic effects unheard of in the church music of his day. When his words mentioned a bird, his running notes suggested winged flight. He was not afraid to use discords to convey the more powerful statements of his verses. In one of his hymns he urged the singers to clap their hands because the text mentioned hand clapping, and in another he simulated the effect of laughter to accompany the words "shall laugh and sing."

He was the object of a good deal of ridicule in his own time, both for the way he looked and lived and also for the kind of music he wrote. What his musical contemporaries objected to most violently was his discords and the way he so freely broke conventions of counterpoint. "I do not think myself confined to any rules of composition laid down by any that went before me," he announced defiantly in the preface to his first publication. One day, as a symbol of resentment, several musicians hung up a live cat by its tail on a signpost outside his house, its squealing intended to reproduce the sound of Billings's music. Billings's reaction was typical. He replied by writing "Jargon," a short piece for four voices that from beginning to end was filled with jarring discords. Another instance of his sense of humor was a piece named "Modern Music." In his text he amusingly explained how a piece of music should be conceived in order "to tickle the ear." The music painstakingly follows out his own instructions.

His contemporaries might ridicule him and his compositions. Nevertheless, well before Billings died in Boston on September 26, 1800, he had the satisfaction of having his psalms, hymns, and anthems sung in churches throughout the thirteen states and included in numerous anthologies of church music published in his time.

More significant by far as artistic creations are the songs of Charles Ives (1874–1954), one of the most extraordinary composers America has spawned. This strange man lived two separate lives simultaneously. In one, he pursued a highly successful career as an insurance broker in New York City. In the other—which he kept secret from all except his wife, adopted daughter, and a few scattered friends—he secluded himself either in the study of his New York house or on his farm in West Redding, Connecticut, to write music. The manuscripts began to pile up in his closets and drawers and on his working table. He made no attempt to get his music performed. He never submitted his compositions to a commercial publisher. He never discussed them with professional musicians. He was content just to get his musical ideas down on paper.

And what music he wrote!—music years ahead of its time in experimental idioms, outlandish sounds, and an indigenous identity. Techniques and aspirations with which later and more celebrated composers became identified were anticipated by Ives in those manuscripts, which collected dust for years. Toward the end of his life, the manuscripts were rescued from oblivion to be given important performances and recordings. It was only then that the world was able to recognize both his originality and his power, and to acclaim him not only as America's first significant composer but possibly its greatest.

Despite his passion for anonymity as composer, Ives did publish two works at his own expense for distribution among his closest friends. One was a piano sonata, the *Concord* (1915). The other was a collection of all of his songs, to which he assigned the title of *114 Songs*. The first of these, ''Slow March,'' had been written when he was only fourteen; the last, ''Majority,'' came in 1921. He presented his songs in reverse chronological order, so that the last song appeared first in the volume, and the first song, last.

With a levity and whimsy that characterized him both as man and composer, he explained in the preface to his songs: ''Various authors have various reasons for bringing out a book. . . . Some have written a book for money; I have not. Some for fame; I have not. Some for love; I have not. . . . In fact, gentle borrower, I have not written a book at all—I have merely cleaned house.''

In ''cleaning house,'' Ives gathered some of the most original and finest American songs ever written. ''One knows oneself to be in the presence of a composer of imagination, a real creator,'' Aaron Copland has written. They range across a wide gamut of both styles and content. Some songs are romantic, some are war songs, some are songs of protest, some are cowboy songs, some are street songs, some are in an American ragtime idiom, and some are satiric. ''Majority'' was one of the first published compositions to use ''tone clusters'' in the accompaniment. This is a term applied to chords made up of adjacent half tones, produced by banging a fist or elbow or forearm on the keyboard. In ''Walking Song'' Ives employs unresolved discords. ''Charlie Rutledge'' uses ragtime. Other songs capture the imagination with their delicacy, mood pictures, romanticism, and precision, notably ''The White Gulls,'' ''Berceuse,'' and ''The Children's Hour.''

Since the end of World War I, and continuing until today, American composers have enriched vocal music. Variety is its spice. In choral compositions, some composers have written polyphonically, though basically in a modern manner. Contrapuntal writing characterizes the earlier choral compositions of, say, Roy Harris (1898–   ) and William Schuman (1910–   ).

William Schuman earned the distinction of becoming the first composer to win the Pulitzer Prize for music. He did so with *A Free Song*

THE

Continental Harmony,

CONTAINING,

A Number of ANTHEMS, FUGES, and CHORUSSES, in several PARTS.

NEVER BEFORE PUBLISHED.

COMPOSED BY WILLIAM BILLINGS,

AUTHOR of various MUSIC BOOKS.

Pſalm lxxxvii. 7. As well the Singers as the Players on inſtruments ſhall be there.
Pſalm lxviii. 25. The Singers went before, the Players on inſtruments followed after, amongſt them were the Damſels.
Luke xix. 40. I tell you that if theſe ſhould hold their peace, the ſtones would immediately cry out.
Rev. xix. 3. And again they ſaid Alleluia.

Come let us ſing unto the Lord,	From eaſt to weſt his praiſe proclaim,
And praiſe his name with one accord,	From pole to pole extol his fame,
In this deſign one chorus raiſe ;	The ſky ſhall echo back his praiſe.

Publiſhed according to Act of Congreſs.

PRINTED, Typographically, at BOSTON,
BY ISAIAH THOMAS and EBENEZER T. ANDREWS.
Sold at their Bookſtore, No. 45, Newbury Street ; by ſaid THOMAS in WORCESTER ; and by the BOOKSELLERS in BOSTON, and elſewhere.—1794.

The title page of The Continental Harmony, *a collection of works of William Billings, printed in Boston in 1794.*

A composition in the round of William Billings.

Samuel Barber.

Ned Rorem.

A scene from Bernstein's Mass, performed at
the opening of the Kennedy Center for the Performing Arts
in Washington, D.C., on September 8, 1971.

(1942), a secular cantata for chorus and orchestra to poems by Walt Whitman.

Some composers distinguished their vocal writing with a strong-fibered lyricism with pronounced romantic overtones though occasionally spiced with modern idioms. This holds true for the songs of Samuel Barber (1910–   ) and Ned Rorem (1923–   ). Barber has always had a respect for the voice, being the nephew of one of the foremost opera contraltos of her time, Louise Homer, having studied singing early in his career, and having himself given several song recitals. Songs feature prominently among Barber's earliest compositions, in all of which he maintains a sustained expressive lyricism. Between 1927 and 1928, when he was still in his teens, Barber wrote two beautiful songs, gathered in op. 2: "Daisies," and "With Rue My Heart Is Laden." *Dover Beach* (1931) is also early Barber, an extended work for medium voice (baritone or contralto) and string quartet to a poem by Matthew Arnold. Barber's mastery in writing for the voice and his gift for shaping melodies—but with ever-increasing sophistication in the use of melodic patterns, accentuations, rhythms, and modern harmonies—bring distinction to all his later music, of which the following are representative: *A Stop Watch and an Ordinance Map,* for male voices and three kettledrums and brass (1940), the song cycle *Hermit Songs,* op. 29 (1953), to texts by anonymous Irish monks and scholars between the eighth and fourteenth centuries, and the song cycle *Despite and Still,* op. 41 (1969).

Barber has also interpolated the voice prominently in three important orchestral compositions. *Knoxville: Summer of 1915,* for soprano and orchestra, op. 24 (1947), is a setting of a text by James Agee. *Prayers of Kierkegaard,* for soprano, mixed chorus, and orchestra, op. 30 (1954), draws its text from the writings of a nineteenth-century Danish philosopher and theologian, Sören Aabye Kierkegaard. And *The Lovers* (1971) is an evocative composition for baritone, chorus, and orchestra to words by Pablo Neruda. Barber has composed two operas.

Ned Rorem is a composer of some of the most distinguished songs by an American composer in recent decades. He was born in Richmond, Indiana, on October 23, 1923, and received his musical training with private teachers in Chicago, then at the Curtis Institute of Music and the Juilliard School of Music, with Aaron Copland at the Berkshire Music Center in Massachusetts, and privately with Virgil Thomson. His first bid for success came with a song, "The Lordly Hudson," poem by Paul Goodman, which received the Music Libraries Association Award in 1948. "I began to write for the voice,'' Rorem has said, ''because of a love for words.'' In 1949 he went abroad and for a time lived in Morocco. During the next two years he completed a ballet, *Melos* (which won the Prix de Biarritz in 1951), his first symphony, an opera, and six song cycles, for voice and piano. Among the last were *Penny Arcade* (1949), a setting of six poems by Harold Norse, *Flight for Heaven* (1950), to ten poems by Robert Herrick, *Another Sleep* (1951), to prose poems by Julien Green, and *To a Young Girl* (1951), to six poems by William Butler Yeats. He also completed *Six Irish Poems,* for voice and orchestra (1950).

In 1951, having received a Fulbright fellowship, he established his residence in Paris, where he remained six years and proved highly productive, completing the scores for ballets, a piano sonata, and works for orchestra. His vocal music during this period included *Four Dialogues* (1954), *Five Songs,* for high voice and orchestra (1954), and *The Poets' Requiem,* a meditation on death for chorus and orchestra (1954–55) from the writings of seven contemporary poets. He returned to the United States in 1957 and attended the world premiere of *The Poets' Requiem* in New York on February 15, 1957. Rorem's later song cycles included *Five Songs to Poems by Walt Whitman* (1957); *Poems of Love and the Rain* (1963), a cycle of seventeen songs with texts by American poets; *Hearing* (1966), a cycle of six songs; *War Scenes* (1969), an indictment of war in five songs to poems by Walt Whitman; *Ariel* (1971), a cycle of five poems by Sylvia Plath, for soprano, clarinet, and piano; and *Last Poems of Wallace Stevens,* (1972), for soprano, cello, and piano.

Few musical personalities have made such a deep impression on American musical life and thought as Leonard Bernstein. He was born in Lawrence, Massachusetts, on August 25, 1918. When young, he was often referred to as the ''wonder boy of music.'' Today he is frequently characterized as the ''Renaissance man'' because of his formidable versatility. His prodigious talent for music revealed itself as soon as he began studying the piano in early boyhood with Helen Coates. It came even more forcefully into play during the four years he spent at Harvard, where he attended classes in theory and composition, and involved himself in all of its musical activities, and from which he was graduated in 1939 with a *cum laude* in music.

On the afternoon of November 14, 1943, he made front-page news all over the country when he was called upon, at the zero hour, to direct a concert of the New York Philharmonic orchestra when its scheduled conductor, Bruno Walter, fell ill. Bernstein had to lead that concert without a single rehearsal. Besides, never before had he conducted a major orchestra publicly. That afternoon he proved decisively that conducting was second nature to him. He then went on later to become one of the world's most distinguished and adulated conductors: as music director of the New York Philharmonic (so far, the youngest, and the only American-born, to hold this post). He also appeared as guest with the world's foremost orchestras and opera houses. At the same time he achieved renown as a pianist by playing concertos while directing the orchestral accompaniment himself; as a television personality, particularly in concerts for young people illuminated by his brilliant verbal analyses; as a best-selling author of books on music; and as a composer of both popular music for the Broadway stage and serious music for the concert hall.

His first success as composer came with his first large-scale work, and his initial attempt at writing for an orchestra. It was the *Jeremiah* Symphony (1942), the last movement of which required a mezzo soprano for a verbal text taken from the Book of Lamentations, in which the prophet Jeremiah grieves over the pillaging and ruination of Jerusalem by Babylon. Acclaimed when first performed on January 28, 1944, with Bernstein conducting the Pittsburgh Symphony, this work soon made the rounds of America's foremost orchestras and was then recorded by RCA-Victor and later by Columbia. It also received an award from the New York Music Critics' Circle as the best new orchestral composition of the season.

Among Bernstein's later serious works are two giant choral works, each honoring the dead. *Kaddish* (sometimes designated as Symphony no. 3)—for female narrator, mezzo soprano, chorus, boys' chorus, and orchestra—was commissioned eight years before Bernstein put the final notes on the manuscript. He was working on the concluding "Amen" when he learned that President John F. Kennedy had been assassinated in Dallas, Texas, on November 22, 1963. Since a "Kaddish" is a prayer for the dead from the Hebrew liturgy, Bernstein dedicated his composition to the memory of the fallen President, and conducted its world premiere in Tel Aviv, Israel, on December 10, 1963. The *Kaddish,* then, was Bernstein's memorial service to a man whom he honored as a statesman and loved as a friend.

In *Kaddish,* Bernstein pursued a method previously employed so successfully by Britten in *A War Requiem:* that of combining a centuries-old liturgical text with a present-day one. Britten joined the words of the Catholic Mass with poems by Wilfred Owen. Bernstein wrote his own verses for interpolation within the context of the Hebrew prayer. In his text, Bernstein establishes a personal relationship between man (or, in this case, woman) and God, something that outraged the feelings of those who considered it to be blasphemy. A female narrator, named Lily of Sharon, frequently addresses God as she might another human being. Sometimes she speaks with angry accusations, and sometimes with startling familiarity. "O Holy Father," are her opening words, "ancient hallowed lonely disappointed Father, angry wrinkled Old Majesty, I want to pray." At one point she shouts at Him: "Listen, Almighty, with all your might; there may just be none to say it after me. Do I have your attention, majestic Father?" To the hot accusations that he had been blasphemous, Bernstein quietly explained that a personal relationship between man and God was part and parcel of ancient Hebraic tradition.

Bernstein's music was as unconventional as his text. Whereas in his *Jeremiah* Symphony he quoted synagogal music and at times modeled his own melodies after the intervallic patterns of Hebrew chants, Bernstein made no pretense at all to write Hebrew music in *Kaddish*. His score makes use of the twelve-tone system but is primarily tonal. The discordant music seems alien to an aged Hebraic religious text until we come to realize that Bernstein is speaking for modern man in a modern language. The modernity of Bernstein's writing is enhanced through extensive use of the percussion group and through emphasis on rhythmic effects, even to the point of having the members of the chorus clapping their hands.

More controversial still than the *Kaddish* is the Mass written on assignment for the highly publicized opening of the Kennedy Center for the Performing Arts in Washington, D.C., on September 8, 1971. Bernstein rose to the occasion with a huge work taking two hours for performance. (There is no intermission.) The basic words of the Catholic Mass are combined with additional textual material by the composer and by Stephen Schwartz. Written once again in memory of President John F. Kennedy, this exciting project was described by its creators as a "theater piece for singers, players, and dancers." Two hundred performers were put through the rigorous paces of numerous rehearsals not only by the conductor but also by a stage director and choreographer. A pit orchestra, made up of strings, percussion, and organ, was supplemented on the stage by a blues band, a rock group, and a street chorus. Loudspeakers amplified and spread musical sounds from tracks of prerecorded tapes throughout the auditorium.

Once again, as in *Kaddish,* a narrator (this time a male) is used as commentator. He is assigned the unique name of "Celebrant." The Celebrant portrays "everything from Everyman to Christ," explains Bernstein, "from simply a 'priest' to a representative of Youth . . . that element in every person without which you cannot live." He is the central figure. He is first seen and heard after the opening Kyrie (which is electronically amplified), dressed in blue jeans and a denim work shirt. He sings "A Simple Song" in praise of God, accompanying himself on a guitar. After that, words, music, dance, and theater explore the place of religion in a world torn asunder by hatred and violence. The Mass touched upon such contemporary events as the assassination of President Kennedy and such then current problems as the war in Vietnam and (by implication) the pacifism of the Berrigan brothers. A shattering climax comes when the Celebrant, disillusioned by religion, and disenchanted with his followers, goes berserk and smashes the sacramental vessels. But in the end the Mass spreads the message of faith, love, and peace. The boys' chorus marches down the aisle of the auditorium to touch members of the audience as a token of love and peace. The audience is expected to join in the ritual. Then from a recording comes the simple words of farewell spoken by Bernstein himself: "The mass is ended. Go in peace."

Bernstein's music embraces every possible style and idiom: the sounds and textures of jazz, the blues, rock; ecclesiastical music and revivalist hymns; show tunes and marching songs; ballads. The avant-garde techniques embrace electronic music. Its eclecticism, as Bernstein has explained, is the essence of the score in its effort to find suitable material for the rapidly changing experiences and messages of the text. "But it had to be very carefully handled," says Bernstein, "so that the eclecticism worked positively and not negatively, as a pastiche. . . . It's a matter of timing, which is very difficult, and a matter of making certain key moments work. . . . By 'key moments' I mean those moments when there is a sense of shock, where the eclecticism is most apparent. . . . Someone told me that, for him, the mass was two hours of constant shocks, surprises that were always surprising and never became predictable after a certain point. . . . But actually I never used these 'surprises' for their sheer shock value; they all came from somewhere very deep."

Some who have heard the Mass regard it as not only Bernstein's greatest composition but one of the most significant in the twentieth century. Others felt it was too pretentious, contrived, and given to histrionics. Time alone can decide wherein lies the truth. But there is no question that this Mass is a powerful and unforgettable spokesman for our turbulent, confused, and divisive times, speaking in the language and symbols of our times, and addressing itself forcefully to the young and the old of our times. Within one of the oldest forms of choral music, the mass, Bernstein has produced a vital art form that is as contemporary as this morning's headlines. Thus the distant past joins the present in anticipating what may well be a musical art form of the future.

Glossary

Absolute Music   Music with no literary, pictorial, or programmatic interpretation, deriving its interest exclusively from musical content and structure, as opposed to program music.

A Cappella   Unaccompanied vocal music.

Alto, or Contralto   The lowest range of female voice, rising about two octaves from E or F below middle C.

Anthem   A sacred composition for chorus or mixed solo voices from Anglican church services, utilizing a text from the Scriptures or prayer book, but not part of the prescribed liturgy. It originated in 1662, when Queen Elizabeth I demanded inclusion of hymns and songs in the prayer book.

Antiphony   A method in choral music in which a line of music is sung by one choir (or part of a choir) and sung in alternation by a second choir (or part of a choir).

Aria   *See* Concert Aria.

Arioso   A lyrical style of recitative, more songlike than speechlike.

Art Song   A musical setting of a poem (called the lyric) for solo voice   *237* and accompaniment created by a single composer for concert presentation. *See also* Folk Song; Lied.

Atonality   Absence of a key center, music without a basic tonality.

Ave Maria   A prayer of praise to the Virgin Mary in the Catholic liturgy often set to music, sometimes for chorus, sometimes for solo voice and accompaniment.

Ballad   An extended art song dealing with a historical, legendary, or fantastic subject. See discussion in Chapter 5.

Ballet   A species of madrigal. See discussion in Chapter 2.

Baritone   A male voice with the approximate range of two octaves upwards from the A a tenth below middle C. The baritone range lies between those of the tenor and the bass.

Bass, or Basso   The lowest range of male voice, rising two octaves above E, an octave and a sixth below middle C. A singer with a slightly higher range is a bass-baritone; one with a lower range, a basso profundo.

Bel Canto   "Beautiful song, beautiful singing." A type of singing emphasizing beauty of tone, purity of texture, elegance of phrasing, virtuosity, and agility.

Berceuse   A cradle song or lullaby.

Bravura   Brilliant and technically demanding vocal passage.

Canon   A choral composition using the contrapuntal technique of "imitation" in which a voice begins with a melody and continues it while a second voice enters with the same melody, overlapping the first, and so on for three or more voices. A canon in which the voices immediately repeat the original melody without a break is called a round.

Cantata   An extended work for chorus or one or more soloists, or chorus and soloists, and orchestra on a religious or secular text, similar to but smaller in dimension than the oratorio. See discussion in Chapter 3.

Cantilena   A smooth and melodious vocal number.

Canzonetta   A short, light, and cheerful song.

Carol, or Noël   A Christmas song, generally religious in character, said by some to have originated in Grecia, near Assisi, where Saint Francis built the first Christmas "crib" in his church and urged that hymns be sung around it.

Cavatina   A song simpler in style and structure than a concert aria.

Chorale   A hymn of the German Protestant Church developed during the Reformation in the sixteenth century, under the encouragement of Martin
Luther, to promote congregational singing. The words were German li-

turgical texts or psalms set to simple folklike melodies, in the singing of which the congregation would join during the services. See further discussion in Chapter 3.

Chord   Combination of three or more tones sounded simultaneously.

Classical Period   An epoch beginning roughly in the middle of the eighteenth century and ending in the first decade of the nineteenth. See discussion in Chapter 4.

Concert Aria   The concert equivalent of an opera aria, an extended vocal composition with a recitative preceding the main melody.

Consonance   An agreeable combination of musical tones.

Contralto   *See* Alto.

Counterpoint   Simultaneous combination of two or more independent melodic lines.

Declamation   Vocal music that follows the inflections of speech and in which the text assumes greater importance than the melody.

Dissonance, or Discord   A discordant chord or chords that are not resolved into consonance.

Dodecaphony   *See* Twelve-Tone Technique.

Duet   A vocal number for two voices.

Durchkomponiert   *See* Through-Composition.

Elegy   A musical composition in a melancholy or pensive mood, or a song expressing sorrow, especially for a person who has died.

Embellishment   A decorative figure in melody.

Expression   Nuances of dynamics, phrasing, and other elements left to the judgment of singer or singers, too subtle to be indicated in the music.

Expressionism   A twentieth-century art idiom. See discussion in Chapter 10.

Falsetto   Singing by a male performer in a high range with a quality and texture resembling that of a female voice.

Fioriture   Ornamentations and decorations either provided by the composer or improvised by the singer.

Folk Song   A song representative of a race or nationality, handed down from generation to generation, the composer or composers lost in anonymity. It is the oldest form of known music. Folk songs are simple in structure and emotional appeal and reflect the culture, feelings, backgrounds, customs, and at times superstitions of the people.

Fugue   A complex contrapuntal form generally for three, four, or five parts, called "voices." The subject theme is presented by each voice in turn. Stated in the first voice, the subject is repeated a fifth higher or a fourth lower by the second voice, while the first voice continues with that subject; the third voice enters an octave higher or lower than the first voice, as do subsequent voices. A free development follows.

Harmony   The science of combining notes into chords and chords into progressions.

Homophony   A style emphasizing single melody and its harmony.

Hymn   A religious song in metrical or stanza form intended for congregational singing.

Imitation   *See* Canon.

Impressionism   A term borrowed from painting. Music of this style suggests the sensation or impression aroused by any given subject. Subtle nuances, colors, effects, and atmospheres are emphasized, rather than structure or substance. See discussion in Chapter 9.

Intonation   Adhering to correct pitch.

Kapellmeister   Current German term for conductor. Originally it meant a choirmaster.

Lied   German for "art song." More specifically it connotes a German art song where melody and words are so closely related that they become a single artistic entity. See discussion in Chapter 5.

Madrigal   A musical setting of a poem on a pastoral, amorous, or satirical subject. It is the secular equivalent of a motet. It is contrapuntal in style, for three or more unaccompanied voices. See discussion in Introduction.

Maestro di Cappella   An Italian term used in an earlier period, meaning "master of the chapel." The leader of a choir, a conductor, a composer, or all three combined. The French equivalent term was *maître de chapelle*.

Magnificat   A musical setting of the song of the Virgin Mary from the Gospel According to Saint Luke. It became a part of the Vespers services in the Roman Catholic Church.

Maître de Chapelle   *See* Maestro di Cappella.

Mass   The most important ritual of the Catholic liturgy. Its music makes up one of the earliest-known forms of choral music, originally for unaccompanied voices, but later for solo voices, chorus, and orchestra. See discussion in Introduction.

Mattinata.   A "morning song" of love sung under a lady's window.

Mélodie   French art song. See discussion in Chapter 6.

240   **Melody**   Succession of single tones in a logical and pleasing pattern.

Mezza Voce   Literally, "half a voice." Singing with diminished volume.

Mezzo Soprano   The range of female voice between soprano and alto, usually rising about two octaves from A below middle C.

Missa Brevis   A short mass. See explanation in Chapter 4.

Mode   A church scale antedating the major-minor modality.

Motet   A polyphonic setting for unaccompanied voices of a biblical text, generally in Latin. The religious equivalent of the madrigal.

Neo-Romanticism   An extension of the Romanticism of the nineteenth century following Brahms and Wagner, usually with philosophic or ideological implications. See discussion in Chapter 7.

Neumes   Earliest decipherable form of notation. See explanation in Introduction.

Noël   French name for a Christmas carol.

Obbligato   A background motif, or a part subordinate to a solo part.

Oratorio   A large work for solo voices, chorus, and orchestra utilizing a text dramatizing a part of the Bible but performed without costumes, scenery, or staging. See discussion in Chapter 3.

Organum   Earliest form of polyphonic music in which two voices in long notes move in parallel lines. See discussion in Introduction.

Ornament   *See* Embellishment.

Parlando, or Parlante   Literally, "speaking." An indication for a singer to simulate speech.

Part Song   A song in contrapuntal style for two or more voices.

Partita   An eighteenth-century term used interchangeably with "suite" for a several-movement composition made up mostly of dance movements.

Passion   An oratorio whose text is based on the story of the crucifixion (Passion) of Christ according to the Gospels. See discussion in Chapters 1 and 3.

Plainsong, or Plainchant   Earliest form of religious music; a simple unaccompanied melody in long notes. See further explanation in Introduction.

Polyphony   Two or more different melodies sounded simultaneously.

Portamento   Carrying the voice from one note to another while gliding over the intervening notes.

Prelude   A piece of music played as an introduction to a liturgical ceremony or to another composition, such as a suite. With the Romantic composers it became an independent composition for the piano that established a mood.

Program Music   Music depending on a literary program, or describing a specific scene or mood—in short, music with extramusical interest, as opposed to absolute music.

Psalm   A sacred song of praise for solo voice or for chorus. It was the predecessor of the hymn or chorale. It refers specifically to a setting of any one of the 150 psalms in the Book of Psalms in the Old Testament.

Quartet   A vocal number for four voices.

Quintet   A vocal number for five voices.

Recitative, or Recitativo   Declamation accompanied by music in an oratorio or Passion.

Register   The compass of a vocal range, and the colorations and voice production suitable for that range.

Requiem   A mass for the dead. It utilizes the liturgical text of the mass, but begins with an Introit ("Requiem aeternam"), omits the Gloria and Credo, and substitutes the sequences of a Dies Irae and other sections varying with different requiems. See discussion in Chapter 4.

Romance, or Romanza   A song romantic in feeling, or concerned with unfolding a narrative rather than with dramatic expression.

Romantic Period   Period in music history beginning roughly with the late Beethoven and continuing through the nineteenth century. See discussion in Chapter 5.

Roulade   Florid vocal passage.

Round   *See* Canon.

Scale   Formal succession of notes within an octave, such as diatonic and chromatic scales.

Scena   A voice number more extended and dramatic than a song or aria.

Secular Music   Music of a nonreligious nature.

Serenade   An "evening song" of a lover sung under his lady's window.

Sextet   A vocal number for six voices.

Song   *See* Art Song; Folk Song; Lied; Part Song.

Song Cycle   A group of songs with unifying mood or common theme. See discussion in Chapter 4.

Song Form   A form made up of two or three parts. When in two parts it consists of subject and countersubject; in three parts, the third part repeats the first.

Song-Speech, or Sprechstimme, or Speech-Song   A kind of melodic line in atonal music resembling speech. See discussion in Chapter 10.

Soprano Highest range of female voice, usually a little over two octaves from B-flat below middle C. Sopranos fall into three categories: lyric, dramatic, and coloratura.

Sotto Voce Literally, "under the voice." Singing in an undertone, or in an "aside."

Stabat Mater A hymn of the Roman Catholic liturgy. Many musical settings have been made of the text describing the Holy Mother at the Cross.

Strophic A song structure in which each stanza of the verses uses the same melody.

Te Deum A part of the Roman Catholic liturgy; a hymn of praise. It subsequently became a choral song of thanksgiving celebrating a festive event. See discussion in Chapter 6.

Tenor The highest range of male voice, extending two octaves above the C an octave below middle C.

Tessitura Literally, "texture." The approximate range of a song.

Through-Composition, or Durchkomponiert A method of songwriting, as opposed to strophic, in which the melody changes continually with each verse. See discussion in Chapter 5.

Trio. A vocal number for three voices.

Twelve-Tone Technique, or Dodecaphony A system developed and popularized by Arnold Schoenberg utilizing the twelve tones of the chromatic scale without repeating a note before using the others. Expressionist composers create a "row" of these twelve notes, which becomes the basis of their composition. See discussion in Chapter 10.

Unison Singing the same note or notes by more than one performer.

Whole-Tone Scale A scale consisting entirely of whole tones used extensively by Debussy. See discussion in Chapter 9.

Index

248

256

258